The Middle Colonies
And The Coming Of The
American Revolution

Kennikat Press
National University Publications
Series in American Studies

General Editor
James P. Shenton
Professor of History, Columbia University

John A. Neuenschwander

The Middle Colonies And The Coming Of The American Revolution

National University Publications
KENNIKAT PRESS   1973
Port Washington, N.Y.   London

Library of Congress Catalog No. 73-83267
ISBN: 0-8046-9054-5

Manufactured in the United States of America

Published by
Kennikat Press, Inc.
Port Washington, N.Y./London

973.3
Neu

*To Patti, Jeff,
and Sara*

CONTENTS

ACKNOWLEDGMENTS

Carl Ubbelohde was not only responsible for calling my attention to this long-neglected aspect of the American Revolution but he often helped me to return to the main road when I had become lost on one of the innumerable backroads in the Middle Colonies. Bertram Wyatt-Brown, Neil Stout, Arthur Jensen, Robert Weir, Nelson Peter Ross and John Bailey deserve a special mention for their timely criticism and encouragement. A general word of thanks must also go to the staff members of New York Historical Society, New York Public Library, Historical Society of Pennsylvania, Library of Congress, New Jersey Historical Society, Western Reserve Historical Society and the Delaware Historical Society who did everything possible to make my brief stays productive. Finally, I owe an immeasurable debt of gratitude to my wife Patti, who not only was a constant source of strength but endured without complaint the countless nights and weekends that I spent in scholarly seclusion.

J.A.N.

The Middle Colonies
And The Coming Of The
American Revolution

INTRODUCTION

On March 4, 1815, as John Adams reflected on the American Revolution he was so overwhelmed by the seeming inscrutability of that great event that he dolefully asked: "Who shall write the history of the American Revolution? Who can write it? Who shall ever be able to write it?" Many actors in the American Revolution like Adams were skeptical that their deeds would ever receive the kind of scholarly attention they deserved. Adams would undoubtedly be surprised, if alive today, to see the thousands of books and articles that our academic and publishing industry have produced in pursuit of that elusive event. Each generation of American scholarship has added its measure to the enterprise, and yet somehow the subject remains unexhausted and as enigmatic as ever. Thomas Jefferson certainly shared Adams' pessimism and in reply to the New Englander's query attempted to elucidate the major reasons for future naiveté:

All its councils, designs and discussions having been conducted by Congress with closed doors, and no members, as far as I know, having even made notes of them, these, which are the life and soul of history must for ever be unknown.[1]

3

Jefferson's answer does not fully explain the continuing am-
biguity of this event, for the absence of materials about the
Founders' deliberations is not the only lacuna. A major difficulty in understanding the Revolution also stems from the
inadequacy of the traditional two-section view of the movement
toward independence. In almost all of the Revolutionary his-
tories to date, New England and the South have received the
bulk of attention. Although their leadership of the independence movement certainly warrants extensive historical attention, one can never fully understand any national struggle by
merely studying the forces that prevailed. What is needed is a
broader comprehension of the pivotal role of the Middle
Colonies in the creation of the American nation.

Despite such unbalanced treatment historians of the Revolution from the Reverend William Gordon to Merrill Jensen
are in agreement that New York, New Jersey, Pennsylvania
and Delaware were the last provinces to commit themselves to
separation. According to George Bancroft the Middle Colonies
"sighed for reconciliation" until the moment that independence
was declared. Such agreement on "external facts" has not
brought in its train any satisfactory explanation of why they
acted as they did. To be sure historians have suggested that
prosperity, political instability and greater attachment to the
Empire were some of the factors that held them back. A few
historians, notably John M. Head and Merrill Jensen, have
even hinted that sectional feeling among the Middle Colonies
might account in large part for their renitence. Yet no one as
yet has studied the coming of the Revolution in the Middle
Colonies to determine whether sectional feeling really did
exist and if so whether it significantly colored their attitude
toward independence.

The reason for this neglect is not hard to locate. Historians have long acknowledged that the American colonial ex-

perience produced two sections: New England and the South. The four colonies that separated these two sections somehow never became distinctive in any collective sense. This middle region has thus been a kind of no-man's land in the shadow of two politically sophisticated and dynamic sections. In fact historians have sometimes turned their attention to this area only to deny its very existence. With a trace of wounded pride, Frederick Tolles, one of the foremost scholars of the Middle Atlantic States, recently noted that "A question might even arise in some minds whether there was a Middle Atlantic region in any other sense than that it was left over between New England and the South."[2] Richard Shryock, another expert, sadly concludes that because New York, New Jersey, Pennsylvania and Delaware never shared in a sectional outlook the area has long been "The Forgotten Region" in terms of scholarship.

Since the beginning of the nineteenth century the propensity to consider the Middle Colonies in nonsectional terms has been so commonplace, it is understandable that historians have looked elsewhere for sectional behavior. Terms like Middle Colonies and Middle Atlantic States have been geographical reference points and nothing more. Viewed across the entire sweep of American history there is no question that this is a sound interpretation. The Middle Atlantic States were never able to develop a sense of area kinship and defensiveness comparable to what New Eng'and and the South experienced. But sectionalism is much too intricate a concept to be accurately defined by means of simple reference to New England or the South. Moreover, the disappearance of New England's sectional consciousness in the twentieth century raises a very important question. Have great national crises and major shifts in the pattern of American life fostered and/or destroyed other sectional impulses? In other words, have there been heretofore unrecognized instances of sectional behavior which have substantially influenced the course of American history? Because of their focus on the long-term perspective American historians have not only neglected to ask this question but they have consistently overlooked the sectional posture that the Middle Colonies assumed during the apocalyptic years from 1774-1776.

The process by which a section evolves is still a little understood phenomenon. For sections do not come into existence in a vacuum nor do they emerge full-blown following a standard incubation period. The process by which an area or region comes to realize its sectional identity is very complex. The first stage generally involves little more than an intuitive sense of common interest and goals. If this feeling continues to be reinforced both from within and without, an inchoate sectional identity begins to take shape. In this second stage a name or term vaguely connoting certain traits peculiar to the emerging section may come into occasional usage. In both of these initial stages only a small percentage of the population of the area is directly involved. The more literate and wealthy members of society are the ones who generally dominate the conceptualizing and articulating processes. For it is not until the third stage that the sectional "concept receives explicit statements as an abstraction," and the general populace begins to think in sectional terms.[3] When the difficult third stage is at last reached, a section can be considered to have reached maturity.

The appearance of an outside threat may sometimes dramatically speed up the unfolding of a section. Although the nature of an external threat may vary, it has often been a real or imagined drive by an older section to expand its political and socio-economic control. According to William Hesseltine such regional imperialism is both the root cause and sustaining force of all sectionalism. In the years from 1774-1776 the specter of New England imperialism certainly played a major

role in raising the level of sectional feeling in the Middle
Colonies from an intuitive to conscious plane.

Until the meeting of the First Continental Congress in
September, 1774, the thirteen colonies had never possessed a
suitable organization or governing body in which sectional
attitudes could be readily identified and reinforced. For the
variegated background of the American Colonies had led the
British to treat each of them as separate administrative units.
To be sure the absence of such an intercolonial organization
in the years before 1774 had not deterred the four New England Colonies from attaining a full measure of sectional consciousness. Whether they were referred to as "Yankees,"
"Eastern Men" or "New Englanders," the sectional character-
istics of these "descendants of Cromwell's elect" were well
known from Georgia to New York.[4] There were many indica-
tions in 1774 as well that a Southern section encompassing
Virginia, Maryland and the colonies to the southward was
rapidly taking shape. From the first days of the Continental
Congress the term *Southern delegate* was in common use and
its sectional implications were clearly understood. Only the
delegates from New York, New Jersey, Pennsylvania and
Delaware seemingly entered the First Continental Congress
without any sectional ties. Despite such appearances it is now
apparent that the delegates to the First Congress from the four
Central Provinces did indeed possess an intuitive but largely
unarticulated sense of their common social, economic and
political attributes. In the difficult months ahead, as the American Colonies searched for measures to combat British policies,
the Middle Colonial leaders found that they agreed on two
fundamental principles: the need to preserve the Empire and
to resist New England expansionism. Since the "Yankees" were
the aggressors in both instances, they became the major threat
in the eyes of the Central Provinces. Fearful that New England
might destroy the Empire and subsequently come to dominate

the other colonies, Middle Colonial leaders moved rapidly to the second stage of sectional awareness. For almost nineteen months they waged a spirited but, in the end, unsuccessful campaign to avert a complete separation from the mother country. That historians have skipped over the sectional dimension of Middle Colonial resistance to independence for so long underscores the doubts shared by John Adams and Thomas Jefferson.

chapter one

POOR RICHARD'S SCHOOL:

The Middle Colonies on the Eve

"Between New England and the Middle States was a gap like that between Scotland and England," was how Henry Adams described the division between the two regions in 1800.[1] Although this analogy was somewhat overdrawn, thirty years before the turn of the century colonials were already cognizant of a distinction between the "Yankees" of the northeast and the inhabitants of the Central Provinces. While New England's sectional image was much better defined in the early 1770's, a few perceptive contemporaries also noticed that a singular culture was slowly emerging amongst the Middle Colonies. To begin with, the very diversity of inhabitants and religious groups was an easily identifiable trait in itself. But the multiformity of the Central Provinces created only a part of their cultural image. The Germans, who were the largest non-English group, were scarcely observable to outsiders. Their agrarian ways, initial separatism, and clannishness set them apart as a state within a state. In this condition they exerted only limited influence in shaping the culture of the Middle Colonies. It is only when an ethnic group freely proliferates within its host culture that significant cross-pollinization takes

9

place. The second and third largest non-English groups in the
Middle Colonies, the Scotch-Irish and the Dutch, were able
to make a more substantial cultural impact for this reason.

Overall, Middle Colonial culture still revealed a decidedly
English cast. The most significant architects of this image were
the groups that represented dominant economic interests or
types. Contemporaries tended to equate the industrious Quakers with Pennsylvania, the wealthy merchants and landowners
with New York and plain farmers with New Jersey and Delaware. In particular, thoughtful eighteenth-century observers
detected a marked similarity between the way New Yorkers
and Pennsylvanians conducted their business in the market-
place. Andrew Burnaby, for example, was quite explicit about
the common business ethic:

> The inhabitants of New York, in their character, very much
> resembled the Pennsylvanians: more than half of them are Dutch,
> and almost all traders: they are, therefore, habitually frugal, in-
> dustrious, and parsimonious.[2]

In 1775 John Adams took a less charitable view of this outlook: "There are some Persons in New York and Philadelphia,
to whom a ship is dearer than a City and a few Barrells of
flower, than a thousand lives—other Mens Lives I mean."[3] In
sum Pennsylvania and New York bore the unmistakable im-
print of the businessman, and their culture symbolized the
entrepreneurial spirit of the Middle Colonies in general.

The northernmost province of the Middle Colonies, New
York, was a colony of sharp contrasts. Here a mercantile and
landed aristocracy dominated the economic, political and social
life of the colony in a manner reminiscent of the bluebloods
of Charles Town. Yet the New York scions had a pronounced
bourgeois aura. They showed the results of a century-long
campaign of selective assimilation and extirpation waged
against the entrenched Dutch culture of the original settlers.

One of the Dutch traits that New Yorkers could not resist embracing was the aggressive pursuit of material wealth. Patrick M'Roberts expressed the common stereotype in his treatment of Long Islanders:

A great many of the old settlers here are of Dutch extract, and very rich, said to be great hoarders; for if a piece of gold or a dollar fall into their hands, it is ten to one, ever it sees the air again in their day. This hoarding disposition is natural to all Dutch in this Country.[4]

In the decades before the Revolution fellow colonials generally viewed New Yorkers as "men on the make" and with good reason. During the third quarter of the eighteenth century the colony underwent a remarkable economic acceleration. In the short space of twenty years New York's population grew from approximately 68,000 souls to 168,000. Wartime prices and trade practices during the Seven Years War accounted in part for the economic takeoff, while New York's slow rate of development during the first half of the century meant that opportunities for expansion were in good supply. Judge Thomas Jones, a New York Tory historian, referred to this boom period as a "Golden Age."

In 1774 Governor William Tryon was able to inform the colonial office that Kings, Queens, Suffolk, Richmond, New York, Westchester, Dutchess, Orange, and Ulster counties "are all well inhabited, and not many large Tracts of Improveable land are left uncultivated."[5] Albany and Tryon counties to the northwest of New York City he classified as in the process of agricultural development whereas the northern counties of Charlotte, Cumberland and Gloucester (encompassing most of the future state of Vermont) were little more than frontier outposts. Prior to 1750 New York had been at a disadvantage in attracting settlers because of the policy of granting huge tracts of land to wealthy gentlemen who in turn often en-

deavored to people their estates with tenants rather than freeholders. Despite widespread opposition to this practice it
continued down to the Revolution. A review of the most significant patents granted from 1700-1775 shows that of the
211 grants bestowed, 86 tracts contained 10,000 or more
acres. After 1750, however, a substantial number of large
landholders apparently liberalized their sale policies to entice
small farmers.

Not all areas of New York were dominated by huge
landed estates. The three prosperous Long Island counties of
Kings, Queens and Suffolk were dotted with small and
medium size farms with only an occasional large patent.
Orange and Ulster counties on the west bank of the Hudson
River were predominantly made up of small farmers. It was
in the counties of Richmond, Westchester and Dutchess on the
east bank of the Hudson that the baronial estates of the
Phillipses, Livingstons, Bayards and Van Rensselaers were
concentrated. Further west, Tryon and Albany counties contained a number of large estates as well. The fertile soil of New
York enabled big and small farmers alike to secure a high yield
from various grain crops despite generally primitive farming
practices. Flour, wheat and sundry grains constituted the major
exports of the province.

Increased agricultural production during the third quarter of the century facilitated the commercial expansion of New
York City. This growth enabled New York to pull into a virtual
tie with Boston in terms of trade volume and narrow the gap
substantially with Philadelphia by the early 1770's. New York's
balanced trade pattern was an important factor in this surge
forward. Whereas Boston's predominant trade area was coastal
commerce and Philadelphia's the West Indian trade, New
York merchants had almost equal commercial involvement in
West Indian, British and North American commerce.[6] The

development of manufactures during the "Golden Age" was not as rapid, but the production of pig and bar iron showed a slight increase. Flour milling and distilling also grew rapidly.

Between 1756 and 1771 New York City's population rose from about 13,000 to 22,000. Patrick M'Roberts found the city in the early 1770's to be well laid out, with distinguished churches and public buildings. As for the inhabitants, they were ". . . in general brisk and lively, kind to strangers and dress very gay. . . ."[7] The lateness of its development placed it well behind Boston and Philadelphia in regard to cultural activities. Yet New York could claim a distinction that neither of its two rivals had: British influence and customs were more strongly entrenched there than in any other urban area in the thirteen colonies. The presence of the headquarters of the British Army in North America and the northern district post office filled the city with large numbers of officials whose habits, style and money were infectious. The structure of New York City's municipal government was also distinctly British in that the mayor and the recorder were appointees of the royal governor. The Anglican Church was the established religion in the city and numbered among its parishioners most of the merchant princes, landed scions and crown officials. The munificent patronage of these individuals as well as that of the royal governors amounted to "Ecclesiastical Imperialism."[8] The social customs of prominent New Yorkers were slavishly copied from London models. New York not only had replicas of the most prominent London public entertainment halls but even named its resorts Vauxhall Garden and Ranelagh.

Provincial politics in New York was the preserve of the merchant princes, landed aristocrats and affluent lawyers. By means of an intricate network of family relationships the leading families of the province—the DeLanceys, the Livingstons,

the Crugers, the Wattses, the Waltons, the Van Cortlandts, and
the Morrises—constituted themselves as the fountainhead of
all appointed and elected officeholders. A survey of the back-
grounds of all supreme court justices, provincial council members and assemblymen from 1750-1776 reveals that ten of
thirteen judges, twenty-five of twenty-eight members of the
council and fifty-two of seventy-seven assemblymen were
minimally classifiable as landed gentry. This classification was
limited to those with holdings of 1,000 acres or more.

Carl Becker's seminal interpretation of New York colonial
politics as a rivalry between aristocratic families has withstood
more than a half century of scrutiny. To be sure historians have
expanded his treatment of political motivation to give greater
weight to religious strife and ethnic clashes. But his explanation
of New York provincial politics before the Revolution as a
quarrel between the landholding, predominantly Presbyterian
Livingstons and the mercantile, largely Anglican DeLanceys
has survived without serious modification.

New York politics also had an urban-rural aspect. The
assemblymen from neighboring counties like Westchester,
Richmond, Kings and Queens regularly advocated anti-urban
measures and usually managed to shift the tax burden to city
residents. The annual tax contribution of New York City
amounted to one-third of the total provincial receipts although
the city possessed only about one-fifth of the total population.
Although New York City and Albany often banded together
in self-defense they were usually not very successful against
the rural interests.

During the 1750's and 1760's New York supplied a
sizable portion of the combatants on both sides of the controversy surrounding the proposed Anglican bishopric for the
American colonies. Relations between Church of England men
and dissenters were far from idyllic before this prolonged

struggle, but afterwards a virtual religious war erupted. By
the early 1770's the Presbyterians were the most numerous of
the religious denominations with sixty-one congregations. Because their church hierarchy was based in the colonies the
Presbyterians had a clear advantage over the Anglicans who
were forced to refer most matters to London. Though out-
numbered by the Presbyterians (the Anglicans had only thirty
congregations in New York) the established church was still
a formidable foe, owing to its wealth and official status. The
Dutch Reformed Church had more members and churches
than the Anglicans but its political influence was negligible
save in Albany. The Lutherans with twenty churches, the
Quakers with twenty-six and the Baptists with sixteen formed
the second echelon in terms of power and prestige.[9]

While New York was in the midst of a great leap forward
in 1774, Pennsylvania was working to retain its ascendency.
Though scarcely a century old, William Penn's colony could
boast of prosperity, religious freedom, and the largest city on
the continent. Eighteenth-century observers like Andrew
Burnaby marveled at the flourishing state of the province:

Can the mind have a greater pleasure than in contemplating the
rise and progress of cities and kingdoms? Than in perceiving a
rich and opulent state arising out of a small settlement or colony?
This pleasure every one must feel who considers Pensylvania
(sic).[10]

Like New York the Quaker Colony experienced a period
of rapid economic growth during the third quarter of the
eighteenth century. Aided by the continuing waves of German
and Scotch-Irish immigrants, agricultural production grew so
rapidly that in 1775 Governor John Penn asserted that Pennsylvania had more acres under cultivation in proportion to its
geographic area and vintage than any other colony on the
continent. Agricultural expansion supplied the impetus for the

rapid commercial and industrial development of Philadelphia. By the early 1770's the city had left its two closest rivals, New York and Boston, far behind in commerce, manufactures, population and cultural attainments. On the eve of the Revolution Pennsylvanians pointed with pride to their many accomplishments and contemplated the future with satisfaction.

The farmers of Pennsylvania engaged in the mixed agriculture that prevailed in the other Middle Colonies. Although Pennsylvania's agricultural potential was rated by contemporaries as superior to that of its neighbors:

The agriculture of the province is not equal to what the preceding productions would admit of; and to which they might be encouraged by soil, climate and getting labour more plentifully than many other colonies.[11]

Only the German farmers with their superior farming techniques came close to securing optimum yields. Farms in the colony ranged in size on an average between 100 and 400 acres. Larger farms were common, especially in the older agricultural regions of Bucks, Chester and Philadelphia counties. The moderate land prices established by the proprietary government enabled small holders to acquire land easily. Nevertheless, squatting was a common practice, especially among immigrant groups. By 1726 it is estimated that there were about 100,000 squatters engrossing 670,000 acres in the province.[12] Grains and livestock were the chief agricultural products of Pennsylvania with flour the major export commodity.

The rise of Philadelphia to commercial dominance was the result of enlightened local regulation, good business sense and a favorable geographic location as the entrepôt of the Delaware River district. Farmers from West New Jersey and Delaware sent their produce to Philadelphia for export and in turn were supplied with imports and manufactured goods. By the early 1770's Philadelphia was the busiest port on the North American continent and the third largest city in the entire British Empire. Only London and Liverpool were more populous. During the years 1764-1772 Philadelphia's West Indian trade was double that of New York and a third larger than Boston's. Philadelphia's greatness was not built solely on commerce. Shipbuilding had become an important industry by the 1770's and the various crafts (i.e., silversmithing, carpentry) taken together represented the largest single concentration of skilled artisans on the continent.[13]

Philadelphia's economic success ushered in a new urban way of life. By 1776 the population of the city stood at close to 40,000. The well-ordered colonial seaport on the Delaware was fast becoming the first American metropolis. Its size, activity, diverse population and insufferable pride made it repulsive to many visitors. Silas Deane, a delegate to the Continental Congress from Connecticut, apparently deemed the city a challenge to his critical ingenuity. He found Philadelphia's produce market inferior to those of Connecticut while he thought the women of the city were devoid of beauty. Deane did not, however, venture to criticize the culture of the city, because literary clubs, theaters, lending libraries and scientific societies abounded. The large concentration of able printers in the city was another indication of Philadelphia's intellectual development. In essence Philadelphia was the harbinger of the America that was still to come.

The amalgam of ethnic groups in Pennsylvania was more pronounced than in any other Middle Colony. Benjamin Franklin maintained that before the Revolution the Germans and English Quakers each constituted a third of the population while the Scotch-Irish and remaining ethnic minorities made up the final third. The English Quakers were generally clustered in the three older counties (Bucks, Chester and

Philadelphia) adjacent to the City of Brotherly Love. The
counties further west and north of Philadelphia like Berks,
Lancaster and York were thickly settled with Germans while
Cumberland was predominantly Scotch-Irish and Northampton an ethnic potpourri.

As one might suspect the religious situation was more
complex than the ethnic divisions. The German settlers were
either "Church People" encompassing members of the traditional Lutheran or Reformed Churches or "Sectarians" like
the Mennonites, Dunkers and a host of minor sects. The
"Church People" did not actively strive for cultural separatism
and non-involvement in the affairs of the world as did the
"Sectarians." The Presbyterians constituted the largest single
denomination in both Philadelphia and Pennsylvania. As in
the other Middle Colonies Presbyterians were mostly small
farmers, mechanics and tradesmen, many of whom were of
Scotch-Irish descent. While the Presbyterian Church continued
to grow, membership in the Quaker Society dropped sharply
in the quarter century before the Revolution. Whereas in 1750
about twenty-five percent of the citizens of Philadelphia had
been on its rolls, by 1776 the number had shrunk to fifteen
percent. With this sharp numerical slippage in the City itself
the Quaker's center of strength had shifted to the surrounding
counties of Bucks and Chester. Despite this evidence of de-
cline the Quakers still represented a formidable economic and
political bloc in Pennsylvania. The fastest growing church in
Philadelphia was the Anglican. Led by the astute Dr. William
Smith, Christ Church and St. Peters were becoming, so to
speak, the cathedrals of the respectable and affluent.

Despite Pennsylvania's widespread prosperity and reputation for enlightened government, politics in the Quaker
Colony was still the exclusive province of the upper class. Two
factions drawn from the elite dominated politics until the Revo-

lutionary movement sapped their strength. The Quaker faction, made up of eastern county Friends, Germans and a small clique from western Pennsylvania, gained the upper hand during the mid-1760's. Much of their success was due to the careful distribution of patronage posts and the policy of keeping the western counties underrepresented.[14] In contrast the Proprietary faction drew to its banner most of the major officeholders, Anglicans and disgruntled ethnic groups. The stakes were so high in the struggle between the two factions that in the 1760's the Quaker faction sought to rid Pennsylvania of the Proprietors by urgently pressing for a royal charter.

Suffrage qualifications in Pennsylvania were based entirely on the fifty-acre freehold provision. County tax books reveal that generally about sixty percent of all white, male residents were eligible.[15] In Philadelphia all taxables were ostensibly eligible but the dearth of voting records makes it impossible to determine the percentage of actual voters. Suffrage habits probably were the same as those in the other Middle Colonies with only a small percentage actually exercising their franchise.

From the early years of the eighteenth century New York City and Philadelphia were intense commercial competitors because of the similarity of their exportable commodities and the limited trade patterns open to them under the Navigation Acts. In spite of their rivalry a close relationship evolved between the merchants and wealthy citizens of the two cities during the three decades prior to the Revolution.[16] Business contacts, improved transportation, family alliances, common recreational outlets and geographical proximity all played a part in deepening the relationship between the two metropolises.

On the business front, merchants from the two cities

increasingly aided one another in such matters as currency exchange, debt collection and business forecasting. Intercity partnerships, though still not commonplace, were on the rise. Francis Lewis, a merchant and later a delegate to the First Continental Congress, was only one of a number of men participating in such arrangements. Family ties through intermarriage were becoming more and more customary as well. For example, the powerful DeLancey family of New York had several important marriage links with the formidable Allen family of Philadelphia. Other forms of intercity and interprovincial contact between the affluent classes included travel and recreational pursuits. A number of wealthy denizens from New York and Philadelphia took waters together at such popular resorts as Berkley Warm Springs, Pennsylvania, and Perth Amboy, New Jersey. The sport of kings also attracted sizable numbers of Middle Colonial aristocrats. New Yorkers, especially, were avid racing fans. Racing tracks flourished in New York City, Philadelphia, and in three New Jersey locations: Elizabeth Town, Paulus Hook and Perth Amboy.

Closer ties between New York and Philadelphia also served to align New Jersey more closely with its powerful neighbors. A British nobleman in the 1760's likened Connecticut "to a cask of good liquor tapped at both ends" by the two neighboring provinces.[17] This description is certainly applicable to New Jersey as well, for its economic spirits were sustenance for the New York City and Philadelphia merchants. Both cities established spheres of influence in the areas of New Jersey adjacent to them. In 1774 Governor William Franklin noted the commercial vassalage of his province, "New York and Philadelphia are in Reality the Commercial Capitals of East and West Jersey; and almost all the Articles we import for Home Consumption are from one or other of those cities."[18] Indicative of the economic hegemony exercised by the two cities was the growth stimulus they provided the towns in central New Jersey. The development of Perth Amboy, Elizabeth, New Brunswick, Trenton and Burlington was directly related to their location astride the major overland route between New York and Pennsylvania.[19] Correspondingly, the remarkable expansion in the number of ferries, roads, and turnpikes in New Jersey during the 1750's and 1760's reflected the desire of Jerseymen to encourage the commercial traffic between the two provinces.

Today New Jersey is widely known as the Garden State and the origins of the appellation go back to the eighteenth century. For with the exception of the merchants of Perth Amboy, the prosperous ironmasters of Morris, Bergen and Sussex counties, and a scattered group of traders, New Jersey was a land of farmers. In the 1770's the Reverend John Witherspoon, President of Princeton College, proudly spoke of "New Jersey being generally settled by farmers, with a great equality of rank and even possessions. . . ."[20] Social equality was an attribute in which Jerseymen themselves took pride. Philip Vickers Fithian, a young tutor amidst the Virginia planter-aristocracy in the early 1770's, was surprised by the class consciousness he encountered. In his diary he recalled that well-to-do families in New Jersey freely associated with men of more humble station, and he likened his native province to ancient Sparta, where equality of the citizenry was essential to government and defense.

Contemporary accounts about social equality and an all-pervasive yeoman farmer class must be judged in light of existing social conditions and land distribution in neighboring New York and Pennsylvania. Eighteenth-century probate court and tax records indicate that the East Jersey counties of Morris, Essex, Bergen and Monmouth were inhabited almost entirely by small farmers. Nevertheless, large farms (four

hundred acres or more) were commonplace in the West Jersey
counties of Burlington and Gloucester.[21] Wealth and family
were the general qualifications for officeholding as in the other
Middle Colonies. The landed gentry of New Jersey may have
had good rapport with their less fortunate neighbors, but they
still exercised the privileges that came with their station in
colonial society.

The soil of New Jersey was on the whole less fertile than
that of New York or Pennsylvania although agricultural practices showed no marked differences.[22] Nonetheless, Jersey
farms were moderately productive. In 1748 Governor Jonathan Belcher remarked that "It is the best county I have seen
for men of middling fortunes, and for poor people who have
to live by the sweat of their brows."[23] The principal agricultural
products of the colony were wheat, Indian corn, flour, livestock and flaxseed. New Jersey's major agricultural export was
wheat. For a few years prior to 1750 the colony actually produced more wheat than either New York or Pennsylvania.
Hunterdon County in West Jersey was an especially rich wheat
growing area. New Jersey's only sizable industry grew out of
the discovery of substantial deposits of iron ore in the three
northernmost counties. On the eve of the Revolution New
Jersey was an important producer of pig and bar iron.

A sometimes overlooked feature of colonial New Jersey
was its ethnic diversity. Just prior to the outbreak of the Revolution a little less than half of its 150,000 inhabitants were of
English origin. Slightly more than one-sixth were Scotch-Irish
or Welsh while another sixth were of Dutch origin. Germans
made up a tenth of the population with small groups of Swedes,
French and Finns also represented. Although both East and
West Jersey were roughly equal in population, a larger percentage of the non-English elements were concentrated in East
Jersey. Bergen and Somerset counties were Dutch enclaves,

and German settlers were numerous in Sussex and Hunterdon counties. Scotch-Irish farmers were most prevalent in Morris and Hunterdon counties.

The study of provincial politics in New Jersey has been handicapped by the paucity of historical materials. It was one of the few colonies without a newspaper of its own and would-be polemicists thus never had a medium for their invective. What little evidence there is seems to indicate that New Jersey politics was dictated by numerous factions rather than more regular parties. Religious affiliation, land policy and family ties seem to have often determined assembly alignments. Anglicans, Presbyterians, Quakers and Dutch Reformed all angled for political power in the assembly. On occasion the assembly-men even divided along historic East vs. West lines. Despite unification of the two sections in 1702, complete integration had not been achieved by the early 1770's. The memory of distant clashes and independent decision-making still lingered in the minds of both East and West Jerseymen. In 1774 Governor Franklin informed London that the dual capital arrangement (Burlington and Perth Amboy) ". . . is . . . disadvantageous to the Public, as it keeps up an idle Distinction between the two Parts of the same Province. . . ."[24]

The franchise in New Jersey was limited to freeholders who either possessed one hundred acres of land or fifty pounds of real or personal estate as calculated by the value of provincial monies. Because of the large number of small Jersey farmers the potential size of the electorate was quite large. Nevertheless, the election procedures, coupled with the absence of serious challenges in most elections, dictated small voter turnouts. In West Jersey, especially, initial election often insured virtual life tenure.[25] On occasion, however, controversial county elections brought out the voters in droves. In 1754 almost 700 freeholders cast their ballots for assemblymen in

Middlesex County—a number which just about equaled the
total number of freeholders listed.

In the battle for men's souls colonial New Jersey churches
compiled an excellent record. John Rutherford, a revolutionary
leader, estimated in 1776 that only about 14,000 inhabitants
did not belong to a church. The Presbyterians formed the
largest single denomination with fifty congregations and about
36,000 members. The founding of New Jersey College (later
Princeton) in 1748 contributed substantially to their growth.
The College provided trained ministers and also strengthened
the interprovincial ties with Presbyterians in neighboring
colonies. The Quaker and Dutch Reform churches ranked next
in size with forty and thirty congregations, respectively, and
about 24,000 members each. The Baptists, German Lutherans
and Anglicans all had memberships in the neighborhood of
13,000.[26]

The influence wielded by the various religious groups,
however, was not always in proportion to the size of their
membership. For example, the Anglican church was far more
powerful than its limited membership would admit. For their
part, the Quakers maintained a preponderant influence in
West Jersey despite continued numerical slippage in relation
to the total population.[27] This was the case even after the
termination in 1764 of the biennial rotation of the Quaker
Yearly Meeting between Burlington and Philadelphia.

If New Jersey resembled a cask of liquor tapped at both
ends, Delaware, in comparison was a small keg tapped almost
exclusively by Philadelphia. The ploughmen of Delaware
considered the City of Brotherly Love to be both their cultural
and commercial capital. The only sizable town in the province,
New Castle was ". . . a place of very little consideration;
there are scarcely more than a hundred houses in it, and no
public buildings that deserve to be taken notice of."[28]

In 1774 Delaware was a colony in search of its identity. Legally it became a semi-independent colony in 1701 with the establishment of its own assembly, though still remaining under the executive control of Pennsylvania's governor. In the years immediately following Delaware inquired about securing a royal charter. When it became known that several British noblemen were intent upon securing Delaware as a proprietary grant the interest in a new charter abated quickly. It was deemed better to be lightly bound to the Penn Family without benefit of an official name and separate charter than to gain such trappings at the risk of falling victim to a more demanding executive. Thereafter Delaware retained its shadowy existence down to the Revolution.

The farmers of Delaware produced wheat, Indian corn, assorted grains, and garden vegetables. New Castle County was the earliest to be settled and generally contained larger farms and more wealth than the two lower counties. The aggregate agricultural wealth of New Castle County on the tax assessment lists of the 1780's was two to three times larger than that of Sussex County. The same assessment list indicated that large farms were virtually nonexistent in Sussex.[29] Kent County had fewer wealthy farmers than New Castle but was not as completely dominated by small farmers as its southern neighbor.

The inhabitants of the "three lower counties on the Delaware" (a prevalent reference to Delaware used by contemporaries) were largely of English descent. A sizable minority of Scotch-Irish and small pockets of Dutch, Swedes and Finns comprised the remainder of the population. The Anglican church, though nonestablished, had the greatest number of inhabitants on its rolls. Kent and Sussex counties were centers of Anglican strength. The Presbyterians were second in terms of membership and their stronghold was New Castle County.

Quakers were present in small numbers as were Baptists, Methodists, Lutherans and a few Catholics.

The political life of Delaware was a tangle of religious rivalries, intercounty jealousies and family feuds. During the summer of 1774, the political leaders of Kent and Sussex counties almost balked at joining the movement of an intercolonial congress because of New Castle's preemptive action on this matter. In Kent County Caesar and Thomas Rodney continually had to guard against church politics interfering with the selection of Patriot committees. Though limited in size and wealth, a circle composed of merchants, country gentlemen, clergy and lawyers formed a small upper class in Delaware. Through intermarriage it became a tightly knit society and generally supplied most of the provincial officeholders. In Delaware all fifty-acre freeholders were eligible to vote for their betters.

On the eve of the Revolution the four Middle Colonies possessed a definite community of interest but this fell far short of sectional feeling. A sense of subconscious regionalism was all that bound them together in 1774. The merchants and lawyers of Philadelphia and New York, as well as the landed gentry of New Jersey and Delaware, were just beginning to intuit that in most fields of human endeavor their colonies were quite distinct from both the Southern and New England Colonies. From mid-century on increasing intercolonial contacts stemming from general economic expansion, the development of a nascent leisure class, and improved transportation had fostered a heightened awareness among Americans of their regional differences. Since the primary increase in intercolonial contacts occurred between neighboring colonies, rather than distant ones, the Middle Colonies thus attained an intuitive perception of their common identity.

Given the extreme variation in the size and influence of

the four Central Provinces, there could be no effective regional understanding unless Pennsylvania and New York joined hands. For Delaware was but a tiny appendage of Pennsylvania and New Jersey was dependent upon both the Quaker Colony and New York. This is what happened.

By 1774 it was clear that Pennsylvania and New York were becoming more closely aligned than they had ever been before. The longstanding commercial rivalry between New York City and Philadelphia was giving way to a new spirit of entrepreneurial cooperation. If the thirteen colonies had been allowed to continue as members of the British Empire for a few more decades the Middle Colonies might have developed a conscious sectional outlook by the simple reinforcement of the trends already described. This was not to be, however. Instead, the Middle Colonies made the transition from the first to the second stage of sectional development in two short years from 1774-1776.

chapter
two

AN OCCASION FOR UNITY:

The Intolerable Acts and the First Congress

In 1774 the Middle Colonies were enjoying more wide-spread and sustained prosperity than either of their neighbors to the north or the south. Wheat was the mainstay of their economy and the source of the epithet "The Flour Colonies." Through complementary commercial and industrial development the region was sufficiently diversified to cushion it against economic downturns. Philadelphia and New York were the two largest commercial centers on the continent, and the Middle Colonies were the colonial leaders in the production of iron and the milling of flour. During the years from 1764-1775 greater world demand for grain and flour helped to maintain the prosperity of the Middle Colonies.[1] A succession of poor harvests in England led Parliament to alter the Corn Laws in 1766, to permit the duty-free importation of grain from the colonies. In addition, European grain shortages during the late 1760's occasioned more demand for grain from "The Flour Colonies."[2]

In the midst of prosperity, Middle Colonial leaders tended to be less receptive than their counterparts in the other sections to measures and actions that could threaten their economic position within the Empire.[3] Prosperity alone, however, did not dictate cautious behavior. A deeper, more intangible feeling was at work. The Middle Colonial leaders were beginning to sense that the Empire favored their interests more than the other two sections. The wealthy business classes in New York City and Philadelphia, especially, were certain that they would be the heirs of the Empire when the colonies eventually passed into manhood.[4] This nabob mentality also affected many prominent political leaders such as John Dickinson and Joseph Galloway of Pennsylvania, James Duane of New York, William Livingston of New Jersey and George Read of Delaware. "If I am an *Enthusiast* in any thing," wrote John Dickinson in 1767, "it is in my zeal for the *perpetual* dependence of these colonies on their mother country. . . ."[5] But lest Britain become too complacent about American goodwill, Dickinson warned at the same time that

Fifty or Sixty years will make astonishing alterations in these Colonies, and this consideration should render it the business of Great Britain more and more to cultivate our good dispositions towards her.[6]

Years later when William Livingston looked back on the American Revolution he recalled how difficult it had been for the Middle Colonies to cut their ties with the Empire for

They had themselves suffered little, if at all, from the English government. Under it they had prospered and multiplied. It required of this part of the people great intrepidity, wisdom, and generosity to join their cause with men already stigmatized as rebels.[7]

General prosperity coupled with a deeper sense of loyalty to the Empire had kept the Middle Colonies from being fervent supporters of the various protest measures during the first decade of the Anglo-American dispute. As long as the intercolonial association continued to be very informal and the running feud with Britain did not reach crisis proportions,

the individual Central Provinces were able to keep their support to a minimum. The more zealous Patriot leaders both in
New England and the South lacked a channel and the issues
to pressure them into taking a more decisive part. The precipitous withdrawal of New York City and then Philadelphia
from the anti-Townshend Act boycott in the summer of 1770
well illustrates the freedom of action that the individual
Middle Colonies had enjoyed. During the winter and spring
of 1773-1774 the actions of a handful of Massachusetts radicals and British ministers changed all this. Confronted with
a major crisis in the British "Intolerable Acts" the colonies
drew together for council. The Middle Colonial leaders may
not have realized it at first, but, with the meeting of the First
Continental Congress, the autonomy they previously enjoyed
would soon be sharply restricted.

The Boston Tea Party on the night of December 21, 1773
was the most brazen of the colonial attempts to foil the Tea
Act. The participants felt justified because they viewed the
Tea Act of 1773 as a thinly veiled attempt to secure American
admission of the right of Parliamentary taxation. Fear of
British-sponsored monopolies, because of the special market-
ing concessions accorded the agents of the East India Company, and the machinations of unemployed tea smugglers also
fostered opposition. Philadelphia, though not previously noted
for its forwardness, actually initiated the tea resistance movement in the fall of 1773. In November, the popular leaders of
the city summarily ordered the tea ship *Polly* to return to
England with its entire cargo. At New York City a clash over
the Tea Act was delayed until April, 1774, when the first tea
ships finally arrived. On April 22, the sons of liberty staged a
tea party after Captain James Chambers of the tea ship *London*
admitted that he lied about the presence of dutied tea on his
vessel.

In the spring of 1774 the colonists waited for the British response to their actions. Reports received from England in March and April were encouraging. The ministry apparently was not contemplating any harsh retaliatory measures. The news that Parliament had approved the draconian Boston Port Act caught the colonists by surprise. Some men were quick to perceive that equally onerous penalties could be directed against any American colony in the future. A New York essayist reminded his readers that coquets of tea graced the bottom of their harbor as well and Philadelphia also had obstructed the Tea Act. John Dickinson, who had won intercolonial acclaim in 1767-68 for his writings as a "Pennsylvania Farmer," again took up his pen. In the first of four letters addressed to the inhabitants of Pennsylvania, Dickinson took the view that the Boston Port Act represented the culmination of the British design to enslave the colonies. Since 1763,

. . . a plan has been deliberately framed, and pertinasciously adhered to, unchanged even by frequent changes of Ministers, unchecked by an intervening gleam of humanity, to sacrifice to a passion for arbitrary dominion the universal property, liberty, safety, honor, happiness and prosperity of us unoffending, yet devoted Americans.[8]

The arrival in late May of Lord North's speech in support of the Boston Port Bill left no doubt that the people of Boston would not be treated lightly. In his speech he had informed Parliament that inhabitants of Massachusetts, and especially Boston, were wayward dependents and it was time to take remedial action. Lord North admitted that he hoped military measures would not be needed to convince them to obey Parliament, but should it come to that he would not hesitate to use the armed might of Britain. He closed by righteously declaring, "If the consequences of their not obeying this act are likely to produce rebellion that consequence belongs to them, not us. . . ."[9]

On May 12, 1774, several days after receipt of the news
of the Boston Port Act, the Boston committee of correspondence met to determine what action should be taken. A circular
letter drafted by Sam Adams was quickly approved and
dispatched to all the colonies. The letter explained the provisions of the Boston Port Act and asked the colonies to support Boston by stopping all trade with Great Britain. Sam
Adams, Joseph Warren and other radical Whig leaders in
Boston realized that support from Philadelphia and New York
was essential to their plans. They no doubt were aware that
many merchants and political leaders in these two cities harbored strongly antipathetic views towards New Englanders in
general. It would not be until the meeting of the First Continental Congress, however, that the New England radicals
would fully comprehend how common such views were among
both Southern and Middle Colonial representatives. In the
meantime, Sam Adams and Joseph Warren urged radical
Whigs like Charles Thomson and Thomas Mifflin in Philadelphia and Alexander McDougall and Isaac Sears in New York
to push for acceptance of nonimportation.[10]

In New York and Pennsylvania the contests to determine
the nature of the response to Britain's acts and Boston's appeal
were long and arduous. The DeLancey faction in New York,
with support from the merchant community and a handful of
the more conservative Livingston faction members, was strongly opposed to any expression of support for Boston.[11] At a
meeting of the city merchants on May 16, this group secured
the nomination of a majority of conservatives and moderates
to a proposed fifty-member committee of correspondence. In
protest Alexander McDougall and Isaac Sears, the radical
leaders of the popular wing of the Livingston faction, established a committee of mechanics and nominated a rival slate
of candidates. On May 19, the radical and conservative groups

confronted one another at a popular meeting called to select
the members of the committee of fifty. The DeLancey faction,
led by Isaac Low who chaired the meeting, garnered enough
votes to elect their entire slate as well as one extra nominee.
Lieutenant Governor Cadwallader Colden noted that the committee of fifty-one,

. . . have a number of the most prudent persons of the Place . . .
in what they are sensible is an illegal Character, from a consideration that if they did not the Business would be left in the
same rash hands as before.[12]

Four days after the election the new committee met to
consider what response should be given to the Boston letter.
The conservative majority on the committee of fifty-one
quickly saw to it that Boston's appeal for an antitrade boycott
was sidetracked and a meaningless expression of support
adopted in its place. Before adjourning the committee also approved a resolution calling for a general intercolonial congress.
The adoption of this proposal by the committee of fifty-one
was doubtless intended to put off consideration of a nonimportation agreement by shifting final responsibility to an intercolonial body.

Although the DeLancey faction dictated New York's response to Boston's plight, another struggle loomed over the
question of who should represent the colony at the general
congress and under what instructions they should act. During
the month of July the committee of fifty-one and the committee
of mechanics clashed over these issues. On July 6, a mass rally
engineered by McDougall and his lieutenants gave enthusiastic
support to proposals for a trade boycott, a provincial congress
and a free hand for the congressional delegation.[13] The committee of fifty-one countered by censuring the mass meeting
as an insidious attempt to undermine its authority. McDougall
and ten other members of the committee resigned in protest the

next day. When the DeLancey faction found itself unable to muster enough votes to elect its congressional slate at an outdoor meeting on July 19, an impasse ensued. In order to break the deadlock over the selection of New York City delegates to the general congress, the committee of fifty-one reluctantly agreed to the city-wide election plan proposed by the mechanics. Although the five candidates originally put forward by the committee of fifty-one (Philip Livingston, John Alsop, Isaac Low, James Duane, and John Jay) were elected, four of these men under public pressure pledged their support for a nonimportation agreement should Congress take up the matter.

In essence New York's response to the "Intolerable Acts" was almost entirely determined by New York City. Early in June the committee of fifty-one had sent a letter to all the counties in the province urging the creation of committees of correspondence. The conservative members of the committee were hopeful that the agrarians would aid them in their struggle with the city radicals. To their surprise and disappointment only scattered townships in Suffolk, Orange and Cumberland counties took any action. To make matters worse these rural gatherings generally favored immediate stoppage of trade. The response of the counties to the committee of fifty-one's second letter, late in July, was also disappointing. Only Kings, Orange and Suffolk counties bothered to elect their own delegates to serve in the First Continental Congress. Albany, Westchester, Dutchess and Ulster all endorsed the New York City delegation while six counties made no reply.

In Pennsylvania the contest to determine that colony's response to Boston's plight also provoked an intense radical–conservative struggle. Most of the merchants, Quakers, Anglicans and Proprietary partisans joined hands in Philadelphia to prevent the radicals from aligning the province with Boston.

Thomas Wharton, a wealthy Philadelphia merchant, admitted to his brother that he abandoned his usual aloofness from politics and agreed to serve on the committee of correspondence only ". . . to keep the transactions of our city within the limits of moderation and not indecent or offensive to our parent state."[14] Charles Thomson and Thomas Mifflin led the mechanics and sons of liberty who favored an immediate trade stoppage as recommended by the Boston circular letter. Working in concert with this group were moderate men like John Dickinson, Joseph Reed and Thomas Willing. They allied themselves with the radicals and engaged in popular politics because this seemed the only way to pressure the conservative-dominated assembly headed by Joseph Galloway into adopting supportive measures for Boston.

That John Dickinson and Joseph Galloway should be heading opposing parties was only fitting. Almost from the moment that Dickinson entered Pennsylvania politics he found himself arrayed against Galloway. Both men were wealthy lawyers and landowners, but in the political arena they were inveterate foes. Dickinson never outgrew his early Quaker training even after three years of study at the Inns of Court and the amassing of an immense personal fortune. In politics as in life Dickinson always sought the middle way. Galloway, in contrast, was a man who thrived on strife. The positions that both men assumed during the Stamp Act crisis set the stage for their struggle in 1774. While the riots and street politics had aroused Galloway's aristocratic ire, Dickinson used his pen to support the Patriots. Thus in 1774 the two men were studies in contrast. Galloway was the hardbitten, Tory-tinged political boss of Pennsylvania. Dickinson, though a lesser light in provincial politics, was the most respected Whig spokesman in all the colonies.

On May 20 the merchants and politicians met at the City

Tavern to decide on a response to the Boston letter. Adroit maneuvering by Thomson, Mifflin and Dickinson resulted in the acceptance of the resolves put forward by the radical–moderate coalition, which tendered full support to Boston. The conservatives, however, managed to have Dr. William Smith draft the official letter from the Philadelphia committee to Boston. It urged that petitions be sent to England before any other measures were adopted and implied that the Boston Tea Party was a bit of misguided zeal.

Disgruntled by this minor trickery the radicals promoted a mass meeting before the State House on June 8. Letters from the New York committee of mechanics were read and a similar committee established to offer alternate proposals to the merchant-dominated city committee. The newly formed committee of mechanics urged relief measures for the inhabitants of Boston and the formation of a more representative committee of correspondence. They also called upon the speaker of the assembly, Joseph Galloway, to summon a special session in order to select the delegates to the general congress.

On June 18 upwards of 8,000 inhabitants gathered to consider the resolves of the committee of mechanics. The crowd gave strong endorsement to the major resolutions of the mechanics and voted in a new committee of correspondence with a distinct radical flavor. To the consternation of the conservatives the meeting also voted to entrust the committee of correspondence with the authority to determine the manner in which Pennsylvania's delegation to congress would be selected. Several days later the new committee dispatched a letter to the counties calling upon them to send delegates to a provincial convention which would select and instruct the delegates to the general congress. The conservatives suddenly realized that they had misjudged the temper of the province. Governor John Penn's assessment of the situation expressed this view:

The general Temper of the People, as well here, as in other Parts of America, is very warm. They look upon the Chastizement of Boston to be purposely vigorous, and held up by way of intimidation to all America; and in short that Boston is Suffering in the *Common Cause*.[15]

Galloway apparently shared the Governor's concern for the assembly convened in mid-July to ride herd on the provincial convention.

Unlike New York all the counties in Pennsylvania, including the frontier outposts of Bedford and Northampton, responded to the Philadelphia committee's call to form committees of correspondence and select delegates to the provincial convention. On July 15 delegates from all eleven counties began their work by selecting Thomas Willing as chairman. Adhering to proposals drafted by John Dickinson, they affirmed their allegiance to King George III and disavowed any desire for independence. A majority of the delegates favored a petition to the King listing American grievances as the first step that should be taken by the general congress. The congressional delegation was to concur in a trade boycott if a majority of the colonies in congress favored such a measure.

A committee from the convention presented these resolves to the assembly on July 19. In short order the conservative-dominated assembly set aside the resolves of the convention. Likewise, they selected seven of their own members (Samuel Rhoads, Thomas Mifflin, Charles Humphreys, George Ross, Edward Biddle, John Morton and Joseph Galloway) to represent the colony in congress.[16] The instructions for the delegates were penned by Galloway. The Pennsylvania delegation was to enter into general discussions with the other representatives about the nature of the Anglo-American dispute and specifically to

exert your utmost Endeavours to form and adopt a Plan, which shall afford the best Prospect of obtaining a Redress of American

Grievances, ascertaining American Rights, and establishing that Union and Harmony which is most essential to the Welfare and Happiness of both Countries. And in so doing this, you are strictly charged to avoid every Thing Indecent or disrespectful to the Mother State.[17]

The success of the assembly's preemptive action was primarily owing to the acquiescence of moderates like Dickinson. Rather than embroil the colony in another round of mass meetings and popular referenda that might seriously undermine the legal government of the province, they chose to allow the largely conservative delegation to proceed unmolested to the general congress. Without support from the moderates the radicals were unable to carry on the fight.

Although it had taken almost all summer the conservative forces in New York and Pennsylvania had come up with safe delegations to the First Continental Congress. Even Lieutenant Governor Colden was not displeased with the outcome. "Our Delegates to the Congress, at least the major Part of them are moderate Men . . ." he observed, and ". . . Scott, McDougall, Sears and Lamb are all in disgrace. . . ."[18] He also took solace from the reports that the affairs of Pennsylvania were in the hands of sensible men as well.

In both New Jersey and Delaware the absence of sizable merchant communities made for less acrimonious proceedings during the summer of 1774. Without a strong mercantile interest to consider, the farmers in both provinces were quick to advocate a vigorous nonimportation agreement. Essex County in East Jersey was the first area in the province to take action on the Boston circular letter. On June 11, a county-wide meeting endorsed resolutions calling for a boycott and the establishment of a general congress. In quick succession Bergen, Middlesex, Sussex and Monmouth in East Jersey adopted similar measures. The alacrity with which the East Jersey counties responded to Boston's call evoked favorable comment outside the province. A Boston correspondent informed his friend in New York that "New Jersey is very forward, and are on the point of choosing their deputies for the Congress. . . ."[19]

On July 21 the New Jersey provincial congress convened at New Brunswick with seventy-two delegates representing all fourteen counties.[20] Stephen Crane of Essex County was selected to chair the congress. In the two days of sessions eight resolves were adopted *nemni contra dicente*. The congress disavowed any desire for independence, endorsed the trade boycott, and extended thanks to America's champions in Parliament. James Kinsey, John De Hart, Stephen Crane, William Livingston and Richard Smith (the latter three from Essex County) were selected to represent the colony in Philadelphia. Although the ideological temper of the New Jersey delegation was not immediately discernible, all the men proved themselves to be of more moderate sentiments than the delegates from either Pennsylvania or New York.

As in New Jersey, Delaware's first response to the Boston letter originated in a Whig stronghold. On June 22 "A Freeman" exhorted the inhabitants of New Castle County to take up the cudgels against the British. Recalling the past exertions in behalf of freedom he asked,

Shall the people of this large and wealthy county, heretofore the foremost on many occasions particularly in the time of the detestable Stamp Act to oppose all attempts to deprive them of their personal security and private property, be now inactive and silent?[21]

A county-wide meeting held at New Castle Court House on June 29, brought out a crowd of 500 freeholders to decide what action should be taken. With Thomas McKean in the chair the meeting resolved that the Boston Port Act was unconstitutional and that the speaker of the assembly should

call a special session of the assembly. This last resolution was
apparently the result of Governor Penn's initial disinclination
to convene the Pennsylvania assembly.

New Castle's assumption of leadership alarmed the Sussex
County political leaders. The rift was so serious that Caesar
Rodney and the Kent County committee of correspondence
had to intervene as mediators. They urged the Sussex committee to overlook

. . . the Unreasonableness and impropriety of the New Castle
People on this Occasion, in undertaking to dictate to You and us
a mode of conduct Convenient to themselves but very incon-
venient to us. . . .[22]

Their efforts evidently bore fruit, for on July 23 the Sussex
committee informed the Kent committee that given the need
for action, not delay, they would go along with the site and
date as arranged by New Castle.

On August 2, two weeks after the Pennsylvania assembly
adopted its resolves, the Delaware convention met at New
Castle. A list of grievances was prepared which included the
British regulations against colonial manufacturing and the
capricious operation of the local customs house. A moderate
delegation on balance, composed of Thomas McKean and
George Read of New Castle County and Caesar Rodney of
Kent County, was selected "to consult and advise with the
deputies from the other colonies, and to determine upon all
such prudent and lawful measures . . ." to end the "unnatural"
dispute.[23]

As the delegates began arriving in Philadelphia the city
took on a new character. According to William Bradford, Jr.,
their presence made Philadelphia ". . . another Cairo; with
this difference that the one is a city swarming with Merchants
and the other with politicians and statesmen."[24] For the men
who were to determine the nature and extent of the American

opposition to British measures were almost without exception political leaders in their respective provinces. Ten of the delegates were former assembly speakers and another nine had served in the Stamp Act Congress in 1765. They came to Philadelphia, as one essayist described it, knowing that "The weal of America, yea of Britain, too, will very much depend upon their proceedings."[25] It seemed certain that Congress would draft a petition to the King but beyond that only speculation held sway. Would Congress approve a nonimportation, nonexportation agreement? Would it propose a permanent intercolonial organization to protect American rights? These were some of the questions that colonists from the rice paddies of South Carolina to the White Mountains of New Hampshire were asking one another.

Even before all the congressmen were assembled in the City of Brotherly Love, some of the delegates began to take the measure of their colleagues. The Massachusetts delegation led by John and Sam Adams made good use of their travel time. They took political soundings in Connecticut, New York and New Jersey as they journeyed southward to Philadelphia. Arriving on the 29th of August the Adamses immediately began to canvas the delegates already in the city. Great urgency marked their efforts for they had come to Philadelphia for help. Massachusetts, even with the support of the other New England Colonies, could not hope to stand up to Britain for very long. But in order to secure the desired assistance from Congress the New England representatives first had to allay the ancient prejudices against them. Even if they accomplished this they still had to convince the Southern and Middle Colonial delegates that they did not favor either a military solution nor the creation of an independent state as was rumored.

The New Jersey delegation was the first of the Middle

Colonial contingents to arrive and the New England representatives immediately endeavored to determine their sentiments. "I had not, sir, been in Congress a fortnight before I discovered that parties were forming," was how William Livingston described the reception accorded the New Jersey delegates.[26] Two days before Congress held its first session Silas Deane of Connecticut confidently informed his wife, "We spent this day in visiting those that are in town, and find them in high spirits, particularly the gentlemen from the Jerseys and South Carolina."[27]

The New England delegates were not the only ones who jockeyed for position while the delegates were gathering in Philadelphia. Joseph Galloway's mansion was the scene of many lavish dinner parties. For he was determined that Congress should adopt a plan (preferably his) that would permanently resolve the Anglo-American dispute by creating an imperial legislature based on a written constitution. As Galloway fraternized with the delegates he noted that the Massachusetts men were working hard to change their image. "They are in their Behavior and conversation very modest," Galloway observed, "and yet they are not so much as not to throw out Hints, which like Straws and Feathers, tell us from which Point of the Compass the Wind comes."[28] He was still optimistic, however, that Congress would reject the intemperate measures which the New England radicals were advocating.

The last minute arrival of the New York and Delaware delegations precluded their participation in these "sounding-out" proceedings. Nevertheless, the Massachusetts delegates knew from their brief stopover in New York what to expect from the Yorker contingent. In John Adams's opinion Isaac Low and James Duane were untrustworthy, Philip Livingston was a New England phobe, John Alsop fainthearted and John Jay untried.[29]

On September 5 the Continental Congress held an informal preliminary session at the City Tavern to decide upon a regular meeting place and to select a secretary. Although the agenda was devoid of substantive items, the division in the house that day gave a foretaste of the political alignments that would hold true for the entire seven weeks that Congress would be in session. Galloway, as speaker of the Pennsylvania assembly, invited the delegates to use the State House for their deliberations. But when the Carpenter's Association proffered their newly completed hall, Congress decided to defer judgment until they had inspected both buildings. Upon visiting Carpenter's Hall the members were ostensibly so taken with the layout and furnishings that they voted at once to make this their official meeting place despite the opposition of the Pennsylvania and New York delegations. In selecting a secretary Congress again went against the wishes of Joseph Galloway by appointing Charles Thomson, a well-known local radical. After reflecting on these two setbacks Galloway concluded that "Both of these measures, it seems, were privately settled by an interest made out of Doors."[30] He suspected, and rightly so, that John Dickinson's Whig coalition had taken a hand to embarrass his faction in Congress. In the days and weeks ahead Galloway was to find his position in Congress continually upstaged by Dickinson and his cohorts.

Even more disturbing to Galloway, however, was the absence of support from the Southern delegations as well as the New Jersey and Delaware contingents. If these congressmen would not support the New York–Pennsylvania faction on minor matters they would not be in the right column on major issues either. In a moment of despair Galloway admitted that "The Gentlemen from New York have as little Expectation of much Satisfaction from the Event of Things as myself."[31]

The Galloway–Duane clique was just recovering from its first-day setbacks when it suffered another debilitating blow. Shortly before termination of the day's session on September 6, Congress was thrown into an uproar by a report that the British were bombarding Boston. John Adams was elated by the courageous response that this news evoked for "War! War! War! was the cry . . . if it proved true, you would have heard the Thunder of an American Congress."[32] Three days later the report was proven false and Congress resumed its deliberations in a less frenzied atmosphere. The war scare was over but it left a lasting impression on the delegates, especially Messrs. Duane and Galloway.

The bellicose attitude of many congressmen and their apparent willingness to take up arms to defend Boston came as a shock to Galloway. It shattered his initial sanguinity about the predominantly moderate temper of the delegates. Galloway apparently had predicated his earlier optimism on the two-fold assumption that the prejudice of the Middle and Southern Colonies toward New England and their common desire to prevent relations with the mother country from deteriorating further would preclude acceptance of rash measures. On both counts he miscalculated. Although many of the Southern and Middle Colonial congressmen were suspicious and distrustful of the so-called "Eastern Provinces," the depth of their phobia was insufficient to Galloway's purpose.[33] For most of the Southern delegates did not allow their jaundiced view of New England to blind them to the seriousness of the British threat. In the weeks ahead the Southern representatives consistently voted with the Eastern delegates. After the First Congress had concluded its labors Lieutenant Governor Colden observed that almost from the opening session the New York–Pennsylvania faction was in the minority:

How Amazing is it my Lord the Congress should prefer a Method big with Wickedness, Extravagance and Absurdity. The Delegates from Virginia were most violent of any—Those of Maryland and some of the Carolinians were little less so—These Southern Gentlemen exceeded even the New England Delegates. They together made a Majority that the Others could have very little Effect upon.[34]

In the absence of any voting records for the First Congress, it is even more difficult to ascertain how the Delaware and New Jersey delegations positioned themselves. According to Joseph Reed, a Pennsylvania Whig leader, the Galloway–Duane interest was consistently outvoted in Congress by a ten to two margin.[35] It seems improbable, however, that the delegates from New Jersey and Delaware were as consistently opposed to the New York–Pennsylvania faction as Reed suggests. But even assuming that the New Jersey and Delaware congressmen offered intermittent support, their refusal to form a sectional party with New York and Pennsylvania is indicative of Galloway's shortcomings and Dickinson's influence "out of Doors." For the delegates from New Jersey and Delaware did not take kindly to either Galloway's aristocratic demeanor or his heavy-handed attempts to corral their votes. Galloway's personal influence was weakened further by his reputed Tory leanings. Dickinson, in contrast, possessed both the personal touch and stature that Galloway lacked. Until his election to the First Congress on October 14, he actively worked to thwart the Galloway–Duane clique. It was to this shadow delegation headed by John Dickinson that the New Jersey and Delaware delegates looked for leadership.

Although Galloway was chagrined by the political power that the radicals had displayed in the early days in Congress, he was still determined to thwart their plans. In order to defeat them, however, it was imperative that Congress take up his plan of union before the New England delegates were able to force through provocative anti-British measures. But Gallo-

way and Duane were unable to secure immediate consideration of the plan of union because the radicals first saw to it
that Congress took a stand on the question of the legitimacy of
forceful resistance to Britain's recent acts.

This question was embodied in the resolutions of Suffolk
County, Massachusetts, which were taken up by Congress on
September 17. In the preface to the resolves the Suffolk men
boldly declared:

If a boundless extent of continent, swarming with millions, will
tamely submit to live, move, and have their being at the arbitrary
will of a licentious minister, they basely yield to voluntary slavery,
and future generations shall load their memories with incessant
execrations.[36]

They resolved that no compliance was owed any of the "Intolerable Acts," that a complete halt to all trade with Britain
should be immediately initiated, and that a citizens' militia
should be formed to protect the popular leaders from arrest
and the populace from coercion by the British Army. Coming
on the heels of the war scare, the "Suffolk Resolves" were
unanimously endorsed by Congress. With this decision the
program of the radicals seemed certain of winning confirmation. The significance of this endorsement was not lost upon
conservatives both in and out of Congress. The Reverend
Charles Inglis of New York, an Anglican minister, viewed
this action as tantamount to a declaration of open rebellion.
"I once had considerable Expectations from Congress," Inglis
admitted, "but since they adopted the fiery Resolves of Suffolk
in Massachusetts almost all hope of good from them vanished."[37]

In a desperate bid to bring about a volte-face, Galloway
and Duane suddenly introduced the former's plan of union
on September 28. Congress was in the midst of debating nonimportation and the radicals were caught looking the other

way. Galloway began his presentation by asserting that the record of the Congress to date was a constant reminder of how far the delegates had wandered from their instructions. Instead of considering a plan to restore harmonious relations with the mother country, measures were being adopted "which tended to inflame rather than reconcile—to produce war instead of peace between the two countries."[38] Galloway proceeded to excoriate the delegates for their failure to recognize the untold advantages which membership in the Empire had showered upon them. If Congress wished to involve the provinces in a bloody civil war, then a nonimportation, nonexportation agreement, coupled with open contempt for Parliament, were the proper tactics. If, however, they desired reunion with the mother country and protection of their rights, then his plan of union was the answer. Galloway's plan called for the establishment of a British–American legislature. A president-general selected by the King was to preside over the grand council made up of representatives from all the colonies. This intercolonial government was to be entrusted with all matters relating to the colonies in general and between two or more colonies. The grand council, the president-general and the British Parliament would be authorized to initiate and veto legislation. The debate over Galloway's plan was quite rancorous. The radicals were unable to advance any conclusive arguments against the plan, but at the close of the day's session they managed to have the whole matter shelved for future consideration by a vote of six colonies to five, with Rhode Island divided.[39] No record can be found of how the individual delegations were aligned, but it is safe to conclude that on this question New Jersey and Delaware voted with the Galloway–Duane clique. While they did not as yet fully share Galloway's apprehension about the measures which the New England delegates were advocating, neither could they bring themselves to reject a peace plan, even if it did bear Galloway's stamp.

After Galloway's plan of union was sidetracked the New York–Pennsylvania faction never managed to mount any serious challenges to the radical contingent. Early in October a sequel to the Suffolk Resolves pointed up this state of affairs. On October 6 the much traveled Paul Revere appeared at the door of Congress with a letter from the inhabitants of Boston. They informed Congress that British fortification of Boston made them apprehensive that open warfare might soon erupt. What course of action would Congress recommend if it came to that? For two days Congress deliberated in search of a proper response. On October 8 a resolution approving the use of force by the citizens of Boston in the event of a British attack was approved. During the debates on this resolution Galloway and George Ross of Pennsylvania moved that Congress leave Massachusetts to its own plight, but their motion was quickly rejected. In disgust over the passage of this resolution Galloway and Duane exchanged certified statements indicating their opposition to this open invitation to rebellion. Galloway even considered walking out of Congress in protest, but Duane dissuaded him.

The congressional consensus on the advisability of a nonimportation, nonexportation agreement did not preclude some of the delegates from seeking to shape the plan in ways that were least harmful to their individual provinces or sections.[40] The Virginia delegation was adamant about postponing the start of nonexportation until the fall of 1775 so that the planters could get their 1774 tobacco crop to market. Maryland and North Carolina lent their voices to this demand and they carried their point. The South Carolina delegates felt justified in pushing for special concessions for rice and indigo since the livelihood of their province was solely dependent on these two products. In presenting their case they argued that "The Flour Colonies" would reap untold benefit from non-exportation because their foodstuffs could be marketed in Southern Europe and the French West Indies.[41] Four of the five South Carolina delegates stayed away from Congress to dramatize their demands; only Christopher Gadsden remained in his seat. The South Carolina delegation finally accepted half a loaf. Indigo was placed on the nonexportation list, but rice was left off.

The Continental Association, adopted on October 20, was the agreement that spelled out the provisions of nonimportation, nonconsumption and nonexportation and that established the means for enforcement and review. December 1, 1774 was the date set for implementation of nonimportation. The nonconsumption phase, which was to supplement the former by prohibiting usage of British products in order to hold down smuggling, was to go into effect on March 1, 1775. The final phase of the boycott, nonexportation, was set to begin on September 10, 1775. Enforcement of the Association was relegated to local committees on the county, city and township levels. Overall, the Association was more than just an instrument to apply economic pressure on Britain. Under its aegis certain colonials were authorized to exercise complete control over the economic life of their neighbors and kinsmen. It was in essence the first appropriation of sovereign rights from the regular colonial governments to the resistance movement.

On October 26 the First Continental Congress adjourned. Most of the delegates from New England and the South left Philadelphia satisfied that Congress had struck a blow for freedom, at the same time displaying the indivisible unity of America. Most of the supporters of Joseph Galloway went away with a different impression. They had come to Philadelphia in hopes that Congress, by means of temperate conduct, could assuage the wrath of Britain and prepare the ground for a peaceful and lasting settlement. Instead the First Continental Congress had adopted a policy of brinkmanship that seemed destined to further estrange Britain and the thirteen colonies. With the Second Congress already scheduled for May, Galloway was convinced that if the price for continued intercolonial solidarity was steadily worsening relations with the mother country and a minority voice in Philadelphia, then the individual Middle Colonies should come to terms with Britain of their own accord.

In contrast, more moderate Whigs like John Dickinson, William Livingston and Caesar Rodney were well satisfied with the work of the First Congress. "A determined and unanimous resolution animates this Continent," declared Dickinson, "firmly and faithfully to support the Common Cause to the utmost extremity, in this great struggle for the blessing of liberty. . . ."[42] Although these men were just as cognizant as the conservative Whigs of the favorable position which the Middle Colonies occupied within the Empire, they were not yet convinced that the Eastern Colonies intended to disrupt the Empire for their own sectional advantage.[43] While the First Congress had not proven to be an occasion for unity for the Central Provinces, in the months ahead John Dickinson was destined to become the architect of sectional accord.

chapter three

CAUTIOUS UNIONISTS:

From the First Congress to Lexington

With the adjournment of the First Congress the attention of the Whig leaders shifted from Philadelphia to the thirteen provinces and across the ocean to London. The reception to be accorded the congressional resolves at home and abroad would dictate the future shape of the Anglo-American dispute. The congressional radicals were very concerned about the Middle Colonies. The obvious dissatisfaction of certain key men in the New York and Pennsylvania delegations with the congressional proceedings might very well lead them to work against continued association with the other colonies. Even before the adjournment of Congress a report was received from William Lee, a transplanted Virginia lawyer in London, that the ministry was hopeful that it could sabotage colonial unity by detaching New York and Pennsylvania from the continental union.[1] Colonial disunity was considered by Whigs of all shades to be the most dangerous threat to the success of the American protest movement. If Britain could detach a colony or two by whatever means the movement would be lost. Men like John Dickinson and John Adams, who were serious students of history, knew all too well the fate of re-

51

bellious states who fought for freedom with their own houses in disarray. Until the British response was known, argued Dickinson, "The great Point, *at present,* is to keep up the appearance of an unbroken Harmony in public measures, for fear of encouraging Great Britain to Hostilities, which, otherwise she would avoid."[2]

The decision by the First Congress to adopt a hard-line, anti-British policy precipitated the first crisis of state and individual allegiance. Since the Whigs made participation in their program mandatory for all colonists, citizens in disagreement were either forced to suppress their dissent or actively work for the overthrow of the Whigs. The Tories thus became an opposition but hardly a party. Their resistance efforts were almost always localized and sporadic. Interprovincial coordination never developed because Tory groups within the individual colonies scarcely ever cooperated with one another. The men who became Tories were not simply Anglophiles and placemen but often colonists who held membership in the Empire dearer than all else. They favored reason over force and refused to surrender their faith in the fairness of British leaders and institutions. From November, 1774, through March, 1775, Tory pamphleteers worked furiously to convince their fellow Americans to desist from supporting the congressional program. At the same time, Tory representatives in the Middle Colonies also pressed valiantly to have their respective assemblies reject the congressional proceedings and seek redress through direct appeals to the Crown.

The contests in the Central Provinces during the winter months over ratification and implementation of the congressional resolves were waged against a backdrop of confusing reports from London. It was not until April that the colonists learned what the true British reaction was to the congressional program. During this five-month period Americans in the

Middle Colonies vacillated between hope and fear.

Late in October a London correspondent informed New Yorkers,

that the Ministry are so much embarrassed by the firmness of the Bostonians, that they are much divided in opinion about future measures: some are for making a retreat . . . others breathe fire and sword. . . .[3]

Another London reporter alluded to a persistent rumor in the city that Parliament was preparing to repeal the Quebec Act and the King was attempting to secure a new ministry headed by Lord Chatham.[4] Later the same month Thomas Wharton of Philadelphia observed that all the inhabitants of the city were anxiously awaiting the December mail packet:

as we think some judgement may then be found of what [is] to be the fate of these colonies; deep and gloomy are our prospects, and the considerate part of the inhabitants greatly fear our happy days have departed us. . . .[5]

The month of February witnessed a continuation of the confusion about British intentions. The King's speech to Parliament from the throne on December 1, 1774, seemed to indicate that Britain might well prefer coercion to negotiation. King George III expressed grave concern about the treasonous conduct of Massachusetts and the fact that

These proceedings have been countenanced and encouraged in other of my colonies, and unwarrantable Attempts have been made to obstruct the commerce of this kingdom, by unlawful combinations.[6]

He assured Parliament that he would work tirelessly to enforce the recent acts relating to the colonies and resist any attempts to contravene its supreme authority. The King's speech evoked concern among some colonists and brought forth a torrent of angry words from others. But the Lords' Protest against the speech served to dispel the darker implications of the address.

It was very unusual for a division to occur in the House of Lords over a speech from the throne and this clearly indicated that the colonists were not without support in the upper chamber.[7] Towards the end of the month John Dickinson received word from William Lee that the ministry was on the verge of repealing some of the odious acts as a ploy to break apart colonial unity. "If there ever will be a time when union & steadiness can be useful to America; tis now;" concluded Lee, "prepare for War, that you may not be taken unprovided; but I am thoroughly convinced ye non-exportation plan carried into execution will fully settle the business for you next session of Parliament."[8]

In March, colonists in the Central Provinces rejoiced upon learning of the favorable reception accorded the congressional petition to the King and Lord Chatham's January 20th speech in Parliament.[9] The great war leader appealed to Parliament to put out the righteous flames of American discontent by withdrawing the troops and making necessary concessions. "I will not say," Chatham intoned, ". . . if the Ministers persevere in thus misadvising and misleading the king, that they can alienate the affections of his subjects from his Crown, but I will affirm, that, the American jewel out of it, they will make the crown not worth wearing."[10] Reflecting on the general satisfaction in the Middle Colonies, Thomas Rodney of Delaware concluded, "This news will greatly tend to silence that Spirit of opposition (which had hitherto existed in a few factious bosoms) to the united and patriotic measures of the colonies."[11]

In view of the six to eight weeks that it normally took for letters and communiqués to travel across the ocean, the ministry was not guilty of procrastination in formulating its response to the American challenge. Admittedly, however, the unified front displayed by the colonies and General Thomas

Gage's frenzied appeals for more troops and new instructions did call for very careful consideration of all the alternatives. Nevertheless, the ministry was convinced from the start that the only way to proceed was with a firm hand. The mild dissent registered by Lord Dartmouth scarcely slowed the development of this policy.[12]

It must be noted that conservative Whigs like Joseph Galloway of Pennsylvania and Oliver DeLancey of New York, who embraced Toryism after the First Congress, had few doubts about what response Britain would make to the congressional demands. Their decision to abandon the Whig camp was made primarily because they considered the congressional program dictated by the New England radicals to be unrealistic and provocative. Galloway went so far as to charge the Whigs with outright news management in order to keep the populace in line. He believed that they manufactured optimistic reports about upcoming British concessions.[13]

It is doubtful that Galloway's allegations were true. The numerous letters from Britain published in the newspapers of New York and Philadelphia from November, 1774, through March, 1775, show no evidence of Whig editing or fabrication. The single recurring theme in these published letters, and in the private communiqués of William Lee and Benjamin Franklin, was the necessity of continued American unity. If the colonies could maintain their solidarity, then British efforts to incite defection would be discouraged and the economic pressure of the Continental Association would be maximal.

The first contest over ratification of the congressional resolves took place in Pennsylvania. To the surprise of the Whigs and the discomfort of the Tories it proved to be no contest at all. The annual election for assembly representatives in October actually set the stage for the easy Whig victory. A number of the more conservative members were dislodged in this election and, as a result, Edward Biddle of Berks County, a staunch Whig, was chosen speaker of the house over Joseph Galloway. On December 10, with Galloway off in New York nursing bruised feelings, the assembly unanimously endorsed the proceedings of the Continental Congress and reelected the congressional delegation to serve in the Second Congress should it be held.[14] The man most responsible for winning over the assembly was John Dickinson. Thomas Wharton bitterly assailed Governor Penn for not intervening to prevent an affirmative vote, for without this action ". . . Dickinson's politics turned the scale. . . ."[15]

In the city of Philadelphia the radical Whigs replaced the existing committee of correspondence with a new committee of sixty-six. Elected on November 12, the new committee contained fewer Tories and conservative Whigs and immediately showed a strong interest in rigorously enforcing the Association. On December 4 the committee ordered the recently arrived ship *Jamaica* to quit the harbor without unloading its cargo. Elsewhere in the province all the counties established inspection committees with dispatch and began enforcing the Association. At times enforcement was rather extreme. The committee for the borough of Lancaster enjoined a certain Mr. Francis from continuing to operate his recently opened dancing school because it was in violation of the eighth article.

Although the first round went to the Whigs, the Tories were willing to bide their time. They were hopeful that popular disenchantment with the Association, coupled with Whig excesses, would provide them an opportunity to reverse the decision of the assembly. Events outside the colony soon justified their faith. On December 15 the Maryland convention meeting in Annapolis voted unanimously

that a well regulated militia, composed of the gentlemen, free-holders, and other freemen, is the natural strength and only stable security of a free government, and that such militia will releave our mother country from any expense in our protection and defence, will obviate the pretence of a necessity for taxing us on that account, and render it unnecessary to keep any standing army (ever dangerous to liberty) in this province. . . .[16]

Maryland's call to arms represented the first move towards military preparedness outside of New England, and the implications seemed ominous to many inhabitants of the Central Provinces. Some of the radical Whigs, however, began to clamor for Pennsylvania to follow suit. When their entreaties were not heeded they blamed the Quakers. ". . . Pennsylvania seems as if it had expended all its vigor in the time of the Stamp Act," lamented William Bradford, Jr., "or surely it would catch some of the martial fever that is kindled all around it."[17]

In January the Philadelphia committee of sixty-six issued a call for a second provincial convention to meet later in the month for the ostensible purpose of improving the enforcement procedures of the committees of inspection. The specter of burgeoning Tory strength and the likelihood that the next session of the assembly might seek to reverse itself on the congressional resolutions appear to have been important underlying motives for the convention call as well. Another element in the decision was the desire on the part of some of the more radical Whigs to put the province on a military footing.[18] Joseph Reed was persuaded to serve as president of the convention despite his skepticism about its value. Eight counties were represented as the convention opened on January 23. After enthusiastically endorsing the congressional resolves, the convention adopted a resolution to encourage the formation of domestic manufacturing societies to produce common import items like cloth, gunpowder and ironware. The convention gave some consideration to the question of organizing a provincial military force, but the idea was dropped owing to lack of support. A resolve to meet force with force should Britain seek to coerce the colonies was unanimously adopted. Tory leaders in Pennsylvania were quick to interpret the refusal of the convention to approve a military preparedness program as a telling defeat for the radical Whigs. "I heartily wish their Meeting had been delayed," declared John Dickinson, for he was fearful that the refusal to arm would be construed at home and in Britain as a sign of deep internal cleavages.[19] Charles Lee of Virginia, soon to become a major general in the Continental Army, was particularly incensed by Pennsylvania's refusal to take up arms:

but you have always in my opinion been in pursuit of a chimera, absolute unanimity which cannot be expected in a society of any considerable extent, that damn'd slow heavy Quakering Nag your Province is mounted upon ought to be flogg'd and spurr'd though she kicks and plunges. If it had not been for the smart whip of my friend Mifflin I believe she never would have advanced a single inch. Virginia and Maryland ride most noble mettled coursers—but to drop this Jockey metaphor, they are noble spirited people.[20]

Roughly six weeks after the Pennsylvania assembly approved the proceedings of the Continental Congress, the New Jersey assembly followed suit. The task was successfully completed despite the efforts of Governor Franklin and a handful of Tories to block passages. The Governor used all the skill he had acquired in dealing with the legislature for over a decade but to no avail.

It was Essex County that spearheaded the drive to secure implementation of the Continental Association. On November 28 the Essex County committee of correspondence resolved that local inspection committees should be chosen by the freeholders as soon as possible. The freeholders were also asked to select a new county committee which would be empowered to participate in any convention that might be called to choose delegates to the Second Continental Congress. The example set by Essex was quickly emulated by the other New Jersey counties.

As in Pennsylvania, the Tory opposition began to gain in strength because of the stringent enforcement of the Association and the growing fear that New Jersey would soon be placed on a total military footing. The writings of the New York Tory pamphleteers also won converts. A few Jersey Tories availed themselves of the opportunity to reach their fellow citizens through the medium of *Rivington's New York Gazetteer*. A penman named "Z" depicted the Continental Congress as an inquisition established by designing men to subvert colonial liberties. He charged that pious-sounding Whigs "insolently trample on the liberties of their fellow-subjects; and without the shadow of a trial, take from them their property . . . and expose them to the villest [sic] injuries."[21] Incidents like the Greenwich tea bonfire in December, 1774, wherein a consignment of tea was taken from the cellar of the county sheriff and burned by poorly disguised Indians, were precisely what "Z" and his fellow essayists meant.

In high hopes that a conservative wind was indeed sweeping the province, Governor Franklin addressed the legislature on January 13, 1775. He strongly urged both houses to eschew all violent and coercive means in their quest for reconciliation with Britain. Alluding to the dangers of mob rule, the Governor warned his audience that

. . . it is (says one of the wisest of Men) a most infallible Symptom of the dangerous State of Liberty, when the Chief Men of a free Country show a greater Regard to popularity than to their own Judgement.[22]

If the assembly wished to avert a civil war and the destruction of the provincial government, then it had no alternative

but to forsake the wrongheaded Congress and humbly petition the King. Staunch Whigs in the assembly moved quickly
to counter the Governor's eloquent appeal. Acting as a truth
squad, William Livingston, James De Hart and Elias Boudinot
skillfully politicked against the Governor's proposal. With
some timely help from James Kinsey, the speaker of the
house, they convinced the assembly to approve the congressional resolves. For their efforts Franklin angrily dubbed
them the "Junto at Elizth Town."

One of the most telling arguments Livingston and his
colleagues advanced for ratification was that "it would be
a Means of influencing the N. York Assembly, then sitting,
to do the like; for they would not choose to stand single. . . ."[23]
The chance to have an impact on the councils of their over-
weening neighbor must have enticed a number of assemblymen to proceed at once, for the East Jersey men especially
were well acquainted with the habits of their northern neighbor. In their business dealings over the years the Jerseyites
had inured themselves to the avaricious practices of the New
York merchants. As a result they refused to discount the
mid-winter rumor that New York would soon sell out to the
British. If any Jerseyman needed proof that self-interest alone
dictated provincial policy in New York he only had to look
back to the summer of 1770. When word arrived that Parliament had repealed all of the Townshend Duties save the tax
on tea, New York promptly broke the colonial boycott and
resumed normal commercial intercourse with Britain. New
York's shameful act had outraged many Jerseymen: " . . .
we are betrayed and undone by New-Yorkers," had been the
cry.[24] For months afterwards essayists held New York up to
public ridicule and called upon all Jersey farmers to cease
trading with a people so devoid of honor. One writer named
"Neo Caesarienies" urged his East Jersey readers to rid

themselves forever of the money-grubbing New-Yorkers by diverting their trade to Perth Amboy.[25] Many New Jersey men were apparently convinced that nothing had changed by 1774. In the trying months ahead New Jersey would continue to keep a wary eye on her troubled northern neighbor and offer aid and comfort to the anemic New York Whigs.

When it came to a vote only a handful of assemblymen balked at the Whig tactic of ramming ratification through the house in a single day. Thus on January 24 the New Jersey assembly unanimously (to prevent any public awareness of division) approved the proceedings of Congress, reappointed the same five delegates to serve in the Second Congress and instructed them to protect the one colony–one vote rule. Copies of these resolutions were ordered to be sent to the assemblies of Pennsylvania and New York.[26]

Although the assembly voted to align the province with the continental union, Franklin and his supporters tried one last maneuver. Since the house initially agreed to accept the Governor's suggestion and send a petition to the King, Franklin sought to have a clause inserted providing for the initiation of direct negotiations with crown representatives by means of a congress selected by the various assemblies and royal governors. James Kinsey, who William Livingston considered to be " . . . a very good man, though not the best hand upon deck in a storm," apparently agreed to support this clause at the urging of the Governor.[27] Nevertheless, the Whigs had little trouble in turning back this measure. A frustrated Franklin concluded,

I am fully convinced it is the Determination of the principal Demagogues of Faction to oppose every thing which may have even the remotest Tendency to conciliate Matters in an Amicable Way, & to omit nothing which may have any chance of widening the Breach.[28]

When the Governor refused to endorse the petition to the King because it was for all intents and purposes the same as the congressional petition, the assembly sent it off on their authority alone.[29]

Although Governor Franklin had lost this round to the Whigs, it was not his nature to leave the field. Ever since 1762 when he was appointed Governor of New Jersey because of father Benjamin's influence at court, he had been striving to prove his own worth. For twelve years William Franklin had served two masters well. But it was his capacity to see both the colonial and British positions that made the years from 1774-1776 so difficult. Yet in spite of his American upbringing, his father's entreaties and the shabby treatment he had received from the crown for his faithful service, he chose to remain loyal to his oath of office. His years in England had made him more of an Anglophile than even Benjamin realized. William also must have reasoned that if he could keep New Jersey loyal, or at least make a valiant effort, officials in London might at last appreciate his merit.

One major issue that the assembly did not consider was the question of taking up arms. Any discussion of this volatile issue would have jeopardized the cohesiveness of the Whigs and doubtless resulted in Governor Franklin proroguing the house. In any event, at Elizabeth Town and other radical Whig centers, informal military preparations were going forward at the time. Charles Beatty scolded his brother about such activities:

you expect each one is preparing for an unexpected war—believe me we are not such patriots here as you imagine. . . . Yet I must confess it is a laudable design in the Elizabeth Town people to prepare themselves for what is doubtful.[30]

In the wake of the First Congress Tory writers emerged in all the Middle Colonies, but the New York contingent was by far the most prolific and effective. Anglican clerics like Samuel Seabury of Westchester County, Dr. Thomas Bradbury Chandler of Elizabeth Town, New Jersey, and Dr. Miles Cooper of New York City composed the most trenchant anti-Whig pamphlets found anywhere during the winter of 1774-1775.

Although the Tory essayists wrote as individuals, many of their writings played upon the historic antipathy between Yankees and Yorkers. After more than a century of strife the relationship between the two groups had taken on a bitter cast.[31] Suspicious New Yorkers were unwilling to believe that it was only unselfish American patriotism that had prompted the "Eastern Men" to boldly challenge British authority. Regional self-interest seemed to be a more valid motive. In the early months of 1775 only the New York Whigs and Tories seemed to possess a well-developed fear of New England's intentions. During the increasingly troubled months ahead, however, as relations with the mother country continued to worsen and New England's actions became even more menacing, moderate and conservative Whig leaders in Pennsylvania and to a lesser extent New Jersey and Delaware began to understand and eventually share New York's phobia.

"When the present unnatural Rebellion was first beginning," recalled Seabury, "I foresaw evidently what was coming on the Country, & I exerted myself to stem the Torrent of popular clamour, to recall People to use their Reason, & to retain them in their Loyalty & Allegiance."[32] The Westchester cleric's first pamphlet *Free Thoughts on the Proceedings of the Continental Congress,* published in November, opened the Tory counteroffensive. In this pamphlet Seabury appealed to the farmers of New York. He asserted that hard times would surely befall the tillers of the soil once the Continental Association was in full operation. The New York City merchants and

their urban allies had saddled the province with this burden
assuming "that we farmers were utterly ignorant of everything,
but just to drive our Oxen, and follow the plough."[33] The nonconsumption part of the Association would soon bring the
Whig scoundrels into the homes of everyone. Seabury warned,
"Open your doors to them,—let them examine your tea-
cannisters, and molasses jugs, and your wives and daughters
petty-coats. . . ."[34] By concentrating upon the traditional
merchant–farmer split Seabury used the traders as strawmen,
but in a way that certainly did not accord with the shape of
events. This approach, however, was calculated to appeal to
the emotions, not the rational faculties of the agrarians.

In December Seabury wrote a second pamphlet, *A View
of the Controversy, Between Great Britain and her Colonies,*
which was intended for a more general audience. He tried to
elucidate the historical precedents for the obedience owed to
Britain by the colonies. As for the alleged conspiracy by the
King, Lords and Commons to enslave America, it was pure
fabrication. A handful of unethical opportunists were the authors of this malevolent lie. The Reverend Seabury artfully
played upon the provincial loyalty of New Yorkers and their
phobia for New England. "Virginia and Massachusetts mad-
men, met at Philadelphia," he noted and "have made laws for
the province of New-York, and have rendered our assembly
useless. . . ."[35] Unless the New York assembly was encouraged
to assert its former authority, the colony would be led out of
the British Empire by the nose and forced to join a republic
headed by the Eastern Colonies.

Dr. Thomas Chandler's first pamphlet, *A Friendly Address to all Reasonable Americans,* also reached the public in
December. He began by taking exception to the popular contention that Boston's plight was not of its own making. New
York and the other colonies would be foolish indeed to grant

the Massachusetts men a *carte blanche,* for

their modesty is like that of the fox in the fable, who, because he happened to have lost his own tail, requested of his brother foxes that they would all suffer their tails to be cut off too.[36]

Chandler further warned his readers that the New England radicals were intent upon creating an independent republic. Far from being a utopia of freedom it would doubtless be a Puritan-dominated theocracy. All of the religious groups from Lutherans to Quakers would be subject to the ecclesiastical tyranny of the New England divines. "In a word," he predicted, "no order or denomination of men amongst us, would enjoy liberty or safety, if subjected to the fiery genius of New England Republican Government; the little finger of which he should experience to be heavier than the loins of Parliament."[37] In this manner the Tory writers set themselves up as the disciples of fear. For if they could incite the populace against New England, then the Tories might be able to overturn the Whig cause in New York.

In his second pamphlet *What Think Ye of the Congress Now?* published in January, Chandler argued that since Congress completely disregarded the instructions of its constituents, and since the New York delegation was chosen by the most unrepresentative means, no allegiance was due the resolves of this body. Furthermore, since the New York delegates opposed virtually every measure adopted by the Congress, it was apparent that this province held different views about how to resolve the dispute. To remedy the situation, Chandler called upon the New York assembly to chart a separate course which would serve as an example for the wavering colonies.

In addition to these pamphleteers, the editor of *Rivington's New York Gazeteer,* James Rivington, was a constant thorn in the side of the Whigs.[38] He adroitly snipped at their heels by slanting news, fabricating incidents and publishing the works of Tory essayists.[39] Even before the First Continental Congress opened Rivington was under attack. A group of delegates to Congress pledged to discontinue purchasing his paper because of its pro-British disposition.

Whig groups in the Central Provinces were quick to brand the Tory publicists of New York as ministerial sycophants. Moreover, some of the Patriot groups in the East Jersey towns endeavored to suppress the offensive works. For example, on January 9, 1775 the freeholders of Morris County determined that James Rivington, by publishing two ministerial pamphlets,

all containing many Falsehoods, wickedly calculated to divide the Colonies, to deceive the Ignorant, and to cause a base submission to the unconstitutional Measures of the British Parliament for enslaving the Colonies, do unanimously resolve, that they esteem the said _____ an enemy to his Country; and therefore that they will for the future refrain from his Newspapers and from all further commerce with him. . . .[40]

Elizabeth Town in Essex, New Town in Sussex and Freehold in Monmouth also voted sanctions against Rivington's paper and the pamphlets coming from his press. Even men from Philadelphia, no radical hotbed itself, chided their New York City friends about Rivington's unabashed Toryism. We are astonished, wrote one Philadelphia Whig, "that your sons of liberty and committee suffer that base fellow Rivington to continue publishing his vile calumnies of every province in America."[41]

Pennsylvania's speedy ratification of the congressional program, coupled with New Jersey's affirmative action, meant that New York stood as the only possible nonsupporter from the Middle Colonies. Contemporaries certainly realized that New York's attachment to the Empire was closer than that of any other colony. "We are not ignorant of that crowd of place-

men, of contractors, of officers, and needy dependents upon
the Crown, who are constantly employed to frustrate your
measures . . ." wrote the general committee of South Carolina.
"We know the dangerous tendency of being made the headquarters of AMERICA for many years."[42] They went on to
assure their New York brethren that "all these things, though
they necessarily tend to clog the wheels of publick spirit, yet
do not cause us to doubt of your public virtue, as a colony.
. . ."[43] Nonetheless, in light of the New York delegation's
posture in the First Congress, most radical Whigs considered
New York to be the Tory citadel of America. Radicals in
other colonies expressed sympathy for their New York comrades. "I understand by all hands that you have an over
proportion of tories with you to any place on the Continent.
. . ." wrote Thomas Young of Rhode Island. "I heartily pity
you if anything like the above is true."[44]

   Despite all of the foreboding speculation, the initial reception accorded the Continental Association in New York
City gave encouragement to the Whigs. On November 10 a
group of citizens detained a sloop bound for the West Indies
with a consignment of sheep because it was violating the
Association. The owner of the vessel, upon being confronted
by two hundred enforcers, removed the sheep with dispatch.[45]
Several days later the distillers of the city voted to refrain from
distilling any molasses or syrup imported from the British West
Indies and not to sell any rum for use in the slave trade. Even
more heartening to the Whigs was the formation of a new
committee of correspondence at the behest of the committee of
mechanics. The city committee also was displaced, and the
new committee had significantly fewer Tories on its rolls.[46]

   The inaction and lethargy that characterized the rural
counties before the meeting of the First Congress was again
manifested in their inattentiveness to the Association. Only

Albany, Suffolk and Ulster counties bothered to appoint committees of inspection in 1774. In the case of Tryon, Queens
and Dutchess counties, vigorous Tory opposition stayed the
hand of the Whigs. Elsewhere, sheer inertia dictated inaction
and six counties (Kings, Orange, Richmond, Charlotte, Cumberland and Gloucester) made no attempt to set up enforcement machinery until after the Battle of Lexington.

The dismal response which the rural counties made to the
city committee's request for active enforcement of the Association left the Whigs with no alternative but to allow the
assembly to pass on the proceedings of the First Congress.
Given the uncooperative attitude of the agrarians it would
have been the height of folly to have tried to stage a provincial
convention. Besides, the Whigs were hopeful that the assembly,
though dominated by the DeLancey faction, would at least
approve the Association and appoint a delegation to the
Second Congress. Still, James Duane admitted late in December that it was impossible to fathom what position the assembly
would take. Personally, he was hopeful that this body would
consider Galloway's plan of union or a similar proposal for
"We are among those that are thought the most strongly
attached to the parent state and probably from us will be demanded a system of union."[47]

The Tories also looked to the assembly. The Reverend
Samuel Seabury wrote a special pamphlet, *An Alarm to the
Legislature of the Province of New York,* in hopes of influencing its deliberations. He dwelt at great length on the
usurpation of the assembly's powers by the "illegal" Congress
at Philadelphia. With the proud assembly of Pennsylvania
bowing its noble head to this rebel band, "We, Gentlemen,
have no alternative left but either join the other colonies in
war against Great-Britain, or to make the best terms that we
can for ourselves."[48]

The Tory faction in the assembly, led by Isaac Wilkins of Westchester County and Captain James DeLancey of New York City, rode roughshod over the attempts of the conservative Whigs (Livingston faction men) to secure acceptance of the proceedings of the Continental Congress. The Tories beat back all of the bids by Colonel Philip Schuyler of Tryon County and Abram Ten Broeke from Albany County to secure passage of a ratification resolution. Instead the assembly drafted a petition to the King. a memorial to the Lords and a remonstrance to the Commons, "all expressed, especially the Petition to the King, in very moderate decent style."[49]

The Tories were jubilant over the assembly's rejection of the congressional program and the seeming withdrawal of the province from the colonial union. Henceforth, Lieutenant Governor Colden surmised, "The peaceable Disposition of the People of this Province will become every day more evident, and give some check to the Mad Career of their Neighbors."[50] Colden himself was greatly relieved by the outcome and "Worthy Old Silver Locks" was heard to remark, "Lord, now lettest thou thy Servant depart in Peace."[51]

The imperious refusal of the New York assembly to link their colony with the other provinces seemed at first to be a major setback for the American protest movement. Whig leaders in New England and the South were fearful that this decision would encourage the other Central Provinces, notably Pennsylvania, to follow suit. The magnitude of this threat was underscored by the arrival of reports from London in March and April that the ministry was actively seeking to retain New York's allegiance. The Conciliation Proposal, passed by Parliament on February 20, was drafted by Lord North with this end in mind. Under the terms of the Proposal each colony was offered complete exemption from taxation by Parliament if it would provide an annual contribution for defense and civil government. Lord North openly admitted:

he rather imagined this proposition would not be to the taste of
the Americans. . . . However, if but one of them submitted, that
one link of the chain would be broken; and if so, the whole would
inevitably fall to pieces.[52]

Arthur Lee confirmed North's intentions and implored Sam
Adams to do everything in his power to see that New York
was not the first broken link. "It is certain that the Ministry
are bidding for New York. . . ." Lee warned, "Depend upon it,
That Peace or War depends on the determination of this single
Province, & as it is the great maneouvre of the Enemy, nothing
should be left undone to contradict it."[53]

Although the ministry's policy of *divide et impera* was
not directed solely towards New York, the formulation of this
strategy was in large part a response to the information supplied by Lieutenant Governor Colden and Governor William
Tryon. Colden's reports of conditions in New York from May,
1774, through February, 1775, were filled with assurances
that the disaffected were only a small, insignificant group and
that the vast bulk of the people were loyal subjects. During
his stay in London Tryon sought to convince the ministry that
with proper assistance he could save New York for the Crown.
On the eve of his departure for America in April, 1775, he
informed Lord Dartmouth that confirmation of the New York
claims to the Vermont lands would help to preserve the loyalty
of the men of property for "I flatter myself the peculiar importance which the affairs of New York at this Crisis derive
from the effect they may have, on the present American
System. . . ."[54]

During the months of March and April the colonial press
was filled with reports of New York's impending betrayal.
Prominent New Yorkers like Isaac Low, James DeLancey and
John Watts were rumored to have received a thousand pounds
each with more secret service money on the way. And late in

April an unknown Whig publicly accused Messrs. DeLancey, White, Colden, Watts and Cooper of supplying the ministry with false information about the sentiments of New Yorkers.[55]

The stigma which the assembly affixed upon the colony also deeply embarrassed the Whigs. Alexander McDougall, noting that a ship from Scotland was recently ordered back to its home port, commented: "I hope this will convince our neighbors the City is in earnest."[56] In order to undo the work of the assembly the radical Whigs on the committee of sixty at last prevailed on their moderate brethren to opt for a provincial congress. In New York City the Tories endeavored to prevent the election of delegates to the provincial congress. When this failed the Tories asked that the vote on the nominees be postponed until April 20, on the pretext that favorable news from London would be forthcoming. This tactic "allarmed all men, who influenced by party or selfish views, wished to preserve that union. . . ."[57] The Whigs moved quickly to capitalize on favorable public sentiment. On March 18 at an open air meeting the voters approved their entire slate that included the five congressional delegates from the city and six Livingston faction members—most notably Alexander McDougall. The soundings taken in the rural counties indicated that enough support would be forthcoming to hold the provincial convention as scheduled on April 20.

Although most Whigs were troubled by events in New York, Sam Adams was surprisingly confident that the Tory ascendance would prove ephemeral. As he analyzed the situation early in March:

The people of that City & Colony, are infested with Court Scribblers who have labored, perhaps with some Success, to divide them; they are however in general firm. . . . You know their parliament is septennial—and therefore must be corrupted. It is best that the Tories in their house have acted without Disguise. This is their last Session and the house will, I hope, be purged at the next election.[58]

Sam Adams no doubt believed that New York would eventually come around since both Pennsylvania and New Jersey had affirmed their support for the colonial union.

The news that the New York assembly rejected the entire congressional program reached Joseph Galloway shortly before the Pennsylvania assembly was to convene. His initial response was one of jubilation. New York's exemplary stand would serve as a significant point of influence among the uncommitted assemblymen. Even before this news arrived Tory observers in Pennsylvania were encouraged by the growing evidence of a shift in public opinion away from the Whig measures. The adoption by the Pennsylvania–New Jersey Quaker Meeting of a strongly pro-British "Testimony" on January 24 was indicative of this trend. The "Testimony" began with a disavowal of all means of protest used against the King and Parliament which were contrary to the gospel and harmful to the tranquillity of the provinces. In the interest of restoring the bountiful relationship with the Empire, they called for a halt to ". . . all combinations, insurrections, conspiracies, and illegal assemblies," and declared their membership ". . . restrained from them by the conscientious discharge of our duty to almighty God, by whom kings *reign,* and princes decree justice. . . ."[59] The Friends' position statement did not explicitly call for noncompliance with and nonparticipation in the protest movement, but the inference was obvious. Christopher Marshall, a staunch Philadelphia Whig, adjudged that the Quakers were bent upon undermining the provincial support for the congressional program and that they would expel all recalcitrant members to accomplish this.

Another reason for the shifting sentiment was the appearance in February of Joseph Galloway's pamphlet, *A Candid Examination.* This incisive appeal for a more constructive and less provocative approach to Britain was widely read in the

Quaker Colony. He set forth the many benefits and advantages that the imperial connection had bestowed upon the colonists and castigated the Continental Congress for ignoring the people's mandate for constitutional reconciliation. "Nothing has been the production of their two months labour, but the ill-shapen diminutive brat, INDEPENDENCE, . . ." Galloway charged. For the Whigs were seeking to encourage the people "to rush into the blackest rebellion and all the horrors of an unnatural Civil War."[60] He predicted that if the interprovincial jealousies and hatreds did not rip apart the colonial union before it achieved separation from the Empire, the New Englanders would certainly establish religious and political hegemony over the new nation. In addition to Galloway's tract, the works of Seabury and Chandler were well known in Pennsylvania. "They have produced a happy effect in this Province . . ." Galloway noted and "I wish more of them had been for sale in Philadelphia and advertised in our papers."[61]

An interesting aside to Galloway's assessment of the New York pamphlets was his contention that they did not appreciate the legitimacy of most of the American grievances nor did they offer a palatable alternative to the Whig measures. This apparent ideological division between Tories reflects the different routes they traveled. Galloway became a Tory only after his disenchantment with the tactics of the Whigs, whereas Seabury and Chandler never possessed enough American sentiment to condone any real opposition to the mother country.

John Dickinson and the other Whig leaders in Pennsylvania were quite apprehensive about the increasing unpopularity of the congressional measures. The "Pennsylvania Farmer" anticipated that there would be a sizable group of representatives in the upcoming assembly who would work "to stop all vigorous proceedings, by prevailing on the assembly to

give very restrictive instructions to the Delegates appointed
for the next Congress."[62] In order to prevent the Tories from
accomplishing this Dickinson admitted, "a good Deal of
Delicacy will be required in managing the affair."[63]

Governor Penn, in his opening remarks to the assembly
on February 20, urged the house to draft a respectful petition
to the King as the best means to promote reconciliation. Galloway, sensing his chance, began at once to try and convince a
majority of the assemblymen to approve such a petition. During the next two weeks he used his manifold political talents
to make life miserable for the Whigs. Shaken by Galloway's
sudden resurgence, Dickinson resorted to a bit of his own
political legerdemain. On March 8 after Galloway had succeeded in having the speaker of the house appoint a special
committee to answer the governor's request, the Whigs made
their move. They quickly called a secret meeting of the drafting committee and saw to it that the letter which this committee
reported out the next day was harmless. Although Galloway
cried "foul," the assembly approved the Whig letter and this
reversal effectively ended Galloway's bid to lure Pennsylvania
away from the congressional program.

Even before the concluding Whig victory over the Tory
faction, the impending result was communicated to the other
colonies. An anonymous correspondent reported that John
Dickinson had ". . . acquired fresh laurels. . . ." As for the
Tories, they were melting away after their stalwarts in the
assembly failed to throttle the Whigs. "Our Assembly begin
to vie with the Assemblies of Virginia and Massachusetts," he
proudly asserted.[64]

Delaware was the last of the Middle Colonies to pass on
the proceedings of the First Continental Congress. It was not
until March 24 that the assembly approved the program of
Congress and renominated the same delegation to the Second

Congress. Delaware's delayed response was doubtless the result of its own internal divisions and the second-guessing that was taking place in Pennsylvania.

In keeping with its past performance New Castle was the first county to respond to the congressional resolves. On November 18 the committee of correspondence resolved that each hundred in the county should select a committee of inspection to enforce the Association. Several weeks later, on December 5, the freshly chosen committees of inspection gathered at New Castle Court House to coordinate policing procedures. But the meeting went beyond mere consideration of the Association. They resolved unanimously

That pursuant to an intimation given by the said Continental congress, as well as from a full Persuasion that a well regulated Militia, composed of the Gentlemen, Freeholders and other Freemen, is the natural Strength and Stable Security of a free Government . . .[65]

Each hundred was encouraged to form militia units comprising all male inhabitants between the ages of sixteen and fifty.

Kent County followed closely on the heels of New Castle. A county committee of inspection was organized in December to secure compliance to the Continental Association and to collect money for the suffering inhabitants of Boston. Kent County did not, however, go as far as New Castle in recommending the formation of militia units. The third Delaware county, Sussex, apparently took no action on the proceedings of the First Congress prior to Lexington.

As in Pennsylvania the initial enthusiasm shown by the two Delaware counties for the congressional measures began to wane in January and February. The economic burden of the Association and the rumors of impending civil war were potent deterrents. On February 11 a Kent County resident confidently asserted that

The people have not, till lately, considered the consequences of a
Civil War . . . and when people come to tast[e] feelingly of the
hardships, which a suspension of trade will occasion, they will
change sides, nay, I believe, if the King's standard was now
erected, nine out of ten would repair to it.[66]

He noted further that Dr. Chandler's *A Friendly Address To
All Reasonable Americans* as well as ". . . other performances
of the moderate stamp have done much good, in opening the
blind eyes of many. . . ."

The publication of this letter angered the Kent County
committee, which immediately began an exhaustive search to
uncover the author. By making an example of this writer they
hoped to repair the image of their county both in Delaware
and Pennsylvania. A number of moderate Whigs cautioned
the committee to refrain from encroaching on the freedom of
the press lest their actions do more damage to the cause than
the original letter.[67] The committee, however, persevered and
in April discovered that Robert Holliday, a Quaker, had received the letter from an anonymous source and conveyed it
to the printer. Under examination he admitted that his intentions were to contribute to free discussion of the issues and
not to damage the cause.[68]

The Delaware assembly convened on March 13 at New
Castle to consider the proceedings of Congress and decide
upon a slate of delegates for the Second Congress. An incident
that occurred on March 7 doubtless aroused the patriotic
sentiments of the house members. On the day in question Captain George Taylor was aboard his shallop when an inspection
team from the King's armed schooner *Diana* came on board.
When Captain Taylor tried to accompany the search party into
his cabin, as he had several hundred pounds in coin stored
there, "he was immediately furiously attacked and knocked
down, where he was beaten in a most inhuman manner till
the deck was besmeared with blood."[69] For several hours after

the beating Taylor was denied medical assistance because the *Diana* towed his boat about the bay while the schooner's crew behaved like barbarians.

Although the assembly did not issue a protest, the unanimous approval of the proceedings of Congress on March 15 no doubt served in lieu of one. The same three men who served in the First Congress were reappointed and instructed

to concert and agree upon such further measures as shall appear to them best calculated for the accommodation of the unhappy differences between Great Britain and the Colonies on a Constitutional foundation.[70]

On March 29 the final instructions were approved for the congressional delegation. While they were strictly enjoined from supporting any actions likely to be disrespectful to Britain or the King, they were empowered to meet with any peace commissioners His Majesty might send to the colonies. The house completely ignored a petition from a group of Kent County freemen who requested the establishment of a colony-wide militia to protect the province from its natural enemies. In so doing the assembly gave notice that it did not wish to do anything that might impinge upon the prospects of peaceful negotiations with Britain.

With the affirmative action of Delaware the only Middle Colony that had not yet ratified the proceedings of the First Congress was New York. Nevertheless, the Whigs there were confident that the provincial congress coming up in April would quickly assent to the congressional measures and select a delegation for the Second Congress. Their faith was rewarded, as the New York provincial congress did just that on April 20. Joseph Reed had perceived from the beginning that the strong attachment of the Middle Colonial inhabitants to the status quo and the Empire might lead them to balk at accepting the mandates of the First Congress. "The proceedings of Congress have been pitched on too high a key for some of

these middle Provinces," was his conclusion.[71] Although the
Whigs had scored victories in the hardfought engagements
over the congressional resolves in Pennsylvania and New
York, these triumphs carried with them no assurance that
these provinces were fully committed to the colonial union.
The refusal of all four colonies to join Virginia and Maryland
in taking arms bespoke of the cautiousness that still dogged
their councils. They would await the next round in the Anglo-
American dispute before they took another step.

In reaching their decisions the four Central Provinces
also clarified their sectional relationships. After the First Congress adjourned, Pennsylvania and New York had parted company for a time. While Dickinson and his party managed to
have the Quaker Colony endorse the entire congressional
program, New York found it more expedient to listen to the
Tories and stand apart from the colonial union. Yet after New
Jersey cast its lot with Pennsylvania and the Quaker Colony
did not reverse itself (despite Galloway's gallant efforts), the
New York Whigs managed to bring their province into line.
Henceforth, until the colonies passed out of the Empire, Pennsylvania would determine the sectional position of the Middle
Colonies. The New York Whigs balked on occasion, but their
weakness at home coupled with the tarnished reputation of
the province left them little choice but to follow.

New Jersey's decision to join Pennsylvania in support of
the colonial union was not solely the result of the predominantly Whiggish climate in the province. Historically, New
Jersey's relationship with Pennsylvania had been more harmonious than that with New York. In the first place it was not
until 1738 that New Jersey managed to secure a full-time
royal governor, thus bringing to a close thirty-six years of
administrative neglect by a series of New York governors.
Even as late as 1749 some New Yorkers still harbored thoughts

of annexation.[72] Although after mid-century the threat of being absorbed had little currency, New Jersey was still locked in a heated controversy with New York over the location of their boundaries. This dispute, which spanned a century, was finally resolved in 1772 by a crown-imposed settlement that neither New York nor New Jersey was happy with. But it was New Jersey that lost over 150,000 acres.

No one can question that the Tory attempts to detach the Middle Colonies from the colonial union during the winter of 1774-1775 fell short of their objective. But ironically the undertaking served to strengthen sectional accord. The Tory penmen succeeded in propagating the notion that the Middle Colonies held a privileged place in the Empire. They were even more successful in portraying the threat which the New England Colonies posed to the continued peace and prosperity of the Middle Colonies. The seeds of doubt which Seabury, Chandler and Galloway sowed so skillfully would be nurtured by the disturbing course of events from Lexington to the Declaration of Independence. In the minds of most of the Middle Colonial leaders New England became the cause of all their woes. Back in October, 1774, the Reverend Charles Inglis had contended that the only way to deny support to the New England scoundrels was to publicly reveal that in their private conversations

They are for an Independent Republica; & Lord have mercy on those who live under it & Dissent in religious or political Principles from them—For my part I would rather live under a French or even Turkish government. I most ardently wish that all the Colonists to the Southward had just & proper Notions of these People, & their Views; a different Conduct I am sure, would be adopted.[73]

His words were prophetic. Distrust of New England became the cornerstone of the emerging sectional feeling among the Middle Colonies.

chapter
four

MARS ASCENDANT:

The Continental Congress Prepares for War

The uncertainty which dogged the colonists throughout the winter of 1774-1775 showed signs of coming to an end with the arrival of spring. Reports from London observers early in April warned the colonists that the North ministry was determined to bring the rebellious New England Colonies to heel at all costs. To accomplish this end they declared that Massachusetts was in rebellion and dispatched six regiments to Boston escorted by seven ships of the line.[1] The North measures were also designed to chastise those colonies that had aided and abetted the Massachusetts rebels. For this purpose Parliament approved a bill restricting all colonial commerce to the ports of Britain or her dependencies.[2]

The Middle Colonies scarcely had time to recover from their shock over Britain's belligerent response, when word arrived of the bloodletting at Lexington. The news reached New York City on April 22 and immediately the city was plunged into turmoil. The next day mobs led by John Lamb and Isaac Sears armed themselves with six hundred muskets from the royal arsenal and then proceeded to unload ships scheduled to carry provisions to the British Army at Boston.

For a week the mob ruled the city while the helpless royal and city officials tried to keep out of sight. Angry mobs searched for prominent Tories like Dr. Miles Cooper, Oliver DeLancey and James Rivington.[3] Cooper and Rivington fled in terror to a British man-of-war in the harbor. Although Rivington subsequently returned to his newspaper duties, Cooper forsook his presidency at Kings College and became one of the first Tory exiles in the conflict. Outside of the city the emotional response to Lexington was more subdued. Nevertheless, the Tory-dominated New York council sadly concluded that there was ". . . such a change of temper and conduct (which has entirely prostrated his majesty's Government in this Province) . . ." that it would be foolhardy to bring Lord North's February 20th Conciliation Proposal before the assembly.[4] They further concluded that another military clash of any sort would drive an irremovable wedge between Britain and her colonies.

In view of New York City's past history of urban unrest and mob violence, the massive popular response to the Battle of Lexington was not surprising. That tranquil Philadelphia should respond with spirited popular meetings and military preparations was quite unexpected. It clearly displayed the depth of colonial feeling. The news reached Philadelphia late in the afternoon of the 23rd. The next morning some 8,000 people gathered in the state house yard and voted to establish a general military association. Samuel Curwen, a Boston merchant who was soon to side with the British, took alarm at the militarism he witnessed in Philadelphia. "I find the drums beating, colours flying, and detachments of newly raised militia parading the streets, the whole country appears determined to assume a military character. . . ."[5] Even the anti-Patriot Quaker elders, Israel and John Pemberton, made no

move to discipline members of their church who defiantly
served in the two predominantly Quaker militia companies.
Pennsylvania's indignation was infectious as the three lower
counties on the Delaware soon initiated military programs
of their own.

Governor William Franklin informed Dartmouth that the
outpouring of patriotism in New Jersey was equivalent to the
response in the other Middle Colonies. Monmouth County in
particular was so apprehensive about the colonial treasury
falling into British hands that it posted a guard to thwart any
such development. "All legal authority and Government seems
to be drawing to an End here," Franklin observed, and the
supporters of the Crown were reduced to signing the Continental Association to protect themselves from Whig reprisals.[6]

The military clash at Lexington coupled with the full
revelation of the British policy of repression heightened the
spirit of unity and will to resist among the colonies. As a
result of their strong show of patriotism even New York and
Pennsylvania were no longer stigmatized as halfhearted supporters. Radicals like Silas Deane and John Adams were
heartened by the thunderous popular receptions they received
in New York City, sundry places in New Jersey, and finally
in Philadelphia itself. William Hooper, a congressional delegate from North Carolina, concluded that ". . . the character
of New Yorkers is no longer suspicious."[7]

It was in this superheated atmosphere that the Second
Continental Congress began its deliberations. A number of
new faces in the delegations from New York and Pennsylvania illustrated the change in the American mood since the
First Continental Congress. Joseph Galloway, who led the
conservative faction nine months before, was no longer a
member of the Pennsylvania delegation. The decision not to
serve was his own. Galloway, like many other conservative

Americans, wished to have no part in precipitating civil war. Benjamin Franklin scarcely had time to remove himself and his effects from shipboard, following his return from London, before he was chosen to serve in Galloway's place. Although Franklin was initially close-mouthed about his political sentiments, the radicals in Congress thought he was quite an improvement over his predecessor. In addition to Franklin, Thomas Willing and James Wilson were added to the Pennsylvania delegation. Willing was one of the wealthiest men in Philadelphia while Wilson was a rising western lawyer, but both men were members of John Dickinson's Whig clique. The "Pennsylvania Farmer," John Dickinson, stood ready to lead the Pennsylvania delegation.

The New York delegation underwent an even more noticeable ideological face-lifting. Isaac Low, the conservative chairman of the New York City committee of sixty, declined a second trip to Philadelphia doubtless because he viewed his task of restraining the domestic radicals as more important. During the First Continental Congress he had been an active supporter of Joseph Galloway.[8] Another New York delegate, John Haring, declined to serve again for personal reasons. In all, five new delegates were added to the seven incumbent members of the New York delegation. None of the new representatives were destined to become supporters of the radical faction in Congress. Francis Lewis, a wealthy merchant, and George Clinton, an astute young lawyer, tended to side with the New York conciliationists led by James Duane and John Jay. Two of the other new members, Lewis Morris, a prominent merchant, and Robert R. Livingston, a wealthy landowner, turned out to be staunch adherents to the Duane–Jay group. The fifth delegate, Philip Schuyler, was only in Congress a few weeks and then resigned to assume his post as a major general in the Continental Army. Delaware and New Jersey made no changes in their delegations.

The Second Continental Congress began in the same manner as the first, with a stirring prayer delivered by the eloquent Reverend Jacob Duché. He called upon the delegates to weigh carefully each decision and put aside their petty jealousies and prejudices. The first injunction was perhaps taken to heart but the latter fell upon deaf ears. For the Middle Colonial delegates were no longer divided as they had been in the First Congress. Moderate Whigs like John Dickinson and William Livingston were now convinced that the New England Colonies would be satisfied with nothing less than independence. The frightful prospect of leaving the Empire and then falling victim to New England imperialism was a great unifier. While John Adams perhaps did not immediately perceive the outlines of this new sectional party, he was well aware of the strong anti-New England sentiment, "I have found this Congress like the last, when we first came together I found a strong jealousy of Us, from New England, and Massachusetts in Particular."[9]

Two recent historians of the First and Second Continental Congresses, Curtis Nettels and Herbert James Henderson, both agree that three more or less well-defined groups or factions were present. The radical group, they contend, was composed of almost all the New England representatives, plus a small but potent contingent of Southern delegates. During the summer of 1775 the radical faction advocated strong military opposition to Britain and came to full endorsement of secession from the Empire in the fall when Britain's policies became unmistakable.[10] The other two factions were the conciliationists (or conservatives) and the moderates. Although the difference in their positions was very slight, the moderates were evidently more willing to apply military pressure upon

Britain than the conciliationists who feared this means
would destroy the end in view—amicable reconciliation with
Britain.[11]

Despite their agreement on the tripartite party arrangement in Congress, Nettels and Henderson diverge sharply in
their identification of moderate and conciliationist faction
members. Nettels concludes that the balance of power in the
Second Continental Congress was held by the twenty-eight
moderates, because they constituted a majority of the delegates. Henderson's compilation of factional membership lists
the radicals and the conciliationists (or conservatives as he
terms them) as numerically about equal, with the former
having twenty-two and the latter nineteen.[12] Yet it was the
small moderate faction of about ten delegates that generally
determined whether the radicals or conciliationists got their
way. The marked disagreement between these two historians
on the relative numerical strength of the congressional factions
does not call for taking sides but rather for a shift of emphasis.
Instead of trying to make policy considerations the only basis
for factional identification, we need to recognize that sectional attachment was a much more powerful determinant.
The welfare of the home province was the fundamental
decision-making criterion for all delegates, but often the
posture of neighboring colonies determined a colony's best
interest. Both Nettels and Henderson tacitly admit that the
radical faction was virtually indistinguishable from the entire
New England delegation. But when it can be demonstrated
that no less than twenty-eight of the thirty-six men who
represented the Middle Colonies in the Second Congress until
July 2, 1776, were opponents of independence and supporters
of rapprochement, a sectional interpretation of their voting
behavior seems in order.[13] The delegates from the four

TABLE I

Henderson's assessment of the political positions held by the members of the Second Continental Congress
May, 1775–July, 1776

State	Radicals	Moderates	Conservatives
New Hampshire	Langdon Bartlett Whipple		
Massachusetts	S. Adams J. Adams Gerry, Hancock	Cushing	
Rhode Island	Ward, Hopkins		
Connecticut	Sherman, Dyer Walcott, Deane		
New York		Lewis	P. Livingston R. R. Livingston Duane, Jay Wisner, Smith
New Jersey	Sergeant* Clark* Stockton* Witherspoon*	W. Livingston DeHart	
Pennsylvania	Franklin Clymer* Rush*		Dickinson Willing Wilson, Morris
Delaware	McKean Rodney		Read
Maryland	Chase	Paca	Johnson Tilghman
Virginia	R. H. Lee F. L. Lee Jefferson Wythe	Harrison	Braxton
No. Carolina		Penn, Hooper Lynch	Hewes
So. Carolina	Gadsden		E. Rutledge J. Rutledge
Georgia	Bulloch*, Hall* Gwinnett*		Zubly

*New, pro-independence delegates who entered Congress in May or June, 1776.

TABLE II

Nettels' assessment of the political positions held by the
members of the Second Continental Congress
May, 1775–July, 1776

State	Radicals	Moderates	Conciliationists
New Hampshire	Sullivan		
	Langdon		
Massachusetts	S. Adams	Hancock	
	J. Adams	Cushing	
Rhode Island			
Connecticut	Sherman	Deane	
New York	Clinton	P. Livingston	Duane, Jay
		Schuyler	R. R. Livingston
New Jersey	W. Livingston		
Pennsylvania	Wilson		Dickinson
	Morris		
Delaware			
Maryland		Johnson	
Virginia	Jefferson	Harrison	
	R. H. Lee		
	P. Henry		
No. Carolina		Hooper	
		Hewes	
So. Carolina	Gadsden	J. Rutledge	
		E. Rutledge	
		Lynch	
		Middleton	

Middle Colonies began to discover in the First Continental
Congress that they shared a common reverence for Britain,
a distinct life-style and a distaste for New England men and
their ideas. Nine months later in the Second Continental
Congress, with the stakes much higher and John Dickinson
to lead them, the representatives from the Central Provinces
began to perceive more clearly their sectional identity.

Even before the First Continental Congress was called,
some members of the upper classes in the Middle Colonies
were cognizant of a slowly emerging sectional outlook. The

First and Second Congresses, however, proved to be more potent distilleries of this sentiment. During the many months Congress was in session, the delegates from the Middle Colonies had an excellent opportunity to explore their common interests. The countless hours they spent together working, dining, and on occasion carousing enabled them to perceive their sectionality.[14] The presence of the New England delegates also helped the representatives from the Middle Colonies to see what they were not and what they never wanted to be.

From the tenor of the broad-based colonial response to the events of April 19, it seemed a foregone conclusion that the Second Continental Congress would embark upon a general program of military preparedness. But the delegates in Philadelphia, shielded as they were from the direct influence of the citizenry by their closed-door sessions, were too experienced in politics to leap before they looked. Thus on May 15 they formed themselves into a committee of the whole to consider the state of the resistance movement. For a week and a half they examined the available options and finally on May 26 passed four resolutions to guide their future deliberations. The first resolution simply declared that Britain was responsible for the Anglo-American dispute. Resolution number two called for the enactment of defensive measures to protect the colonies from British aggression. The third resolution advocated a petition to the King in the interest of securing a peaceful settlement of the dispute, while the fourth suggested that Congress should enter into direct negotiations with Britain in order to restore harmony to the Empire. Congress voted unanimously for the first three resolves, but the fourth resolve was too controversial to garner such support.

The passage of the third and fourth resolutions was due

primarily to the efforts of John Dickinson and James Duane.[15]
Prior to the opening of Congress the two had collaborated
on an ingenious plan that blended together the reconciliation
interest of the Middle Colonies and the military preparedness
ideas of New England.[16] In presenting this program to Congress during the committee of the whole sessions, Dickinson
admitted that the colonies must be prepared to defend themselves in order to thwart any immediate British military
plans and also to show the ministry that the colonies would
fight as one. Such a show of force might even dissuade the
British from pursuing their coercive program and lead to
meaningful negotiations. Dickinson considered the reconciliation petition to the King as an effective way to alert the
British that what began as a family squabble rapidly was
becoming a civil war. Yet even if the petition was ignored
or scorned by the King, Congress would surely enhance its
domestic support because of such a rebuff. In order to insure
that American terms in the petition would be afforded proper
consideration, Dickinson believed a negotiation team should
carry the petition to the King.[17] Once in London the American
emissaries could quickly ascertain whether there was any
real ground for negotiation. If they found the British committed to resolve the dispute by force of arms the negotiating
team could stall the ministry and thus give the colonists more
time to prepare. James Duane also spoke in behalf of the
two-pronged proposal to work for peace and prepare for war.
A strong defense was needed, he asserted, but preparation for
war should not preclude continued efforts to reach an amicable
reunion with Britain.[18]

The radicals in Congress were quite pleased to have
the leaders of the Middle Colonial bloc lend their support to
military mobilization, but they did not relish the idea of

tying this to a quest for reunion. For even before Congress convened it was apparent that the radicals wanted to put the colonies on a complete war footing. Samuel Chase, the lone Maryland radical in Congress, sought to convince John Dickinson shortly after the Battle of Lexington that

The natural strength of this province cannot be exerted or called forth into action, without assuming the Powers of Government while the present *forms* of Government subsist we can neither raise taxes nor collect taxes sufficient to answer any effectual Purpose. . . .[19]

The radicals warned that peace efforts would only dissipate the resistance efforts and keep the people ignorant of America's dangerous predicament. Yet the efforts of the radicals to sidetrack the Dickinson–Duane program laid bare its deep-seated sectional support. After one particularly stormy debate on the Jay motion to send a petition to the King, John Adams was personally upbraided by the "Pennsylvania Farmer." "If you don't concur with us, in our pacific System," raged Dickinson, "I, and a Number of Us, will break off from you in New England, and We will carry on the Opposition by ourselves in our own way."[20] This outburst, however, made no impression on the New England men and it was only after the South Carolina delegation had lined up with the Middle Colonies that the motions for a petition to the King and a negotiating team to accompany it won congressional approval.[21]

On May 26 Congress had placed itself on record as supporting both aspects of the Dickinson–Duane program, but it was military preparedness that demanded immediate and sustained attention. In fact the continued deterioration of Anglo-American relations during the remainder of 1775 and the first six months of 1776 forced Congress to concen-

trate upon military affairs to such a degree that it became a
virtual council of war. The New York provincial congress
asked Congress on May 12 to outline the proper course of
action to be taken should a sizable British force be landed
in the colony. If this did not provide enough consternation,
Congress was informed on May 18 that because of the gen-
erous efforts of a band of Connecticut and Vermont adven-
turers, it had come into possession of the British forts at
Ticonderoga and Crown Point. Two weeks later, on June 2,
the Massachusetts provincial congress requested Congress to
consider the possible transformation of the New England
militia forces besieging Boston into a continental army.

One by one Congress dealt with these crucial military
questions. Most of the conciliation-minded delegates from the
Middle Colonies were in favor of reasonable military preparations but were chary of going beyond what could be defined
as defensive measures. John Dickinson in particular was in
favor of the colonies being "well armed and disciplined," but
he did not want American armed forces provoking hostile
action. The Middle Colonial bloc, along with some Southern
delegates, was also insistent that if a continental army was
formed it must contain troops from all sections. Thus on
June 14 Congress resolved that a total of six rifle companies
be raised to assist in the encirclement of Boston with Pennsylvania, Maryland and Virginia each supplying two companies.
John Adams viewed the willingness of the Middle Colonies to
supply troops for the Continental Army as indicative of their
deep-seated distrust of New England. "They have a Secret
Fear, A Jealousy," Adams contended, "that New England will
soon be full of veteran Soldiers and at length conceive Designs
unfavorable to the other Colonies."[22] In view of the small
numbers of troops ordered to Boston it seems apparent that

at least some of the delegates from the Southern and Middle
Colonies were more concerned about showing their good faith
than in limiting the build-up of New England troop strength.

George Washington's selection as commander-in-chief of
the infant Continental Army on June 15 also reflected the
sectional realities in Congress. Sam Adams convinced the
radicals that it would be good politics to drop their demand
for a New England man and allow the Middle Colonies and
the South to share the plum instead. The Reverend William
Gordon, a contemporary historian, concluded that "New
York, Pennsylvania, and the other colonies to the southward,
have not such confidence in Massachusetts Bay, as to admit
that one of their own natives should be commander-in-chief."[23]
Certainly, in the eyes of the delegates from the Middle Colonies, New England's flirtation with separation made it essential that one of their men not be entrusted with such a crucial
post.

Congressional consideration of military matters forced
the reunion proposals into the background for a time but did
not completely sidetrack them. On June 3 Dickinson and
Duane managed to have a petition-drafting committee appointed. Dickinson was made a member of the committee
along with John Jay of New York, Thomas Johnson of
Maryland, John Rutledge of South Carolina and Benjamin
Franklin. Only Franklin was a potential opponent of the
petition, but he was too wily a politician to try to sabotage
Dickinson's personal project. Dickinson and Duane did not,
however, solely confine their reconciliation efforts to Congress. The latter endeavored to bring the fourth resolution to
the attention of Congress by means of colonial referral. This
was the tactic which the Massachusetts delegates had used
skillfully on several occasions to prod Congress into making
important policy decisions. Duane apparently encouraged

Benjamin Kissam, a wealthy New York City lawyer who later
became a Loyalist, to bring before the New York provincial
congress a conciliation plan.[24] On May 30 he moved that the
New York provincial congress establish a committee to draft
a plan of reconciliation to be submitted to the Continental
Congress for its approval. The radical contingent led by
Alexander McDougall and Abraham Brasher worked to defeat this motion but were unable to prevent the selection of
a conservative-dominated drafting committee headed by Benjamin Kissam.

Three weeks later, on June 24, the report of the committee on the subject matter of a plan of accommodation with
Great Britain was presented to the New York congress for
consideration. In content the accommodation plan was very
similar to the negotiation terms which John Dickinson set
forth in May. The negotiators were to accept nothing less
than a redress of all the grievances enumerated by the First
Continental Congress as well as the repeal of the recent re-
straint of trade and fisheries acts. Parliament was also to
agree that the revenue received from colonial customs was
to be turned over to the assemblies. Unlike Dickinson's
scheme for a fixed income for the King, the New York plan
stated:

That the Colonists are ready and willing to support the civil
government within the respective colonies; and on proper requisi-
tions, to assist in the general defense of the Empire, in as ample
a manner as their respective abilities will admit of.[25]

However, the procedure to raise these funds was unacceptable
to the radical contingent and in the ensuing floor fight they
managed to strike out the objectional features. Thus, instead
of the colonial assemblies having the authority to select
representatives to a continental legislature "To meet with a

President appointed by the Crown . . ." as the drafting committee proposed, this power was left unspecified by inserting
the word "colonies" in place of "Assemblies."[26] McDougall
and his supporters were not able to emasculate the plan by
further direct alteration but they did manage to tack on two
crippling amendments.

A motion made by Gouverneur Morris to send the plan
to the New York delegation as a testimonial of the desire of
congress for reconciliation, and to be used in any manner
they determined, won approval. The second encumbering
amendment was introduced by Melanchthon Smith, a wealthy
landowner and merchant from Dutchess County, who does
not appear to have been a member of a radical clique. His
resolve declared that

all concerns of a religious and ecclesiastical nature, so far as they
may be under the cognizance and control of civil authority ought
to remain exclusively with the respective Colony Legislatures as
the most inestimable object of their internal police.[27]

Smith may have been influenced to introduce this amendment
by the strongly anti-papist newspaper essays "Remarks on the
Quebec Bill," from the pen of Alexander Hamilton.[28] Hamilton's assertion that Britain was laying the foundations for a
powerful Catholic state in the new province of Quebec under-
layed Smith's amendment. Gouverneur Morris once again
put his facile pen to work and redrafted the Smith amendment.
The result was an even more controversial amendment calling
for complete separation of church and state, whether the
state be Britain or the colonial assemblies. Benjamin Kissam,
Isaac Low, James DeLancey and other conservatives, fearing
the amendment would compromise the entire plan of accommodation, voted against the Morris rendition of the Smith
amendment but were unable to block it. On June 28 the

provincial congress approved a letter of introduction which gave the congressional delegation the option of laying the whole plan before Congress or only those portions of the plan they felt most advantageous.

The New York congressional delegation responded quickly to the plan of accommodation. In a letter written on July 6 and signed by all seven delegates then in Congress, the New York contingent expressed its gratitude to the provincial congress for offering a plan to avert the impending civil war.[29] But the letter made no mention of any intention to introduce the plan of accommodation. In fact it was worded in such a way as to give the impression that the plan would be filed and forgotten.

The gentle diversion of the plan of accommodation was dictated by the inhospitable climate in Congress. Duane's request for negotiation had barely passed in May, and since that time the increasing evidence of Britain's hostile intent had served to cool the spirit of reconciliation. One conservative delegate admitted confidentially that the Second Congress would never send a negotiating team to London because too many members were opposed to giving such a group plenary powers.[30]

Many Southern delegates were still on edge as the result of Governor Dunmore's threat to offer freedom from bondage to those slaves who would forsake their masters for the British standard. The situation on the Northern frontier was also of growing concern to the colonists for Sir John Johnson was reportedly wooing the Iroquois in behalf of the British. The bloody Battle of Bunker Hill fought on June 14, however, evoked the strongest anti-British reaction. Benjamin Franklin noted that in the wake of this event

. . . propositions for attempting an accommodation were not much

relished; and it has been with difficulty that we have carried
another petition to the crown to give Britain one more chance,
one opportunity more of recovering the friendship of the
colonists. . . .[31]

Thomas Jefferson contended that it was only because of Dickinson's great prestige that Congress approved his so-called
Olive Branch Petition to the King on July 5.

The petition which Dickinson drafted was virtually devoid of inflammatory language though not supine in tone.
John Dickinson left no doubt that the present unnatural state
of affairs was directly attributable to the tyrannical legislation
and administrative practices developed since 1763 by a handful of evil ministers. Although the Olive Branch Petition did
not clearly spell out all of the colonial terms for peaceful
settlement of the dispute, the immediate cessation of all British
military activity in the colonies would have to take place before
meaningful negotiations could commence. Another precondi-
tion for diplomacy was that Britain would have to agree to
redress all the grievances enumerated by the First Continental
Congress.

The petition expressed continued colonial fidelity to the
Crown and the British nation but stressed that George III
would have to intervene to preserve these attachments. Dickinson prophetically noted the day after the Olive Branch
Petition was accepted that all the hopes of the conciliation-
minded delegates were riding on this document. A hospitable
reception by the King might very well produce negotiations,
but a curt rejection would only mean full-scale civil war.[32]

Many of the radicals thought the petition foolhardy and
potentially detrimental to the American cause. John Adams
for one did not believe the reports from London that the
ministry was prepared to negotiate because of the unexpec-

tedly stiff colonial resistance at Lexington and the spirited support extended to the American union by New York and Pennsylvania.[33] But he and the other radicals were smart enough to check their impulse to make a precipitous rush for independence. John Adams was aware that the Middle Colonies ". . . like all Bodies of Men must and will have their Way and their Humour and even their Whims."[34] Yet the very next day his patience with the conciliationists wore thin and he angrily impugned their lack of empathy for New England. "Their are some persons in New York and Philadelphia," wrote Adams, "to whom a ship is dearer than a City, and a few Barrells of flower, than a thousand Lives—other Men's Lives I mean."[35]

Despite the frequent attacks that the radicals leveled against the Middle Colonial bloc because of its hesitancy, the significant body of legislation passed during the first eighty-one days of the Second Continental Congress clearly indicates that the statesmanship of reconciliation bowed to the statesmanship of war. The conciliationists in Congress who viewed the formation of a Continental Army as a necessary step soon learned they had opened Pandora's box. On June 22 Congress resolved to issue two million dollars in bills of credit on behalf of the twelve confederated colonies to finance American defensive preparations. Five days later, after a long and acrimonious debate, Major General Phillip Schuyler was instructed to invade Canada in order to prevent Sir Guy Carleton from launching an offensive via lakes Champlain and George. Scarcely two weeks later Congress extended its authority into the realm of Indian affairs by establishing three departments: the Northern, the Middle and the Southern.[36] From Indian affairs Congress turned to home defense and resolved on July 18:

That it be recommended to the inhabitants of all the United
Colonies in North America that all ablebodied effective men,
between sixteen and fifty years of age in each colony, immediately form themselves into regular companies of militia.[37]

Compulsory military service for every colonist was not the
intent of Congress at this time, but within a few months the
individual colonies would see fit to give the July 18th resolution this interpretation.

When the Continental Congress convened in May the
opinion among the delegates was that they would hammer
out some general policy recommendations within a relatively
short time span and either allow the individual colonies to
implement their recommendations or possibly select a small,
interim caretaker committee. Within a month it became clear
to most of the delegates that in lèading the American resistance movement they were assuming more and more functions
that were clearly governmental. The First Continental Congress may have been an advisory body but the Second was
rapidly becoming an intercolonial government. Benjamin
Franklin for instance recognized this emerging state of affairs
and decided to offer a remedy.

Although Franklin seemed ". . . more like a Spectator
than a member . . ." according to one observer of the Continental Congress, his affinity with the position of the New
England radicals soon became apparent.[38] "He does not hesitate at our boldest Measures . . ." wrote John Adams, and he
could have added that Franklin did not shy away from intro-
ducing controversial measures either.[39] For the "Articles of
Confederation" which he presented to Congress on July 23 was
tantamount to a declaration of independence. Basically it was
his old Albany Plan of Union with a number of alterations
to fit the current circumstances. The details of the proposed
government for "The United Colonies of North America"

need not concern us here, for the most important aspect of the plan was the list of unnegotiable demands that it tendered to Britain. Franklin had cast his "Articles of Confederation" in the form of an ultimatum. The intercolonial government established by the Articles was to continue until all of the grievances listed by the First Continental Congress were redressed, Boston received proper remuneration for economic losses resulting from the Boston Port Act, and all British troops were evacuated from the American mainland. If these conditions were not met the Confederation would become perpetual. Franklin admitted to his fellow delegates that his plan was intended to stimulate thought and discussion about the form of government Congress might wish to adopt should that exigency come to pass. But most of the delegates were terrified at the prospect of such a bold step, and they made sure that no entry was ever made in the *Journals* regarding Franklin's proposal.

Many of the Middle Colonial delegates had moved uneasily in their chairs several weeks before when John Dickinson defended the Olive Branch Petition as the last hope of substituting words for bullets. But for Benjamin Franklin, a man who knew the British mind better than any other American, to step forward and espouse what only a handful of the most forward radicals had been whispering in the cloakrooms, was a very sobering experience indeed. Prior to Lexington the topic of independence scarcely came before the public eye save in the writings of Tory pamphleteers. During the summer months of 1775 the Continental Congress and the New York provincial congress publicly denied that their activities were directed towards the achievement of independence. These disclaimers may be interpreted as a sign that the Patriot leaders were themselves beginning to realize that independence could no longer be scoffed at as a specious charge leveled by the British to frighten the American people. The intelligence letters sent to London during the summer of 1775 by such perceptive colonial watchers as Governor Franklin, Governor Tryon and Gilbert Barkly, a British merchant acting as a spy in Philadelphia, expressed alarm over the unmistakable drift towards independence. Almost with one voice these observers pleaded with the ministry to halt all military operations against the colonies and offer creditable terms for negotiation. "I verily believe nothing will bring these unhappy differences to a happy period, but the Appointment of Commissioners from home . . ." wrote Barkly, for "If the wound is continued open, the people's minds will get Corroded and prove ruinous to this Country and hurtful to the Parent State."[40]

On July 31 the Second Congress, wearied by its prodigious labors and wracked by sectional animosity, adjourned until September 5. The last major item of business the Congress transacted on the 31st was symbolic of the record this body had compiled during its first eighty-one days. Congress accepted a resolution prepared by Messrs. John Adams, Franklin, Jefferson and Richard Henry Lee denouncing Lord North's Conciliation Proposal as ". . . Unreasonable and insidious. . . ." This effectively dashed the hopes of some of the conciliationists who wished to use the North proposal as a basis for initiating negotiations with Britain.[41]

As with the First Congress the radical faction departed from Philadelphia in early August having accomplished a number of its objectives. But the gains were more closely contested in the Second Congress because of the emergence of the Middle Colonial bloc as a coherent faction. Since the Battle of Lexington had brought into clear focus the two alternatives of reconciliation and independence the delegates from the Central Provinces no longer suffered from the uncertainty that hampered them in the First Congress. The issues were now unmistakable. Although the Olive Branch Petition represented the only clear-cut victory achieved by the Middle Colonial bloc, it was a very important one. All hope of amicable reconciliation rode on this petition. A warm reception in Britain would enable the Middle Colonial delegates to put a stop to further military preparations and assumption of governmental powers and to begin searching for peace in earnest; a curt rejection would greatly undermine the credibility of their position.

chapter five

"THERE IS NO LITTLE ENEMY"

Military Preparations in the Middle Colonies
April to October, 1775

"[S]urely this Proceeding on the Part of General Gage is not the Olive Branch held up by Government . . .": this incredulous response by an unknown citizen of New York effectively summarizes the confusion and anger which the events of April 19 engendered among colonists of all political persuasions.[1] In every town and village from Lewes Town, Delaware, to Albany, prominent Tories lapsed into pained silence and conservative Whigs bowed to the demands of the radicals for mobilization. Christopher Marshall of Philadelphia happily noted this dramatic change of mood: "It's admirable to see the alteration of the Tory class in this place, since the account of the engagement in New England, their language is quite softened."[2] Neither John Adams nor any radical Whig could have anticipated that the Middle Colonies would begin to arm with such determination. Nevertheless, most radicals did not completely abandon their skepticism about the spirit of the Middle Colonies. And by the end of the summer the Central Provinces were again conducting their affairs like sunshine patriots.

    The transformation of the Middle Colonial protest leagues

into fledgling resistance movements was nowhere better illustrated than in Pennsylvania. While the Quaker Colony's response to Lexington may have lacked the fury of New York's,
in terms of the resulting military preparations and shift in the
balance of power it was far more substantial. The moderate
Whig coalition, which John Dickinson organized the preceding
summer, moved quickly to channel the popular enthusiasm for
military measures into a program that would satisfy the radicals
without completely alienating the conservatives.[3] After Governor Penn's futile attempt to have the Pennsylvania assembly
act independently on Lord North's conciliatory offer was
brushed aside, the question of arming the province came up
for debate. A petition from a substantial number of city residents urged the assembly to allocate £50,000 for defense.[4]
Dickinson and his cohorts realized that such a vast initial
expenditure was out of the question for many conservative
assemblymen were opposed to any allocation of funds whatsoever. Working on the theory that even a modest appropriation would set a precedent for more substantial grants in the
future, the Whig coalition convinced the assembly to approve
a grant of £7,000 for defense before it adjourned on May
13. Even the more radical leaders like Thomas Mifflin and
Charles Thomson did not balk at this amount because they
were intent upon organizing and training the thousands of
farmers and artisans who were already enrolled in the provincial military association. Governor John Penn estimated
that during the month of May alone 20,000 men took up
arms.[5] Even in counties like Bucks, which had previously been
only lukewarm in its support of the cause, the military proceedings won enthusiastic support. In the wake of this favorable reversal a patriotic gentleman from Bucks County
informed a friend in Philadelphia, "I hope [this will] in some
measure wipe off those aspersions we too deservedly lay
under."[6]

By the middle of June it was apparent to most Whig leaders that while the province possessed more than enough volunteers to defend itself, there was a serious shortage of military equipment and a crying need for more coherent organization.[7] The powerful Philadelphia committee led by Joseph Reed sought to remedy both these deficiencies by pressing the assembly to adopt appropriate measures. On June 23 the Philadelphia committee presented the assembly with a petition setting forth the specific military needs of the colony. The petition stressed that war measures should receive top priority in light of Britain's apparent determination to overawe the colonies by force of arms. The city committee urged the assembly to provide adequate defenses for the city and harbor of Philadelphia, to supply the funds for regular compensation of the militiamen and finally to appoint a committee of safety to oversee the affairs of the province when the assembly was not in session.[8] Four days later the assembly appointed a committee headed by such staunch Whigs as Charles Thomson, Anthony Wayne and John Dickinson to draft a plan for putting the city and province into a state of military readiness.

On June 30 the committee presented its plan to the assembly which approved it with only three dissenting votes. News of the fighting at Bunker Hill coupled with the effective leadership of Dickinson accounted for this surprising result. In approving the defense plan the assembly not only committed provincial funds to arm and support the associators (£ 35,000 and 5,000 muskets) but also entrusted its governmental powers to a council of safety composed of both assembly and non-assembly members. In effect this newly formed committee was to be the provincial war council. In deference to the Quakers and "Sectarian" Germans the assembly asked all militia officers to respect the right of conscientious objectors not to serve while encouraging the latter to volunteer other forms of assistance in lieu of service.

The council of safety began its work on July 3 and promptly selected Benjamin Franklin to serve as president. Throughout July and August the committee met on an average of six times a week in the sweltering summer heat of Philadelphia. During this period the council of safety, with the cooperation of the New Jersey provincial congress, began construction of gigantic *chevaux de frises* which were to be sunk at strategic locations in the Delaware River to prevent the passage of British warships.[9] The council also determined to secure a fleet of row galleys to protect the city from British warships. A permanent watch was established at Cape Henlopen to provide advance warning of any approaching British men-of-war and work was begun on the fort below the town of Gloucester to make it a more formidable defensive outpost. By the end of August several of the row galleys complete with cannon were ready for service, and the council quickly drafted a set of regulations to govern the sailors and officers manning these armed boats. Article five of the regulations which prescribed the death penalty for mutiny, cowardice or negligence laid bare the apparent conviction of the council members that Pennsylvania could not fight the British with halfway measures.

During the month of August a number of examples of nonsupport and outright opposition to the military association were brought to the attention of the council. The York County committee informed the council that the special treatment accorded the conscientious objectors was lowering the morale of the associators. A tax on all non-associators was the solution they espoused. In Bucks County a majority of the members of the board of commissioners and assessors voted to ignore the directive from the assembly to procure 300 rifles for the military association. Such examples of discontent were to become commonplace during the fall months. They were symptomatic of the shift in the colonial rationale for military preparedness. Volunteerism was no longer deemed sufficient to maintain the military program in Pennsylvania or in any of the Middle Colonies. The radical Whigs were demanding that military service and support for the cause be made compulsory for all inhabitants.

On July 6 the Continental Congress, in setting forth the cause and necessity for their taking up arms, declared:

the arms we have been compelled by our enemies to assume, we will, in defiance of every hazzard, with unabating firmness and perseverance, employ for the preservation of our liberties; being with one mind resolved to die freemen rather than live slaves.[10]

This statement represented both a claim for justifiable self-defense and an attempt by Congress to change the course of British policy. By making the point that the colonial union would fight rather than disintegrate if challenged in war, congressional leaders hoped to play upon the reported indecisiveness of the ministry. America's most reliable London observers, William and Arthur Lee, consistently implored colonial leaders in June and July to keep the pressure on the ministry. The Lee brothers suggested that only through dogged perseverance could the wavering ministry be forced to make concessions. On June 8, William Lee reported that Britain had reached the bottom of its military man-power barrel. If the colonists stalemated the troops already committed, Britain would have to negotiate.[11] Various unidentified London correspondents in the Philadelphia newspapers echoed the views of the Lee brothers throughout June and July.

Early in August, however, a noticeable shift in the tenor of London news took place. In the August 2 issue of the *Pennsylvania Gazette* an anonymous London reporter indicated that vacillation was no longer dogging the councils of the ministry: "It is a determined measure in Council that neither BLOOD nor TREASURE shall be spared to bring our American

brethren to what is called a sense of their duty."[12] Later in
August William Lee corroborated this view: "The sword of
Civil War is at length drawn & . . . Success alone will determine whether it will be called hereafter a Rebellion or Revolution."[13] Towards the end of September reports that Britain
was preparing to wage a full-scale war of suppression received further confirmation with the news that German mercenaries were being hired for the impending contest. As early
as June rumors were about that the ministry was considering
the feasibility of using foreign troops against the rebellious
colonies. The numerous accounts of mercenary forces bound
for America appearing in September and October were still
unconfirmed, but the absence of any authoritative disclaimers
must have made them seem like more than just hearsay.[14]

The reluctance of the conservative and moderate Whigs
to adopt no-choice military and loyalty measures, even with
the mounting evidence that Britain was planning to make war
on the colonies, was tied to the shape of events within the
colony. On July 20 the New York–Philadelphia Synod issued
a pastoral letter to all congregations calling upon Presbyterians
to support the colonial union and be brave in battle, if war
became a necessity. John Adams rejoiced over the strong
patriotic stance of the Synod and he observed in Philadelphia
that the clergy ". . . are but now beginning to engage in politics, and they engage with a fervour that will produce wonder-
full Effects."[15] The reaction of the Quakers and Anglicans in
Pennsylvania was one of dismay. In their minds the Presbyterian Synod's espousal of the cause meant that they were
little better than the despicable New England Congregationalists.[16]

With full authorization from the Synod to work in behalf
of the resistance movement many Presbyterian pastors became
activists. Their sermons increasingly dealt with war and pa-

triotism. The Reverend John Carmichael delivered a sermon entitled "A Self Defensive War Lawful" to Captain Ross's militia company. For his text he selected Luke 22:36, "Then said he unto them, but now he that hath a purse let him take it, and likewise his scrip, and he that hath no sword let him sell his garment and buy one."[17]

During and after the War for Independence many prominent Tories like Joseph Galloway, Samuel Cooper and the Reverend Charles Inglis charged the Presbyterians with instigating the Revolution. In their view the Presbyterians (as used by contemporaries the term encompassed New England Congregationalists as well) engineered a revolution in hopes of attaining colonial religious domination and a republican form of government. It is thus significant to note that during the summer of 1775 the Pennsylvania Presbyterians were becoming increasingly identified in the popular mind with the New England radicals. James Lloyd, a Maryland provincial congress delegate, was informed that ". . . an itch for independence exists in your Province among Presbyterians, and that they make no secret of it."[18]

In Philadelphia proper many merchants and business men were upset by the closing of the export trade on September 10 as specified in the Continental Association. Personal financial loss formed a large part of their concern, no doubt, but many were also worried about the effect that prolonged unemployment would have on the lower classes.[19] Four days before nonexportation was to take effect Philadelphia denizens were shaken by an act of mob violence. The affair began when a crowd of patriotic inhabitants sought out Isaac Hunt and Dr. John Kearsely, who were avowed Tories. The mob had Hunt in tow and was in quest of Kearsely when the good doctor foolishly snapped a pistol at them. A roar went up from the crowd and it surged forward to pummel Kearsely into submission. At that very moment John Dickinson and James Allen interceded and saved both men from serious physical injury.[20]

The violence and lawlessness surrounding the Hunt–Kearsely incident shocked many conservative Whigs in the city and did nothing to strengthen their commitment to the resistance movement. On the other hand the radical Whigs were disgusted by the city committee's failure to deal firmly with the two Tories. One radical Whig noted that in Maryland a certain Tory "had been fined £500 and banished from the province for the same offense committed by Hunt and Kearsely." Yet at that very moment "...Mr. Hunt and his associates were triumphing in the success of their measures, declaring publickly, that the committee had rendered itself ridiculous...."[21] In the weeks and months ahead John Dickinson and his moderate Whig following were to come under increasing attack from radicals for their seeming willingness to condone the cautious policies espoused by the Quaker–Proprietary interest.

In addition to the deepening internal strife Pennsylvania found its frontiers also in jeopardy. On September 11 a force of Virginia militiamen moved into Fort Pitt in direct violation of a pledge by the congressional delegates of both colonies. Many Pennsylvanians were concerned that the Indians might look upon this interprovincial squabble as a sign of mutual weakness. Likewise, a renewal of this dispute could only serve to polarize western inhabitants at a time when unity was essential.[22] In the northwest sector of the province the Connecticut settlers were showing no inclination to check their rapacious land hunger and thus ease the long-standing Wyoming Valley dispute. Violence was feared.[23] Silas Deane went so far as to maintain that the Proprietary interest was intentionally trying to bring the two sides to blows in hopes of weakening the resistance movement.

Seemingly undeterred by the political friction all around
it, the council of safety endeavored to complete its military
plans for Philadelphia during the month of September. A
permanent lookout was stationed at Lewes Town, Delaware,
and the inhabitants were persuaded to mount six cannon to
thwart any British raiding sorties. The council of safety also
agreed to supply the citizens of Lewes Town with 100 small
arms. On September 16 the council resolved that all Delaware
River pilots should place their boats in drydock and refrain
from frequenting places where British soldiers might be lurk-
ing. Refusal to comply with the recommendations of the council was punishable by publication as an "Enemy to American
Liberty, A Traytor to his Country. . . ."[24]

Two days before the annual election for members of the
assembly, the council of safety presented a memorial to the
legislature requesting additional funds to complete the city
and harbor defenses. The council also informed the assemblymen that unless conscientious objectors were forced to pay a
tax equivalent to actual service, the Pennsylvania forces would
face a dangerous morale problem. Both requests were deemed
urgent because of the growing certainty that Britain planned
to subdue the colonies. In view of the forthcoming elections
and the council's past record of forwardness, Franklin and his
cohorts may have been trying to influence the outcome of the
contests in the city. Although Benjamin Franklin and Thomas
Mifflin were among the eleven new members elected throughout the province on October 1, this moderate turnover did
not alter the essentially conservative character of the assembly.[25]

The forward thrust given to the resistance movement in
Pennsylvania by the military clash at Lexington proved to
have less far-reaching effect in neighboring New York. To be
sure, the radical Whigs did gain ascendancy in New York City

for a short time. While in control they deposed the Tory-in-
fested committee of sixty and replaced it with a more balanced
committee of one hundred. But when the first provincial congress began its labors late in May, the radical dominance
came to an end. A coalition of moderates and conservatives
took control of the congress from the onset and saw to it that
patriotic enthusiasm did not becloud their sense of judgment.

The provincial congress began its deliberations with an
appreciation of the grave difficulties that lay ahead. On one
hand rumors continued to circulate that the ministry still
expected to be able to detach New York from the colonial
union. On May 1 a private letter attributed to Oliver DeLancey appeared in a New York newspaper. His point was that
New York would never forsake the Empire:

"I was born in this City, and am well acquainted with the other
colonies, from whose opposition Government has nothing to fear,
except from New England; and as a dutiful subject to the Crown,
I hope they will meet a punishment suitable to their rebellion.
This Province of New York and Pennsylvania are most attached
to the Crown and Parliament. . . . "[26]

Although such reports of sectional discord were becoming
more and more common, the Whigs were also alarmed by the
prospect of an actual invasion by the British Army. New
York's geographical location at the base of New England,
coupled with Britain's belief in the intense loyalty of most
New Yorkers, made it a likely spot for an invasion whether
by sea or via the time-honored Lake Champlain–Lake George
route.[27]

All of New York's woes did not stem solely from the
British threat. The prospect of New England troops intervening in the affairs of the province on the pretext of averting a
mass defection to the enemy seemed all too real. Lieutenant
Governor Colden claimed that "Every species of public and

private resentment was threatened to terrify the inhabitants
of this Province," after the New York assembly refused to
consider the proceedings of the First Congress.[28] In this same
vein he considered the capture of forts Ticonderoga and Crown
Point as part of a general plan to force New York to become
a more dedicated member of the colonial union. In short the
New York Whigs believed they would be damned if they did
and damned if they didn't.

Home defense was the most pressing problem facing
the provincial congress as it began its deliberations. Although
more than four weeks had elapsed since the fighting at Lexington and the threat of a British invasion still hung over the
colony, little if any military preparations had been started. In
contrast Philadelphia was reported to have 4,000 men under
arms including two companies of artillery.[29] It was not until
the last day of May that the provincial congress took the first
step toward the creation of a provincial-wide militia by
recommending to all inhabitants that they " . . . perfect themselves in the military art. . . ."[30] This congressional directive
surprisingly provided no specific guidelines for militia organization.

The provincial congress had moved none too soon in
initiating military preparations, for trouble was brewing on the
frontier. The Tryon County committee of correspondence
became embroiled in a feud with Colonel Guy Johnson, the
Indian superintendent for the Northern district. The committee charged Johnson with attempting to arouse the Iroquois
against them and that " . . . his design is to keep us in awe,
and oblige us to submit to a state of slavery."[31] The committee
further accused Johnson of disrupting communications between Tryon County residents and Albany as well as illegally
searching travellers on public highways. This rash attack
prompted the Albany City government to try to conciliate

Colonel Johnson. They assured him that no invasion of his domain either by New England forces or local residents was planned and that his service as Indian superintendent was appreciated by all frontier residents. The provincial congress also took precautions to avoid giving offense to Colonel Johnson and his Indian allies. Governor Trumbull of Connecticut was asked to make sure that "every effort to preserve and improve the present peaceable disposition of the Canadians and Indians" was made by the Connecticut forces assigned to assist in the garrisoning of forts Ticonderoga and Crown Point.[32] The Tryon County committee, under pressure from Albany and the provincial congress, wrote to Colonel Johnson on June 2, expressing their hope that he would not allow the Indians to take sides in the Anglo-American dispute.

Faced with the prospect of an Indian war the provincial congress turned to the Continental Congress for help. On June 7 it dispatched a letter to the New York delegates imploring them to do everything in their power to have Congress take a hand in Indian relations. "This importance, the necessity of attention to Indian Affairs, is deeply impressed on our minds," wrote the provincial congress "because our publick is more endangered by the situation of the barbarians to the westward of us, than it can be by any inroads made upon the seacoast."[33] James Duane concurred completely in this assessment of the danger. He discounted the likelihood of a British invasion of New York City and stressed that the province faced an immediate threat only from Quebec and the Six Nations.[34]

Throughout the remainder of the year the New York Whigs were apprehensive about conditions on their frontier. Periodic reports from the far western counties during the summer months told of Colonel Johnson's continuing efforts to enlist Indians in behalf of Britain. Early in July Major

General Philip Schuyler reported that Indian warfare on the frontier seemed imminent. He requested the provincial congress to station two regiments on the frontier in order to overawe the Indians and protect the citizens of New York as well as New Jersey and Pennsylvania.[35] Schuyler's warning was followed by a report from the Tryon County committee in mid-July that Colonel Johnson was mobilizing 800 to 900 Indians for a strike against the county. Although neither this attack nor any other Indian raid materialized in 1775, the fear engendered by the threat of such an occurrence was another good reason for the Whigs to shy away from boldness in any form.

The reluctance of the provincial congress to take decisive action in military matters and Indian affairs carried over into the realm of finance. The first New York congress made no serious attempt to come to grips with the problem of finances until the end of August. During the first two and one-half months of operation the delegates managed to limp along on funds drawn from the regular treasury, the loan office at Albany and the personal bonds of various deputies. For a time many of the delegates were hopeful that the paper money scheme which Gouverneur Morris had convinced the Continental Congress to accept would provide a convenient source of operating funds. This did not prove to be the case. Direct taxation was one possible recourse, but the New York Whigs naturally shied away from such a strong measure. Besides, the Whigs in New Jersey were having a hard time collecting the direct tax they had levied upon a populace that was in general better disposed than New York's to the American cause.

Late in July the provincial congress had attempted to shore up its shaky financial situation with a temporary measure. The New York delegation was urged to try to convince the Continental Congress to authorize the sale of the vast stores of Dutch tea in New York City. The proceeds could then be used for military needs. The provincial congress admitted openly that any attempt on its part to tax the inhabitants would be foolhardy.[36] A week and a half later the situation seemed desperate. Unless the Continental Congress could provide some financial assistance, the New York congress might have to disband its armed forces. This dire prediction never became a reality, however, because the New York congress turned to paper money. On August 30 the report of the committee to study the best modes of securing monies for defense was amended on the floor and the taxation provision replaced by a plan to issue £45,000 in certificates.

In its dealings with the British in New York City the provincial congress showed that it was willing to make almost any necessary accommodation. On June 8, for example, John Morin Scott and Alexander McDougall proposed that congress apply to the Continental Congress for permission to remove the cannon and stores from the vacant British forts in the city. This resolution was beaten down by the conservative Whigs. Even more rankling was the decision to order the return of military stores removed from the baggage carts of a departing company of British troops. This continuing want of resolution was a constant embarrassment to the radical Whigs. Christopher Tappan, George Clinton's brother-in-law, attributed the pusillanimity of the New York congress to their incomplete commitment to the resistance movement and their fear of British depredations against the city. Nevertheless, he was encouraged by the growing intercolonial attentiveness to New York's affairs:

thanks be to God that this Chain now Extended over the American Colonies; think ourselves able to take the Ends and form a Circle therewith, so as to squeeze their very guts out if they have any.[37]

Two months later radicals in New York were still decrying
the cunctative pace of the provincial congress. John Holt,
the Whiggish editor of the *New York Journal,* blamed Tory
sympathizers and lukewarm Whigs, who had been brought
into the revolutionary councils in hope that they might be
converted. Instead of becoming well affected to the cause
these men stymied the resistance movement at every turn.[38]
No better illustration of the province's indecisiveness can be
found than the pitiful plea of the committee of safety in
mid-July:

We have no arms, we have no powder, we have no blankets. For
God's sake send us money, send us arms, send us Ammunition.
. . . If Ticonderoga is taken from us, fear, which made the
savages our friends, will render Ravages on our frontiers will
foster dissensions among us ruinous of the cause.[39]

The return of Governor Tryon to New York City in June
ironically coincided with the arrival of General Washington in
the city, enroute to his command at Cambridge. The provincial congress had no qualms about serving two masters as
it provided escorts for both dignitaries. But aside from the
comic relief of crowds and retinues serving an American general in the afternoon and a British governor in the evening,
the situation typified New York's peculiar position in 1775.
Both the British ministry and the Second Continental Congress
were aware of the immense psychological and strategic importance of controlling New York.

With the arrival of Governor Tryon the contest intensified. In large part this was because the Whigs respected his
abilities as a politician and military officer. During his five
years as governor he had waged a vigorous campaign to vali-
date New York's claim to the New Hampshire Grants and also
maintained good relations with both the DeLancey and Livingston factions. By such acts he won the respect if not the

admiration of many inhabitants. But Tryon, both by training and inclination, was always more interested in military affairs. The greatest success of his career had been his suppression of the North Carolina Regulators in 1771. From his conversations with Dartmouth in the spring of 1775 it is evident that he relished the opportunity of returning to New York to emboss his record with even greater military triumphs. As one fellow Loyalist noted, Tryon was "the pink of politeness, and the quintessence of vanity. . . ."[40] Within two weeks of his return Isaac Sears hatched a plot to cart Tryon off to Connecticut and thus free the colony from his skillful machinations. General Schuyler vetoed the plan because he feared it might goad the British into military retaliation.[41]

General Washington was particularly concerned about the damage to the cause that Governor Tryon might accomplish if he were allowed to go about his business unmolested. Throughout the summer months Washington constantly reminded Schuyler to "Keep a watchful eye upon Governor Tryon, and if you find him directly or indirectly, attempting any measure inimical to the common cause, use every Means in your power to frustrate his designs."[42]

Soon after his return Governor Tryon seems to have cooled on the idea of actively recruiting New Yorkers to fight for the King's standard. He informed Dartmouth that without the backing of British regulars the colonial governors could not hope to withstand the resistance movement.[43] He did, however, assure Dartmouth that many of the so-called Whigs were very phlegmatic. If the Union Jack was raised by a sizable force of regulars, thousands of recruits could be secured in both New York and New Jersey.

Although temporarily thwarted in the military sphere, Tryon found that he could effectively harass the provincial congress and the city radicals by playing upon their fear of a

British attack. After living through two rumored invasions, the inhabitants of New York City were understandably edgy. When the British warship *Asia,* commanded by Captain George Vandeput, briefly bombarded the city on the night of August 23, the result was a mass exodus. The bombardment, which was intended to halt removal of cannon from the fort, actually injured only a handful of men and put a few craters in the town walls. Nevertheless it ". . . disconcerted the inhabitants, who have been moving for two or three days with their effects as they expected a Second edition of Captain Vandeput's politeness."[44] Governor Tryon shrewdly informed the mayor that henceforth, on new orders from Lord Dartmouth, British naval commanders had authority to bombard any seaport they deemed in a state of rebellion.

The radicals on the committee of safety led by Alexander McDougall took it upon themselves to answer the British attempts to intimidate the movement. On September 1 they approved a set of penalties for Tory activities ranging from giving aid and comfort to the enemy to willfully ignoring the authority of the Continental Congress. Guilty parties could have their property confiscated, suffer disarmament or even imprisonment. The spirit shown by the committee of safety was not matched either by the committee of one hundred or the provincial congress. Both bodies had trouble raising a quorum in September and as long as the British cannon menaced the city the situation would show no prospect of improvement.

In contrast to their New York comrades, the New Jersey Whigs encountered little opposition during the spring and summer of 1775 as they exchanged their plowshares for muskets. For after Lexington martial spirit swept the colony in a manner reminiscent of Pennsylvania. "I hear with great concern serious accounts of strange Commotions . . . occasioned by the late melancholy news from Boston," was how one conservative described the sudden appearance of marching men in New Jersey.[45] Even the stolid Dutchmen of Bergen County in East Jersey discarded their customary indifference to outside events and began to arm themselves. In their declaration of association of May 12 they stressed "that the Preservation of the Rights and Privileges of the British Colonies in America, now depends on the firm Union of their inhabitants, in a vigorous Prosecution of Measures necessary for their Safety. . . ."[46] The more excitable inhabitants of Sussex County went so far as to close all the courts.

Despite the multitude of evidence that anti-British feeling was running high in New Jersey, Governor Franklin convened the assembly at Burlington in May to present the February 20th Conciliation Proposal. In his opening speech Franklin endeavored to justify the British quest for revenue from the colonies. He claimed that the colonists should pay their share for the naval and military assistance extended them during the French and Indian War. He admitted that many Jerseymen might disagree with various portions of Lord North's offer but they could at least show their good intentions by giving it a reasonable trial. Outright rejection of the British peace offer could only be interpreted as a sign that the colonists were flirting with thoughts of independence.

Although the assembly welcomed Franklin's address, the members refused to be cooperative. They informed him on May 18 that it was impossible to take up Lord North's offer because "this resolution contains no new proposal: it appears to us to be the same with one made to the colonies the year preceding the passing of the late Stamp act. . . ."[47] Besides, such unilateral action by New Jersey would be detrimental to the colonial union. It should be noted that the governor's effectiveness in this instance was diminished by a purloined letter. One of his epistles to Lord Dartmouth, in which he cast aspersions on the patriotism of certain house members, raised the ire of a number of men who ordinarily might have supported him.[48]

Some eighty-seven delegates representing all thirteen Jersey counties convened on May 26. Among them were nine members of the assembly with seven of these from counties in East Jersey. For over a week the provincial congress occupied itself with a host of minor matters, although it did manage to produce a statement of association and a declaration for taking up arms. The statement of association contained the standard justification of American conduct used by most colonies, with one significant addition. The citizens of New Jersey were instructed to support all laws of the existing government insofar as they did not conflict with the recommendations of the Continental or provincial congress. In other words obedience to royal government was becoming a matter of choice. The justification for taking up arms was also belligerent. The provincial congress admitted to

. . . being apprehensive that all pacifick measures for the redress of our grievances will prove ineffectual, do think it high necessary that the inhabitants of this Province be forthwith properly armed and disciplined for defending the cause of American freedom.[49]

Before a week had passed the congress followed up its strong words with equally strong measures. Each township was to raise a minimum of one company (approximately eighty men) and a direct tax of £10,000 was levied to pay for war supplies. A special committee of safety was established to oversee the resistance movement while the congress was not in session. As the delegates prepared for adjournment on June 3 a mood of confidence pervaded the air. Since Lexington the opposition had been silent. Governor Franklin sadly concluded that: "All Parties are united, at least in appearance."[50] Suspected Tories were being watched closely, especially in East Jersey:

... those who happen and are known to differ in sentiment from the generality? They become a mark at once for popular Fury, and those who are esteemed Friends of Government denoted for Destruction.—They are not even allowed to preserve a neutrality and passiveness becomes a Crime—[51]

Anglican clergymen as well as government officials were the targets of the zealous Patriots. The Reverend William Frazer of Amwell was literally barred from his pulpit for encouraging his congregation to abide by the laws of the province. Governor Franklin could only lament that the Tories of New Jersey were ". . . too scattered to venture forming themselves into a Body, especially as they have no places of Strength or Security to resort to."[52]

Although the Tories posed no real problems during the summer months, the provincial congress still faced a host of important business when it reconvened on August 5. A report that a British task force was about to descend on New York City prompted the committee of safety to call the New Jersey congress back into session. New Jersey's continued readiness to come to the aid of New York during its frequent moments of crisis was tied to provincial self-interest. For if New York was ever taken over by the British, whether voluntarily or involuntarily, the Whigs in New Jersey would be placed in jeopardy as well. Typical of the ongoing concern for New York was the report of the Woodbridge committee (Essex County) in early May:

We have for some time past feared the New-Yorkers would desert American liberty, but are now fully convinced, by their late spirited conduct, that they are determined to support the grand cause.[53]

Some of the problems before the New Jersey provincial congress, such as organization of a minuteman network, were directly related to the situation in New York but others concerned strictly internal matters. Two months of trial and error were enough to convince the congress that there were a number of flaws in the military regulations. For one thing the status of conscientious objectors needed clarification. On August 17 the congress, perhaps following the precedent set by Pennsylvania, ordered that the right of conscientious objectors not to serve in the association should be respected. But in turn they were to give generously to aid the cause. Another source of difficulty was the failure of the general public to pay the special defense tax levied in June. The New Jersey congress instructed all township and county committees to submit up-to-date lists of all nonassociators and delinquent taxpayers but went no further. That this congress made no concerted effort to resolve its fiscal problems was apparently owing to its lame duck status. An open letter to the public on August 12 announced that elections for a new provincial congress would be held on September 21. The delegates explained their action as follows:

Whereas, it is highly expedient, at a time when this province is likely to be involved in all the horrours of a Civil War, and when it has become absolutely necessary to increase the burden of Taxes already laid upon the good people of this Colony for the just defence of their invaluable rights and privileges that the inhabitants thereof should have frequent opportunities for renewing their choice and approbation of the Representatives in Provincial Congress.[54]

With more difficult times ahead the provincial congress thought it advisable to solidify its popular support.

In taking this action the first provincial congress inadvertently precipitated a controversy by its attendant effort to clarify voter eligibility.[55] If the suffrage were limited to those citizens who were eligible to vote for members of the assembly, then many loyal supporters would be denied the franchise. It is difficult to determine whether or not the suffrage restriction laid down by the outgoing provincial congress had any bearing on the election of delegates to the new provincial congress. No extant record of any protest or memorial urging election or defeat of a candidate on this issue can be found. Nevertheless, the election did result in a significant turnover of delegates. Twenty-two of the forty-seven men who came together on October 3 for the first session of the second provincial congress were newcomers. Such a result was no doubt what the old provincial congress had in mind when it informed the public of the dire circumstances that the new congress would have to face. The stouter Whigs had offered the fainthearted a way out. Either by choice or otherwise many of the more conservative Whigs disappeared from the political stage at this convenient moment.

Even before the election conditions in New Jersey were becoming increasingly unsettled. Wedged as it was between two populous colonies, New Jersey began to receive increasing numbers of refugees from New York City and Philadelphia.[56] The New Jersey committee of safety took steps to control the influx by empowering its citizenry to arrest and detain for questioning any strangers who did not offer an acceptable explanation for their conduct. On September 25 Jerseyites were given a taste of British justice. A boatload of marines from the *Asia* committed a "felonious piratical outrage" by stopping the Perth Amboy stage boat and carrying off an officer from General Wooster's command.[57] As autumn deepened such acts of violence and raids by British forces were to become more and more commonplace in the Middle Colonies.

"Saturday afternoon I made a little excursion down to Wilmington. Every little village we passed thro, had Com-

panies of Men exercising," was how John Adams related his
pleasing discovery that New Castle County, Delaware, was
again showing good spirit.[58] If he had proceeded a bit further
south into Sussex County, he would not have enjoyed the
countryside as much for this county was again lagging far
behind its northern neighbors. It took New Castle County only
a week after receipt of the news of Lexington to initiate
appropriate measures. On May 3 the county committee voted
to levy a defense tax of one shilling, six pence on each pound
of assessed value. The spirit in the county was so high that
they ". . . pay it with more cheerfulness than they have been
known to pay any tax heretofore. . . ."[59] By mid-summer New
Castle County was able to field three well-armed and trained
regiments of militia. As one might expect Tory activity in the
county seems to have been virtually nonexistent during the
summer and fall months. Even the lone Anglican minister in
the county, the Reverend Aeneas Ross, was a hearty Whig. On
July 20, the day of "Fasting, Humiliation, and Prayer" called
by the Continental Congress, Ross preached to the multitude
from the Biblical text, "When the House goeth forth against
the enemy, then keep thee from every wicked thing!"[60]

Three weeks after New Castle began to organize its defense effort, the militia officers from more than twenty newly
formed companies met at Dover to lay the basis for the Kent
County military organization. Two regiments of militia were
formed with Caesar Rodney being selected as the colonel for
the upper regiment and another staunch Whig, John Haslet,
receiving the same rank for the lower regiment. The Kent
militia officers pledged their lives and property to defend the
freedom and rights of America against British oppression.
Except for the Reverend Syndenham Thorn, who refused to
observe July 20 as a day of humiliation and prayer, Tory
activity was negligible in Kent County during the summer
months.[61]

In September, however, Dr. Charles Ridgely, one of the county's leading citizens, was brought before the committee for examination. A certain Daniel Mifflin claimed that Dr. Ridgely, a past chairman of the Kent committee, had told him that the row galleys could not possibly offer any serious opposition to the British warships. Furthermore that ". . . we could not defend ourselves against the Powers of England . . . that he did not approve of their taking up Arms, it appeared to him like Rebellion. . . ."[62] In the future military engagements the good doctor predicted that American forces would be humbled by the British and Congress forced to eat its words of defiance. With Thomas Rodney presiding the committee interrogated Dr. Ridgely on September 11. The same day by a vote of eight to two he was acquitted. The two men who voted against acquittal, Dr. James Tilton and John Killen, bitterly assailed Rodney for his defense of Ridgely, who they deemed the leader of the Tory cabal in the county. Thomas Rodney defended his conduct by maintaining that the cause would be ill served if Whigs used patriotism as a bludgeon to settle personal quarrels.[63]

No concerted response to the events of April 19 was apparently made in Sussex County until June 20, when about fifty residents assembled at Broad Creek to organize a committee of correspondence and public safety. The newly formed committee blamed the confusion attendant with the Pennsylvania–Maryland boundary dispute, involving the southern edge of the county, for its tardy attention to the cause. Its members emphatically denied that their reluctance to organize a committee and raise a military force was owing to ". . . the influence of any Tories among us, or any disregard to the common cause."[64] And yet within a month these brave denials came back to haunt them. The committee proved incapable of silencing Thomas Robinson, who openly flaunted his Toryism. Robinson, a wealthy landowner and the acknowledged leader of the Sussex assembly delegation, had first revealed his coolness to the cause in the summer of 1774 when he voted against sending delegates to the First Congress. The Sussex committee was informed on July 18 by several witnesses that Robinson was openly selling tea at his Indian River store and referring to the men who mustered as "a pack of fools" for engaging in such treasonous conduct.[65] Four days later the Sussex committee ordered Robinson to appear before it to answer these charges. Robinson impudently responded that he would be glad to appear if he could bring forty or fifty armed retainers as character witnesses. The committee promptly branded Robinson a traitor to the cause but made no immediate attempt to apprehend him. Thomas Robinson's impunity from Whig justice was comparable to the position enjoyed by Col. Guy Johnson in New York. Both of these Tories were simply too powerful for the Whig organizations to bring to heel without outside assistance.

Throughout the summer months the three counties attended to their individual military programs and made no effort to establish a colony-wide defense plan. A committee of safety for the colony was finally organized on September 16 as the result of an informal poll of Whig groups in the three counties.[66] The inactivity of the Delaware assembly from May until October is surprising in light of the influence which this body wielded in March. Except for agreeing on June 7 to assume its proper share of the cost for raising and maintaining Continental troops, the Delaware assembly remained on the sidelines. The only conclusion that seems plausible is that the Tory sentiment of the Sussex delegates was enough to dissuade the Whigs from looking to the assembly to accomplish their plans.

The newly formed council of safety met for a week at

Dover late in September. It immediately confirmed almost all of the militia officers in the province (save for a few Tories) and selected three brigadier generals for the militia including Caesar Rodney. A set of military regulations were drafted which contained a justification for taking up arms and a resolution praying for peaceful resolution of the dispute. The militia officers were enjoined to prepare lists of all able-bodied freemen and conscientious objectors who refused to associate. No action was to be initiated against conscientious objectors save by the council of safety. By the first of October the revolution in Delaware had proceeded in military preparation and assumption of governmental authority about as far as in New Jersey and Pennsylvania.

In six months time the Middle Colonies had moved from peaceful protesting to armed rebellion. Although the grave implications of this transition were not lost upon the conservative and moderate Whigs, they were initially powerless to check the war fever which swept the Central Provinces after Lexington. In the space of a few short weeks the Central Provinces answered the call to arms. As they went about their military preparations, they soon discovered that cooperation with neighboring colonies was essential in such matters as coastal defense, military supply and Tory control. New Jersey especially cooperated with New York and Pennsylvania in a variety of military matters. Towards the end of the summer the natural falling off in the patriotic enthusiasm coincided with the clarification of British intentions, thus creating sharp rifts within the Whig organizations. The radical Whigs argued that America's bluff had been called. To insure the success of American arms they advocated compulsory military service, imprisonment of dangerous Tories and forceable confiscation of weapons from nonassociators The more cautious Whigs like John Dickinson and John Jay wished to hold back from such strong measures because they would seriously undermine the regular governments and bring the provinces closer to independence. In essence the radical Whigs were willing to concede the wisdom of the Italian adage "there is no little war," something the more cautious Whigs were not yet ready to admit.[67]

On the face of it all four of the Middle Colonies were more securely attached to the colonial union in October than they were in April. The steady tramp of drilling soldiers and the mock battle cries of eager militiamen could be heard throughout the entire region. Nevertheless, one should not conclude that either their affection for the Empire or their repugnance towards New England was abating. In the months ahead the attachment of the Middle Colonies to the colonial union was to become an issue again as it had been during the winter of 1774-1775.

In the fall of 1775 the Middle Colonies also diverged in the amplitude of their individual commitments to the colonial union. The Whigs in New Jersey, Pennsylvania and Delaware seemed to espouse the cause with more conviction than their counterparts in New York. All three provinces had proven very conscientious and resolute in their own military preparations and in fulfilling requests from the Continental Congress. That New York should rank lowest in fidelity is not surprising. With the Indian menace on the frontier, the British threat to New York City, a substantial Tory party within and the New England radicals fulminating to the north, it is no wonder that the New York Whigs acted like men in a trance. Sheer expediency tended to dictate their policy. It was as if they wanted the question of independence or reunion to be decided for them. Although Pennsylvania was in no immediate military danger, its internal situation was becoming quite volatile. The moderate Whig coalition headed by John Dickinson was also reluctant to further compound its rebelliousness but for different reasons. If they gave into the demands of the radical Whigs for stronger measures, many conservative Quakers, Anglicans and Germans would be driven into the arms of the Tories. Without the support of these groups the peace Whigs in Pennsylvania would be hard pressed to prevent the radicals from gaining control of the resistance movement. Once that happened Pennsylvania's leadership of the peace forces in Congress would come to an end, and the New England men could consummate the revolution at their leisure. In New Jersey the absence of serious factionalism among the Whigs and the weakness of the Tories made for a relatively stable domestic situation. Despite this state of affairs the Whigs there were content to follow Pennsylvania's cautious lead. For it was not an easy matter for Jerseymen to suddenly chart their own course amidst a great crisis after more than a half century of dependence upon Pennsylvania and New York. Besides, in the event of an all-out war with Britain New Jersey would be in a very vulnerable position. New York would certainly be the major British objective. If it were taken, New Jersey would be hard pressed to repel the British invaders without extensive assistance from Pennsylvania. It is no wonder that the New Jersey Whigs continued to aid their ailing New York comrades and at the same time remained closely identified with Pennsylvania. As for tiny Delaware, it continued to remain in Pennsylvania's shadow.

chapter six

"BETWEEN HAWK AND BUZZARD"

The Continental Congress Drifts
Towards Independence

Early in September the members of the Second Congress began to straggle into Philadephia for the reopening of sessions.
A few new faces were in evidence, notably in the Virginia
and Georgia delegations, but in general the membership was
virtually the same as before adjournment. The six week recess
also failed to produce any significant change in the status of
the Anglo-American dispute. No word on the fate of the
Olive Branch Petition could be expected before late October
and the outcome of the Canadian offensive was likewise still
to be determined. As for the ideological alignment of the
delegates, nothing had changed. If anything relations between
the Middle Colonial bloc and the New England radicals were
even less cordial. On the morning of September 16 John
Dickinson refused to even acknowledge John Adams' greeting
when the two men passed each other on the streets of Philadelphia. This incident reflected more than just the personal
animosity that Dickinson held toward Adams for having
publicly referred to him in July as "a great piddling genius."[1]

Before the recess in July the radicals had made clear
their contempt for the Olive Branch Petition and disappoint-

ment over the failure of Congress to assume complete governmental sovereignty. John Adams compiled a list of unfinished
business which he brought with him to Congress in September:

We ought to have had in our Hands a month ago the whole
Legislative, executive and judicial of the whole Continent, and
have completely modeled a Constitution; to have raised a naval
Power, and opened all our Ports wide; to have arrested every
Friend to Government on the Continent and held them Hostages
for the poor Victims in Boston, and then opened the Door as wide
as possible for Peace and Reconciliation.[2]

During the fall and winter of 1775-1776 the radicals in
Congress redoubled their efforts to secure the adoption of the
measures outlined by Adams. Since each proposal represented
another step down the road to independence, the Middle
Colonial bloc sought to forestall acceptance of these measures in hopes that some means of rapprochement with the
mother country could be found. In this contest the peace
advocates were hampered by their dependence on British
actions. John and Sam Adams never tired of assuring their
supporters that Britain's shortsighted policies would in time
bring the colonies to the point of independence. According to
Sam Adams, George III and "his Councils and Administration
would necessarily produce the grandest Revolution the World
has even seen. . . ."[3] Yet men like John Dickinson and James
Duane refused to believe that the mother country could be
so insensitive and blind as to force the colonies out of the
Empire at the point of a bayonet.

The Middle Colonial bloc was also handicapped by its
previous commitment to the use of military force as a means
to bring about an accommodation. They could hardly oppose
increments in the military program when the rationale for the
Canadian expedition and the capture of Boston was that the
success of American arms would force Britain to the confer-

ence table. Thomas Lynch reiterated this point in November when he informed Washington that a reliable London observer "assures me that the Destruction of the Parliamentary Army in America will certainly produce Peace and by another that seizing Quebec will produce the same effect."[4]

As Congress resumed its labors the leadership of the Middle Colonial bloc again rested largely on the shoulders of John Dickinson and James Duane. They were assisted by a small group of delegates who were both effective spokesmen and committee politicans. John Jay and Robert R. Livingston from New York, despite frequent and often lengthy absences from Philadalephia, were two such members. The remaining members of the New York delegation (Philip Livingston, William Floyd, Henry Wisner, Francis Lewis, John Alsop and Lewis Morris) functioned as loyal supporters but did not assume any real leadership role. Occasionally one of these delegates did receive appointment to a major committee, but in general they were relegated to the more unimportant posts. In June, 1776, as the debate over independence was reaching its climax, Edward Rutledge of South Carolina lamented that men like Alsop, Lewis, Morris and Floyd "tho' good men, never quit their chairs."[5] The delegation from the Quaker Colony supplied four men who qualified as leaders. Andrew Allen, Thomas Willing, and James Wilson had all seen service in the first session of the Second Congress whereas Robert Morris, a wealthy Philadephia merchant, did not assume his seat until November. Upon entering Congress Morris immediately affirmed his support for the Middle Colonial bloc by pledging himself to favor

every measure that has a tendency to procure Accommodation on terms Consistant with our just claims and if I thought there was any thing ask'd on this side not founded on the Constitution in reason and Justice I would oppose it.[6]

Andrew Allen proved to be such an effective advocate of reconciliation that in March, 1776, a number of radicals in Pennsylvania wished

to get Andrew Allen and a few other good Men removed from Congress for they have stood forth and dared to expose the designs of the Cunning men of the East, and if they continue Members of Congress will prevent this province from falling into their favourite plan of independency.[7]

Except for Benjamin Franklin and Thomas Mifflin, who voted with the New Englanders, the remaining members of the Pennsylvania delegation (George Ross, Edward Biddle, Charles Humphreys and John Morton) seem to have been backbenchers who took little part in the verbal joustings with the radicals and sat on few major committees.

William Livingston, the unofficial head of the New Jersey delegation, was another important statesman representing the position of the Central Provinces. He served on many important committees and frequently engaged in floor debates. His long residency in New York seems to have provided him with a broader outlook than his fellow New Jersey delegates. As for James Kinsey, John De Hart, Stephen Crane and Richard Smith—they were content to be followers.[8] The Delaware delegation continued to be divided as it was in the First Congress with George Read voting with the Middle Colonial bloc, Thomas McKean supporting the New England radicals and Caesar Rodney steering an individualistic course of his own. Since Caesar Rodney and George Read were both very irregular in their attendance the vote of Delaware was often forfeited, for when only one of the three delegates was present the delegation lacked a quorum according to their instructions.[9] On the other occasions Delaware's vote was lost because the third member was not present to break a tie.

Congress occupied itself during its first week with such minor matters as Indian treaties, gunpowder procurement and a proposal to send an expedition against Detroit before turning to the more weighty questions of trade policy and the state of the military. With the nonexportation provision of the Association having gone into effect on September 10, Congress faced a very difficult problem. When the First Congress created the Association, the nonexportation provision was intended to be the sanction of last resort. The delegates realized at the time that if they were forced to implement the nonexportation section, it could not be sustained for very long because it certainly would arouse tremendous popular opposition. Besides, the need for military supplies was so great that procurement was possible only through extensive foreign trade. The secret authorization by Congress on July 15 for licensed merchants to contravene the Association and import arms and gunpowder was only a stopgap measure at best.

As might be expected the Middle Colonial bloc and the radicals diverged sharply in their respective trade policy proposals. The delegates from the Central Provinces advocated a limited resumption of trade. The four colonies that had not been restricted by the British Commercial Restraining Act of April, 1775, would resume normal commercial intercourse. The Middle Colonial delegates envisioned that the merchants from the restricted colonies could participate as well, thus easing the economic pinch of the Association while supplying the union with badly needed war materials. The radicals for their part were insistent that Congress drop all pretenses and unilaterally abrogate the British Navigation Acts. Once this was accomplished the colonies would have all of Europe, Latin America and even Asia from which to draw their war supplies.

On September 22 Congress selected a committee of seven men, representing all shades of the political spectrum, to examine the trade question. This committee submitted its report on October 2, and Congress resolved itself into a committee of the whole to deliberate on the proposals. Throughout most of the month the debate over trade policy droned on. The Middle Colonial representatives recommended that Congress lift the bans which the Whigs in North Carolina, Georgia, New York and Delaware had placed upon their colonies. If this was done the merchants in these colonies could take advantage of the exemption afforded them under the British Commercial Restraining Act. Robert R. Livingston endeavored to show that the alternative plan suggested by the New England delegates was fraught with danger to the union, for foreign merchants would not be so foolish as to put themselves at the mercy of the British Navy if their governments did not have a trade agreement or treaty with the American colonies. And if Congress negotiated treaties, Livingston reasoned that such action would be tantamout to a declaration of independence.[10]

Thomas Willing, James Duane and John Jay also spoke in behalf of the Middle Colonial proposal. Jay was quite caustic in his condemnation of the New England radicals. "It is not from affection to N. York that I speak," he declared, for the nonexempted colonies could easily transfer their commercial operations to the exempted provinces. Jay believed that this would be far better than bringing ruin on all colonies because a number were encumbered by British regulations.[11] Jay's attempt to wrap himself in the mantle of altruism doubtless had little effect. Thomas McKean apparently had Jay in mind when he took the floor to debate the question. The Delawarean charged that the plan to allow the four colonies to trade would incite intercolonial jealousy and possibly be misconstrued by the ministry as a sign of disunity. Furthermore, Britain would most assuredly be putting all the colonies on the same footing before very long.

On October 27, as the debate was nearing its conclusion, Livingston again took the floor to support the Middle Colonial position. The New York scion dwelt upon the widespread distress that a complete embargo on colonial commerce would precipitate:

Cloathing will rise tho Provisions will fall. Labourers will be discharged. One Quarter Part of R. Island, N. York and Pensylvania (sic) depend upon Trade, as Merchants, Shopkeepers, Shipwrights, Blockmakers, Riggers, Smiths. . . .[12]

After more than a month of debate neither the New England radicals nor the Middle Colonial men could garner enough votes to pass their respective proposals. As a result, Congress voted on November 1 to continue the existing state of affairs. Total nonexportation was to remain in effect until March 1, 1776. By expanding the number of loopholes in the exportation embargo Congress did ease the economic squeeze somewhat. On October 26 Congress determined that individual colonies could license their own merchants to export goods to the foreign West Indies in exchange for powder and shot. Likewise on November 8 Congress empowered the secret committee of correspondence, which was established in September to procure military supplies for the colonies, to authorize trade voyages to the foreign West Indies.

The lengthy debate on trade policy did not preclude Congress from making a number of important decisions dealing with military affairs. John Adams observed that Congress felt "the Spirit of War, more intimately than they did before adjournment."[13] General Washington's appeal for congressional assistance in shaping up the sadly deficient Continental Army moved Congress to select a three-man commission on September 29 to consult with the General and the New England Colonies on the needs of the army. Three days later Congress instructed Benjamin Harrison of Virginia, Thomas Lynch of South Carolina and Benjamin Franklin to inform Washington that it looked with favor on the idea of an all-out attack on Boston. Congress refrained from ordering him to carry out the attack but rather left the decision to his discretion, with the proviso that the authorization expired the last day of December, 1775. If Washington failed to launch an attack within the prescribed time period Congress advised him to reduce his forces. Congress no doubt justified this recommendation to Washington in the same way that it had the Canadian expedition—every success scored by American arms would bring Britain that much closer to the conference table.[14]

After taking action on Washington's request regarding the condition of the Continental Army, Congress addressed itself to another petition from the general involving a scheme to capture two British powder vessels soon to be in American waters. Up to this time all military preparations undertaken by Congress had involved only land-based forces. If this mission were approved the thirteen colonies would be taking the first step toward the creation of an American navy. This prospect was very unsettling to the Middle Colonial delegates because it smacked of belligerency. Moreover, to the commerce-conscious Central Provinces it held out the danger of inviting more severe British restraints on commerce than were already in force.[15] The radicals, however, won their point. On October 13 a committee was formed to secure two armed ships to undertake the mission.

The items considered by Congress were often determined by events in the provinces and so it was on October 18 when the New Hampshire delegation presented an appeal for congressional assistance in maintaining proper government in the colony. As a result of Governor John Wentworth's recent departure the regular government in the province was no longer legal under the provisions of the charter. John Adams and the radicals viewed New Hampshire's request as an opportunity to have Congress set forth a general recommendation for all colonies to renounce their existing governments and institute new governments on the authority of the people. The committee chosen on October 26 to take up the New Hampshire request contained three New England radicals, one Southern radical and only one conservative, John Rutledge of South Carolina. Adams no doubt put forth his best effort, but the committee's report did not go as far as he would have liked. For one thing it retained the words "province" and "colonies" which he found very objectionable.[16] Nevertheless, the people of New Hampshire were authorized to set up a government of their own choosing which would be the legal government until the Anglo-American dispute was resolved. This went a step beyond the governmental recommendation extended to Massachusetts in June.

Since the beginning of October the members of Congress had gone about their business with one ear cocked for news from England. No group of congressmen were more impatient than the peace advocates. A favorable response by the King to the Olive Branch Petition would enable the Middle Colonial bloc to put a halt to the piecemeal escalation of the dispute. Whether the American superstition that bad news always comes in clusters has any long-term validity is questionable, but this old wives' tale was certainly applicable to the turn of

events in the first two weeks of November. The nightmare
began for the reunionists on November 1, with General
Washington's account of the burning of Falmouth, Maine,
by a British squadron. The general termed it "an outrage
exceeding in Barbarity and cruelty every hostile Act practiced
among Civilized nations."[17] Within a few days Congress was
again beset with unwelcome news, but this time it was from
London and carried far more serious implications. King
George III had issued "A Proclamation For Suppressing
Rebellion and Sedition" on August 23, which had declared
all thirteen colonies had "proceeded to open and avowed
rebellion. . . ."[18] By way of retaliation the King called for
the stoppage of all further correspondence between Britain
and the colonies. One can imagine the sudden paralysis of
thought and spirit that must have afflicted many congressmen
upon receipt of this news. They had looked to George III as
the last hope of the colonies and to have him trample upon
their faith by proclaiming every colonist who supported the
resistance movement a traitor was a terrible shock. On November
8, Congress received a letter from Richard Penn and
Arthur Lee in London which elucidated the fate of the Olive
Branch Petition. The King had not even seen fit to receive it.
With this one cavalier stroke the peace offer that Dickinson
and the Middle Colonial delegates had fought so hard to
secure was rebuffed. Moreover, they were now without their
most effective deterrent. The delegates from the Central
Provinces could no longer urge postponement of radical-
sponsored measures with the argument that Congress should
not plunge further into civil war until Britain's responses to
the Olive Branch Petition was known.

The peace advocates were still reeling from these calam-
itous events when word came from Virginia on November 10

that Lord Dunmore had made official his previous threats to
offer freedom from bondage to all slaves who would join the
King's forces. The halls of Congress must have rung with
profane oaths and fearful denunciations as the delegates
contemplated the serious implications of Dunmore's emanci-
pation proclamation. This incident and the burning of Falmouth lent credibility to the reports that the ministry was
planning to dispatch at least 20,000 troops in the spring to
crush the rebellion. For if the ministry could condone servile
insurrection and destruction of defenseless seacoast towns,
it could certainly send a vast army of redcoats and foreign
mercenaries to suppress the colonists.

   As a consequence of these developments the New England radicals no longer had to flinch when accused of aiming
at independence. A few newspaper essayists began to broach
the subject, including the Philadelphia printer Robert Bell.
Bell advertised James Burgh's *Political Disquisitions* to the
public with the comment that this work would be of
great value in helping the colonists with "the new erection
which must be constructed if the infatuated ministry of Britain
continue to persist in the ignominious attempt of making
FREEMEN SLAVES."[19] Such sentiments frightened the already badly shaken Middle Colonial delegates and served to
intensify their efforts to come up with a plan to stymie the
radical drive toward independence. The resignation from
Congress of John De Hart and James Kinsey of New Jersey
in mid-November was bitter testimony of the sense of hopelessness that prevailed among many supporters of reconciliation. In his letter of explanation De Hart indicated that in
view of his demonstrated inability to carry out the wishes of
the assembly for a peaceful resolution of the dispute and since
the "prospect of procuring an accommodation, by Constitu-

tional measures, seemeth to be nearly at an end," he preferred to be relieved of his duties so that he might attend to his much neglected family.[20]

Although John Dickinson grasped at the fact that the King had not totally rejected the Olive Branch Petition since he never consented to officially receive it, such unsupported assertions regarding Britain's ultimate good intentions could not be expected to carry any weight in Congress. With all congressional avenues closed the "Pennsylvania Farmer" shrewdly turned to the Pennsylvania assembly for assistance. This body still retained its conservative outlook and was a willing tool for Dickinson's scheme. He managed without difficulty to secure his own nomination to the committee charged with drafting the instructions for the congressional delegation. The set of instructions reported out on November 9 showed his handiwork. The report of the committee, which the assembly readily accepted, candidly admitted that it was impossible for individual colonies to do anything more than to lay down certain general precepts for their delegates. But on one point the committee was very explicit:

Though the oppressive measures of the British Parliament and administration have compelled us to resist their violence by force of Arms, yet we strictly enjoin you, that you, in behalf of this colony, dissent from, and utterly reject, any propositions, should they be made, that may cause, or lead to, a separation from our Mother Country, or a Change of the form of this government.[21]

It is highly unlikely that Dickinson would have advanced this restrictive clause if he thought that the radicals stood any chance of overturning it. He was also confident that the other Middle Colonies would follow Pennsylvania's lead as they had in the past. If this turned out to be the case, the peace advocates would once again have grounds for opposing separation.

The success of Dickinson's maneuver was borne out by the angry denunciations heard from the radicals and the subsequent adoption of similar instructions by New Jersey, Maryland, and Delaware. General Charles Lee concluded that Pennsylvania's action would be construed by the ministry as a sign of internal division within the colonial union. In his estimation the "Pennsylvania Farmer," whom he considered to be the architect of the new instructions, could no longer be looked upon as a great American Patriot. If Lee had his way he would "kick the Assembly from the seat of representation which they so horribly disgrace and set 'em to work making Germ Town stockings for the Army—an employment manly enough for 'em."[22]

New Jersey was the first colony to follow Pennsylvania's lead.[23] On November 28 the New Jersey assembly approved the following stricture against independence:

That the said Delegates be directed not to give their assent to but utterly reject any propositions, if such should be made, that may separate this Colony from the Mother Country, or Change the form of Government thereof.[24]

Governor Franklin was instrumental in convincing the assembly to take this action. The governor doubtless perceived that the spate of news during the first two weeks in November had sharply diminished the prospects of reconciliation and that there was a noticeable backlash in New Jersey. Addressing the assembly on November 16, Franklin challenged the representatives to do their "country an essential service" by expressing their opposition to independence.[25] He also implored the assembly to take the initiative and unilaterally send a petition to the King requesting him to intercede and restore the colonies and the mother country to their former state of harmony. The governor's words touched a responsive chord. On November 28, the assembly appointed a committee to draft the petition to the King. When word of these transactions reached Philadelphia, Congress immediately acted to head off the proposed petition. On December 4 John Jay, John Dickinson and George Wythe of Virginia were dispatched to consult with the New Jersey assembly on this matter. The selection of Jay and Dickinson seems to point up the contemporary recognition of the sectional feelings amongst the Middle Colonies. All three addressed the assembly, but Dickinson delivered the major speech. He began by attempting to persuade the Jerseymen that the only hope of resolving the dispute lay in "unity and bravery." If the individual colonies submitted petitions, they would be playing right into the hand of the ministry for "It would break our union . . . we would become a rope of sand. . . ."[26] In deference to Congress the assembly subsequently abandoned its petition plan. Dickinson's performance in Trenton revealed the essential position which the Middle Colonial bloc would seek to maintain in the months ahead. They still believed that if the ministry could be brought to realize how ruinous a full-scale civil war would be to both sides, it would relent rather than fight. In order to accomplish this Dickinson, Duane and the other Middle Colonial congressmen hoped to hold back the New England fire-eaters long enough so that Britain could gain a true understanding of the situation.

New York gave some thought to adopting instructions comparable to those of Pennsylvania but did not follow through. John Alsop was the chief exponent of this because he believed the majority of New Yorkers opposed independence. He was also confident that the New York provincial congress would raise few objections to accepting instructions which ruled out independence.[27] Although the beleaguered

New York congress did not get around to changing the
instructions as Alsop desired, their actions in December
indicated that they shared the sentiments of the other Middle
Colonies.

The batch of unsettling news early in November momentarily slowed the torrid pace which Congress had maintained
since September. Few of the delegates would have disagreed
with Joseph Hewes's evaluation, "We grow tired, indolent,
captious, jealous, and want a recess."[28] By the end of the
month, however, the pace picked up again. On November
25 Congress resolved that all valuables and cargo aboard
captured British transports or warships would become the
property of the united colonies. A strong indication was also
given that Congress was ready to establish a full-fledged
navy.[29] On November 28 Congress did in fact adopt the rules
and regulations for the Continental Navy. Although Congress
had in effect gone out to sea without any ships, this incon-
gruity was corrected on December 13 when a plan to have
thirteen warships ready for service by March won approval.
Almost half of the projected fleet was to be fitted out by the
Middle Colonies with New York supplying two vessels and
Pennsylvania four.[30] The fleet that John Adams considered
an impossibility in October was now going to be a reality.

The radicals continued to win congressional approval
of other important measures in December. For example, an
expedition to dispose of Lord Dunmore's fleet in Chesapeake
Bay and an expansion of the naval confiscation clause to
include British ships as well as their cargo won approval.
Nevertheless, the Middle Colonial bloc managed to prevent
enactment of a number of measures that would have moved
the thirteen colonies very close to an open break with Britain.
On December 19 a motion made by George Wythe to make

all British vessels liable to capture anywhere on the high seas was defeated by a vote of five to four with two colonies divided.[31] The Middle Colonial bloc also made sure that the congressional letter to the colonial agents in London and the proclamation to the King contained no mention of independence. The congressional proclamation prepared by James Wilson, Richard Henry Lee and William Livingston was highly censorious of the language in the King's Proclamation and the unbending position it assumed. After promising to respond in kind to every new British military measure, Congress timidly suggested a truce:

We mean, not, however, by this declaration, to occasion or multiply punishments: Our sole view is to prevent them. In this unhappy and unnatural controversy, in which Britons fight against Britons, and descendants of Britons let the calamities immediately incident to a Civil War suffice.[32]

In view of the many radical successes in November and December and the absence of good news from London, the peace advocates in Congress contemplated the new year with despair. James Duane asserted that he would labor in Congress night and day as long as there was even a faint hope of securing reconciliation, but he admitted in mid-December "this is at present too distant and uncertain to Give me Encouragement, or keep up my spirits. . . ."[33]

Congress began the new year with a rousing debate over what treatment should be accorded known Tories. In preceding weeks several counties in New Jersey and Maryland had conducted Tory roundups and a congressional committee was considering a letter from the New York congress requesting military assistance to suppress the Tories on Long Island. Some sort of general policy statement was clearly needed. Quickly Congress supplied one by recommending on

January 2 that all identifiable Tories be disarmed and the
more dangerous ones imprisoned. The committee assigned to
look into New York's request presented an affirmative report
on January 3. It recommended that the disaffected citizens
of Queens County be denied all trading privileges with their
fellow New Yorkers, be forced to carry certificates if they
wished to travel outside the county and have their names
published for a month. More importantly, companies of
minutemen from New Jersey and Connecticut were ordered
to make a sweep across Long Island disarming all citizens
who voted against sending delegates to the New York congress and jailing their leaders.[34]

If the new year ushered in a harsh policy against Tories
and nonassociators it also brought forth the first hope of peace
since the dispatch of the Olive Branch Petition. The eccentric
British nobleman, Lord Drummond, left England in September determined to be an apostle of peace to the obstreper-
ous colonies. After stopping briefly at Halifax, Boston and
New York City he arrived in Philadelphia just after the first
of the year. He managed to confer informally with several
congressional delegates including James Duane, James Wilson
and Thomas Lynch. That his lordship was able to obtain
any hearing at all was because he was "so much with Lord
North and others of the Administration before his Coming
away, that he appears to know all the Designs of the Ministry
respecting America."[35] Although Drummond admitted to the
congressmen that he was not an official representative of the
ministry, he spoke with confidence about the overriding desire
in London to end the unhealthy dispute on amicable terms.
He gave substance to his contention about the good intentions
of the ministry by predicting that commissioners would accompany the British armed forces in the spring and "before

any blow is struck terms will be held out by the Generals which will be mild, but if not accepted, every Exertion is to be dreaded—"[36]

Drummond's visit gave encouragement to the peace advocates at a time when the New England radicals were mounting a formidable drive for independence. The congressmen who were pushing for separation were naturally upset by his lordship's visit and suspicious of his motives. They depicted him as a ministerial spy. As events were to prove the radicals' concern was justifiable, for the Middle Colonial bloc and its Southern allies immediately began to argue against independence on the grounds that commissioners were about to offer satisfactory peace proposals.

The timing of Drummond's visit also proved highly fortuitous for the peace forces, because on January 8 Congress received some very disturbing intelligence. From London came word of a strongly anti-American speech which King George III had delivered to the House of Commons on October 28. In the speech His Majesty reviewed the steps which a small group of malcontents had taken to assume full governmental power. He discounted all of the peace feelers offered by the Continental Congress as mere tactical maneuvering to buy more time for their wicked designs to mature. "The rebellious war now levied is become more general and is manifestly carried on for the purpose of establishing an independent empire, . . ." the King charged and he promised "to put a speedy end to these disorders by the most decisive exertions."[37] The anti-British feeling aroused by the King's strong words was compounded by the news that Lord Dunmore had attacked and burned the port of Norfolk, Virginia, on January 1.

The next day James Wilson arose in Congress to propose

"that the Congress may expressly declare to their Constituents and the World their present intentions respecting independency, observing that the King's Speech directly charged Us with that Design."[38] In offering this motion he was trying to place a roadblock in front of the independence movement and thus buy time for the commissioners. Sam Adams and some of his radical cohorts were so alarmed by the prospect of such a declaration that they bent all efforts to have the motion postponed.[39] During the weeks that followed the radicals sought to win approval of measures that were increasingly tinged with independence. On January 12 a proposal to open American ports to the world after March 1 was debated and postponed. Four days later they moved to have Congress consider Franklin's plan of confederation once again. John Dickinson delivered a rambling oration against this idea, arguing that no such move was possible until the people specifically granted such authority to Congress.

As the two factions skirmished with one another preparatory to considering Wilson's motion, the peace advocates received assistance of a most unwelcome kind. The long-awaited outcome of the Canadian expedition was at last revealed on January 17.[40] Montgomery and Arnold's combined force was repulsed before Quebec on December 21, with frightful losses. General Montgomery died in the first assault and Colonel Arnold was forced to relinquish command because of a serious battle injury. After the easy capture of Montreal late in November, Congress envisioned that the Northern Army would have little trouble securing Quebec. Now Congress faced the enormous task of mounting a second Canadian expedition in order to strengthen its bargaining position and restore confidence in American arms.[41] Thomas Lynch admitted that he had been ready to support a peace plan after conferring with Lord Drummond, but with the costly defeat in Canada he favored launching another expedition so that the colonies could negotiate from a position of strength.[42]

On January 24 Congress resumed consideration of Wilson's motion and expended most of the day in debating the pros and cons of independence. When all the oratory had ceased, the Middle Colonial bloc emerged with an authorization for a drafting committee. The unbridled appeal for independence contained in *Common Sense* and the smashing defeat before Quebec apparently frightened a number of Southern delegates into giving their support to the Central Provinces. The Middle Colonial leaders also had taken precautions to insure that Delaware's vote would be cast. George Read was pointedly requested to be present in Philadelphia for this crucial vote.[43] In the selection of delegates for the drafting committee the Middle Colonial bloc made sure that its interest was well represented by packing the committee with such familiar figures as Dickinson, Duane, Wilson and William Hooper of North Carolina.

The supporters of reconciliation had scant time to savor victory. The New England radicals continued their relentless drive. Governor Franklin of New Jersey, who must rank as one of the most perceptive commentators on the progress of the resistance movement from protest to rebellion, noted in January that popular discussion of separation was becoming quite commonplace. Although he did not feel that a formal declaration of independence was about to be approved "...the danger seems to be that the design will be carried on by such Degrees, and under such pretences, as not to be perceived by the People in general till too late for Resistance."[44] This was precisely what the Middle Colonial delegates were fighting against in Congress.

Early in February Congress received a report from
Colonel Nathaniel Heard of New Jersey regarding the success
of his mission in Queens County. Nineteen Tory leaders were
taken into custody and a large number of weapons confiscated.
The decision made on January 10 to exclude the Connecticut
minutemen from the expedition because of New York's aversion to New Englanders apparently proved to be a wise one.
An officer under Colonel Heard reported that "even the
delinquents expressed themselves well pleased that a detach-
ment of Jerseymen (and not of New-England) were sent to
disarm them."[45]

While Congress was occupied with such matters the
committee charged with drafting an address to the inhabitants
of the colonies on the state of the dispute was putting the final
touches on its report. On February 13 the draft address came
before Congress with both the Middle Colonial bloc and the
New England radicals ready for this important test of strength.
According to the ever-present Mr. Smith of New Jersey it
proved to be strictly "no contest." For the address, which was
"very long, badly written and full against independence," was
withdrawn by James Wilson when it became apparent that
a large majority of the congressmen would not support the
document.[46]

A careful reading of Wilson's address reveals that the
only stricture it contained against independence was a statement that in taking up arms to defend their rights Americans
did not harbor secret designs for an independent empire. He
further asserted that the ultimate decision as to whether the
colonies would remain within the Empire rested with Britain.
Although Wilson's address does not appear to have been "full
against independency" as Smith claimed, there is little question
that its approval would have greatly assisted the peace advo-

cates. The public at large would no doubt have interpreted this address to be a repudiation of the sentiments expressed in *Common Sense.*

Historians have generally concluded that Wilson's address was passed over because the public had gone beyond its mild sentiments.[47] This may well be part of the answer, but it fails to take into account more practical considerations. Two days before the debate on Wilson's address an urgent appeal for more troops came to Congress from General Charles Lee in New York City. One of the first men to step forward was John Dickinson. He volunteered personally to lead his battalion to New York City. What is significant about Dickinson's display of martial spirit is that it probably meant that he was out of Philadelphia on the day of the crucial debate on Wilson's address. If this was the case, the Middle Colonial bloc was without its most effective spokesman.[48] Another possible explanation for the failure of the Middle Colonies to put up a stiff fight is that they were reluctant to push matters to extreme lengths for fear of disrupting the colonial union. Several weeks later when the question of independence came up again in Congress, the debate was quickly terminated when the delegates from five or six colonies indicated that it was improper for them to discusss the issue since their hands were tied.[49]

During the remaining two weeks in February the radicals kept on the attack. On February 16 George Wythe suggested that Congress already possessed the authority to negotiate alliances with foreign nations. Although a motion to have his proposal considered by a committee initially won approval by a vote of seven colonies to five, the matter was finally postponed.[50] Even an oration delivered in memory of brave General Montgomery became a matter of contention between the two factions. On February 21 William Livingston requested that Congress transmit a letter of appreciation to Dr. William Smith and make copies of his oration available to the general public. A heated debate ensued with John Adams, Samuel Chase and Oliver Wolcott on one side and James Duane, James Wilson and Thomas Willing on the other. The radicals contested Livingston's request because Smith's oration contained a statement to the effect that Congress desired reunion and nothing more. Having already grounded Wilson's address they were in no mood for a substitute.

Since the latter part of 1775 Congress had begun to concern itself with the problem of raising fortifications and organizing regional defense operations in the Middle and Southern Colonies. On February 27 Congress gave its approval to the report of the committee which dealt with the question of setting up military departments south of New England. Under this plan New York, New Jersey, Pennsylvania, Delaware and Maryland were placed in the Middle department which was to be commanded by a major general assisted by two brigadier generals. The colonies from Virginia southward were grouped into the Southern department with the same command provisions. Not all of the delegates were pleased with this alignment which generally adhered to sectional guidelines, save for the inclusion of Maryland in the Middle department. The New England bloc, perhaps noting the inclusion of a Southern colony in the Middle department for what were apparently strategic considerations, proposed that New York be included in their military department.[51] This arrangement would have given the New England Colonies ample justification for interfering in the domestic affairs of New York whether to cow the Tories or implant some backbone in the Whigs. The Middle Colonial delegates saw to it that this request was denied.

Although the New England bloc failed to bring New York into their orbit, the news that Parliament had by means of the innocuous-sounding Prohibitory Act, passed in December, made all American vessels liable to capture and confiscation must have gladdened their hearts. Early in 1776 George Washington had surmised that the colonies were teetering on the brink:

A few more of such flaming arguments, as were exhibited at Falmouth and Norfolk, added to the sound doctrine and unanswerable reasoning contained in the pamphlet 'Common Sense,' will not leave numbers at a loss to decide upon the propriety of a separation.[52]

The Prohibitory Act did not prove to be the event that brought down the Empire, but it did have an adverse effect on the already ebbing hopes for peace. The orderly retreat, which the Middle Colonial bloc had been conducting in the face of the radical offensive, now began to take on the appearance of a rout.

Even so, however, the Middle Colonial bloc made a last gesture in the interest of peace. The opportunity for this effort was provided by none other than General Washington. Early in February Lord Drummond had dispatched to Washington a copy of a letter he wrote to General Robertson at British headquarters in Boston regarding the procedures to be followed should a congressional delegation be dispatched to London for negotiations. By this time the general was already convinced that the dispute could only end in American independence. Nevertheless, he forwarded Drummond's letter to Congress lest he incur the wrath of the reunionists. The radicals frowned on Washington's fairmindedness. John Adams contended that Drummond's proposal for an American negotiating team gained added stature simply because Washington

had seen fit to transmit it. The Middle Colonial bloc realized
it "was a fine Engine to play Cold Water on the fire of independence. They set it in operation with great Zeal and Activity."[53] William Livingston's motion to have Lord Drummond
appear before Congress failed to win approval, however, and
the peace minded lord was not heard from again until August.
The day after this vote was taken James Allen of Philadelphia
made note of the mood in Congress: "The Plot thickens;
peace is scarcely thought of, independency predominant."[54]

With the Middle Colonial peace bid laid to rest, the
month of March belonged to the New England radicals. On
March 14 Congress approved a general order to disarm all
disaffected persons and nonassociators. Six days later the
instruction for the commissioners bound for Canada contained
a recommendation that the Canadians form a new goverment.
In the debate that preceded this action John Jay and several
other supporters of reconciliation had objected to this clause
because it bespoke of independence.[55]

On March 23 Congress approved the issuance of letters
of marque and reprisal to enable American privateers to prey
on British shipping. Surprisingly New York voted with the
majority on this radical-sponsored measure while only Pennsylvania and Maryland stood in opposition. Both New Jersey
and Delaware were unable to cast their votes because their
delegations lacked a quorum.[56] Now only the open-ports
resolution and the continental constitution remained of the
unfinished business that John Adams had brought with him
to Congress in September, 1775. On April 6 Congress reduced
the number to one by voting to open American ports to the
ships of every nation save Great Britain.

By the spring of 1776 it was apparent that the balance of
power in Congress had shifted to the radicals. The peace

advocates were not yet ready to give up on the commissioners, but some of them expressed their doubts in private that a settlement could be reached even if the British agents had plenary powers. With Britain poised to expand the civil war and the colonists preparing to completely divest themselves of their regular governments, it did not seem possible that the clock could be turned back. Nonetheless, what may seem irrational to some men often makes good sense to others, and so it was with with the Middle Colonies in the spring of 1776. They were not yet convinced that the hour had arrived for the united colonies to make their grand exit from the Empire. Thus in the months ahead they proved to be the last outposts of resistance to independence.

In retrospect one must ask what if anything the Middle Colonial bloc accomplished by holding up independence for six months. Would a declaration of independence in January or February have substantially altered the course and outcome of the American Revolution? The answer seems to be yes, for the Middle Colonies probably would have seceded from the colonial union. Without them the American Revolution might have been nothing more than a New England rebellion. Early in 1776 the ascendant Whig Leaders in the Middle Colonies still believed that membership in the Empire was better for their interests than embarking upon a perilous experiment with the treacherous New England provinces. In their minds Britain had not yet proven herself to be a completely unworthy parent. But by sending foreign mercenaries, promoting guerrilla warfare and declaring all American vessels liable to seizure Britain was actually helping the Whig leaders in the Central Provinces to see that the Empire they cherished could never be restored.

chapter seven

A WINTER OF INDECISION:

1775-1776

"This Winter will decide the Question," prophesied William
Smith of New York early in October, "whether Great Britain
and her Colonies, are to be happily reunited, or to prosecute
their animosities to an eternal separation."[1] For the Middle
Colonies the winter of 1775-1776 was not quite everything
that Smith predicted it would be. The conservative and moderate Whig leaders in New York, New Jersey, Pennsylvania and
Delaware did find to their consternation that neither the
British ministry nor the radicals in Congress would permit
them to continue with their halfway measures. The ever-
increasing British military pressure along with the decisive
measures of Congress forced the Central Provinces to divest
their old governments of authority, adopt punitive measures
against nonsupporters and organize for war. As spring ap-
proached a number of Whig leaders, notably in New Jersey,
began to lose all hope of remaining in the Empire. But despite
such defections most of the Middle Colonial leaders still shared
the sentiments of Pennsylvania's Robert Morris:

Where the Plague are these Commissioners, if they are to Come
what is it that detains them; it is time we should be on a Cer-

tainty & know positively whether the Libertys of America can be established & Secured by Reconciliation, or whether we must totally renounce Connection with Great Britain & fight our way to a total independence.[2]

Autumn was just beginning to descend on the foothills of New York when the provincial congress managed to raise a quorum on October 4. With limited enthusiasm the delegates began to shift through the old business which poor attendance had forced them to shelve in August. The actions of the committee of safety that had served in their absence were also to be reviewed. On October 7 a problem of major proportions presented itself. The provincial congress was informed by President John Hancock that it could henceforth "arrest and secure every person . . whose going at large may in their opinion endanger the safety of the Colony or the Liberties of America."[3] Even the slowest delegate realized that the Continental Congress had Governor Tryon in mind when it passed this resolution. The frightened provincial congress made note of the Congressional recommendation and then hurried on to other matters. Nevertheless, the provincial congress could not shut itself off from the continuing reports of the governor's nefarious activities. On October 12 intelligence was received detailing Tryon's role in devising an invasion plan for New York to be carried out by Tory cadres and British regulars.

In the meantime Tryon boldly asked the committee of one hundred for a guarantee of personal safety. The governor apparently offered a promise of protection from bombardment in exchange. The committee refused to bargain with Tryon because they sensed that they would be violating the spirit of the continental union.[4] When the desired pledge was not forthcoming, Tryon transferred his headquarters to the *Dutchess of Gordon.* His sudden departure sent a tremor of fear through the city. A bombardment seemed imminent and hundreds of

families began fleeing the city. The lameduck provincial congress, having issued a call for a second provincial congress on
the grounds that short terms insured popular control, hurried
to conclude its business. Reflective of the nonassertive congressional mood was the decision on October 24 to rescind
the resolution passed by the committee of safety in September
to disarm all nonassociators and public enemies. The retiring
Congress had no stomach for such repressive measures.

The first provincial congress finally expired on November
4, largely because its membership had all but vanished. In its
haste to be gone the congress appointed no committee of
safety to serve until the next congress convened.[5] Perhaps the
retiring delegates felt that a committee of safety was unnecessary since the newly elected congress was to assemble on
November 14. If this was the members' rationale, they were
soon to discover that a quorum was still a hard item to secure
in New York "owing to the Timidity of Creatures call'd Whigs,
but, who are neither Whigs nor Tories, in reality a Sort of
political Maphrodite. . . . "[6]

It was not until December 6, more than three weeks after
the date set for organizing the second provincial congress,
that enough delegates were present to accomplish this task.
And this came about only because a rump session of delegates
wrote a letter on December 1 to a number of members not in
attendance spelling out the unpleasant alternatives New York
would face should the provincial congress fail to meet. Without a congress the colony would either be ruled by a mob or,
if the Continental Congress took a hand, a major general supported by Continental troops.[7]

That the rump assemblage should have mentioned the
possibility of a governmental take-over by the Continental
Congress points up the sorry state of the Whig party in New
York. On one hand it reveals the sense of hopelessness that

seemed to shadow even radicals like Alexander McDougall, while suggesting that the Continental Congress deemed New York so crucial to the colonial union that it would be willing to make it into a virtual protectorate rather than allow it to fall into British hands. During the latter part of November the self-exiled New York radical, Isaac Sears, proposed to the Connecticut delegation that the Continental Congress should send a force of 500 men into New York to clean out the Tories. He was of the opinion that time was of the essence:

For if the matter should not be carried into execution this winter, it is my opinion that one half of the people of the City and Province of New York will be ready to take up arms against the country next spring, and we have little else to do this winter but to purge the land of such Villains.[8]

The difficulties encountered in bringing the second provincial congress into session must have seemed minor as the delegates turned their attention to the gargantuan problems facing the province. While radicals like John Morin Scott initially hailed the new congress as an improvement over its predecessor, for "Those from New York you will see by the papers are changed for the better—all staunch Whigs now," their enthusiasm was destined to wane quickly.[9] One of the thorniest problems confronting the congress involved the recent raid into New York City by a band of Connecticut irregulars led by Isaac Sears. In broad daylight the Connecticut raiders had apprehended the well-known Tory editor, James Rivington, and then brazenly destroyed all his printing equipment. To top off his incursion Sears stopped in the borough of Westchester long enough to abduct several prominent Tories including the Reverend Samuel Seabury.[10]

Most New York Whigs reacted rather ambivalently to the news of Sears' raid. John Jay for one did not question the value of silencing Rivington or putting the fear of God into the

Tories, but he considered "it as an ill compliment to the Government of the Province: and another mark against New York's already maligned reputation."[11] Alexander Hamilton did not share Jay's essentially sanguine outlook about the raid. He viewed the incident as setting a dangerous precedent. Hamilton foresaw that if New York failed to take steps to thwart any future encroachments by New England men and continued to display irresolution, then the province might well forfeit its autonomy. He attributed a goodly portion of New York's Laodicean attitude to the fact "that antipathies and prejudices have long subsisted between this province and New England."[12]

The response of the New York provincial congress showed more backbone than might have been expected. In a letter of protest to Governor Trumbull the delegates admitted their willingness to interpret the raid as the work of a few headstrong individuals. But it voiced concern that any repetition of such actions would do great harm to the resistance movement in New York. The New York congress went on to reprimand the raiders for suppressing freedom of the press. They also asked for Seabury's immediate release because his continued imprisonment might "be subject to misconstructions prejudicial to the common cause" among Anglican laymen.[13] No plans were laid to lodge a formal complaint with Congress, but the New York congress promised it would ask for a ruling on intervention into the internal affairs of one colony by another. Although Jay speculated the provincial congress had "too much Christian meekness" to put Connecticut in its place, the protest lodged by New York was probably as strong as the situation could bear.[14] Radical Whig leaders like Alexander McDougall and John Hobart did not wish to offend Connecticut and thereby run the risk of losing the military assistance that this northern neighbor could provide. For New Yorkers were most apprehensive that a full-scale British attack would be forthcoming after the first of the year. At the same time the growing militancy of the Tories in Westchester County and on Long Island was a source of grave concern.

While congress was pondering the proper response to Sears' raid it also had under consideration a proposal for New York to initiate a peace petition. William Smith was apparently the man responsible for this entertaining maneuver.[15] He had been waiting since July for the proper opening to launch another peace bid. He saw his chance when news arrived that Pennsylvania, and then New Jersey, had instructed their delegations to refrain from supporting independence. After conferring with Governor Tryon it was decided to use much the same approach with which Governor Franklin was proceeding so successfully in New Jersey. Governor Tryon thus wrote a letter to the provincial congress on December 4 expressing his disappointment that the inhabitants of New York had not been given a chance to voice their sentiments on the February 20th Conciliation Proposal. After meeting with a number of provincial congress delegates at Simon's Tavern, William Smith turned the management of the operation over to his brother, Thomas. On December 8 the latter proposed a set of resolutions intended to implement the governor's request. Essentially these resolutions asked the provincial congress to disavow independence and call upon the governor to convene the assembly so that that body could take up the British peace offer.

A triumvirate of radicals—John Morin Scott, Alexander McDougall and John Hobart—managed to sabotage the entire project. They saw to it that all of Smith's resolutions were amended out of existence. The Smiths especially resented John Morin Scott's part in all this for he had introduced a

resolution on December 14 that castigated the February 20th
Conciliation Proposal as an invidious document intended only
to shatter colonial unity. The New York Whigs must have
taken considerable pride in their accomplishment, particularly
in light of the situation in New Jersey where the Whigs had
needed the assistance of a special delegation from Congress
to thwart a similar attempt to breach the colonial union.

The matter, however, did not end here. William Smith
persuaded Governor Tryon to test the Whig resolve. The governor quietly dissolved the old assembly and began making
preparations behind closed doors for new elections on February 1.[16] Such a large secret could not be kept very long and
by the middle of January the Whigs were campaigning hard for
members of their party. Whig writers aided the cause by ex-
posing and vilifying Tory candidates wherever they were
found. "The Monitor" ascribed New York's miserable reputation among the united colonies to the low conduct of the
past assembly and he called upon the people to throw the
rascals out. The committee of safety even took precautions
against the possibility that a Tory-dominated assembly might
be selected. It called upon all the delegates to the second
provincial congress to reconvene on February 1 to "effectively
awe a Corrupt Assembly."[17] In the face of the elaborate Whig
preparations Governor Tryon did not waver in his determination to have a new assembly. He must have reasoned that even
a Whig-dominated assembly would still be a legal house and
as long as two governments existed the rebels would be dis-
comforted.[18]

Meanwhile, congress had to divert some of its energy to
countering the busy movements of the Tories. On December
13, congress received word that boats from the *Asia* were
regularly landing arms and ammunition at Hempstead on
Long Island for the use of local Tories.[19] To make matters

worse the Whigs in Suffolk County professed their helplessness in the face of the Tory buildup and called for assistance from congress. Two days later a letter arrived from the Richmond County committee affirming that no delegates would be sent to congress. A recent vote of the inhabitants in Westchester had gone against sending representatives, and with the prospect of peace fading rapidly the committee decided the county should not be represented. This was too much even for the fainthearted provincial congress to let pass. On December 21 congress declared all disaffected individuals in Richmond and Queens counties beyond its protection and all commercial and personal intercourse with them was to cease at once.

Mere interdiction without attendant force could hardly be expected to overawe the Long Island Tories, and the provincial congress at last resigned itself to this conclusion. Three months after the committee of safety proposed that dangerous Tories be arrested and nonassociators disarmed, the first hesitant step in this direction was at last taken. On December 21, the provincial congress cleared the way for the Continental Congress to use military force against the Long Island Tories. In taking this action the provincial congress admitted that it did not wish to employ New York militia units because such action would more than likely provoke a bombardment of the city at a time when the province was short of powder.[20] As a last resort the provincial congress authorized the committee of safety to take whatever action it deemed necessary in the event that no help was forthcoming from Congress. As already noted Congress moved quickly to assist New York and by the end of January the Tories on Long Island had lost some of their leaders and possessed far fewer weapons.[21]

With the prospects for peace diminishing rapidly as the year 1775 came to a close, radical Whigs in Congress and the military were becoming more and more concerned about the fate of New York. Pleas for congressional intervention from New York radicals were being heard more frequently. Late in December Hugh Hughes concluded,

It is quite time that the Jersey Troops were in New York and under the sole Direction of the Commander in Chief, as the Asia; the Dutchess of Gordon; the Packet, are Nothing but Granaries, & Magazines for Howe & his Followers.[22]

Such pleas, along with the formal request for military assistance issued by the provincial congress, seemed to indicate that New Yorkers would welcome outside assistance. Only the radical Whigs, however, were willing to turn to the New England provinces for such aid.

Men like Washington and Lee, who had been clamoring for months for repression of Tories, were more than willing to lend a hand. When General Lee proposed that a force of Connecticut volunteers be stationed on Long Island to thwart any Tory buildup, Washington was quick to approve the project. On January 11 Washington apprised Congress that General Lee was recruiting volunteers in Connecticut as he journeyed southward to prepare New York City to withstand a British attack. In order to prevent the inhabitants of New York from giving aid and comfort to the enemy, Washington authorized Lee to disarm all citizens of questionable loyalty.[23]

For some reason General Washington's explanatory letter to the New York committee of safety did not arrive before General Lee. Thus his coming caused many inhabitants to depart post haste, anticipating that a major battle was in the offing.[24] After recovering from its own shock, the committee of safety dispatched an urgent letter to General Lee on January 21 imploring him not to enter the city. The committee claimed that a shortage of powder and the absence of adequate defense works made the city indefensible. They attempted to justify this request by alluding to the numerous defensive

measures in progress which would be ready by March:
"We therefore ardently wish to remain in peace for a little
time.[25] The bitter dispute which ensued, first over the question of merely entering the city and then over the question
of who had final authority over Lee's forces, showed that the
New York Whigs had no intention of letting the reins of
power slip from their hands. In light of Lee's flair for acting
first and obtaining proper clearance later, the provincial congress was doubly suspicious of his intentions. During his recent
tour of duty in Rhode Island he ferreted out the Tories by
means of a test oath and then had them post good conduct
bonds. Few New York Whigs doubted his intention to use
the same tactics in their province.

General Lee was very secretive in discussing his plans
with the provincial congress, but he did try to reassure the
delegates that he would not initiate hostilities. He did, however,
give fair warning that he could not compromise his orders to
save the city from destruction for "The sea-port towns are
the only holds they the British have in America; they are
considered as the pledges of servitude; the menacing destruction of them must extinguish all hope of success."[26]

To resolve the impasse between General Lee and the
committee, Congress dispatched a three-man commission
composed of Benjamin Harrison, Thomas Lynch and Andrew
Allen. After several lengthy conferences the congressional
commission produced a compromise. The incoming forces
would be placed under the direction of the Continental Congress itself. With the way cleared the Connecticut volunteers
entered the city on February 4. Once inside Lee quickly forgot
even the limited assurances he had given the committee of
safety and immediately drew the British into a game of brinkmanship. After issuing a call to Congress on February 9 for
reinforcements, which gained him a regiment from Pennsyl-

vania and Lord Stirling's regiment, the mercurial Lee set about to provoke the British. He ordered his men to remove the cannon from the shore batteries under the very gaze of the look-outs on board the British warships. Captain Henry Parker did not, however, make good on his earlier pledge to shell the town if the cannon were removed. The British commander tried to justify himself by claiming that he kept his guns silent because he did not wish to play into the hands of the New England men who wanted the city destroyed. General Lee wryly observed that "the people here laugh at his nonsense, and begin to dispise [sic] the menaces which formerly use[d] to throw them into convulsions."[27]

Toward the end of February General Lee took another decisive step to rid the city of its royal jailers. He cut off all intercourse with the British men-of-war in the harbor. The provincial congress warned Lee that while the Hudson River remained icebound the British could starve the city into submission by halting the provisions ships from New Jersey and Connecticut. The general duly lifted the intercourse ban but a short time later, on March 1, he again interdicted all intercourse with the British ships.

At the same time the provincial congress learned to its dismay that some of the Connecticut riflemen were daily firing upon vessels in the harbor with the apparent approval of their commander, Colonel David Waterbury. Apparently the Connecticut commander was an outspoken exponent of making New York into a New England dependency.

On March 6, after word arrived from General Washington that the British were preparing to evacuate Boston. Lee strongly urged the provincial congress to employ the methods he had used in Rhode Island to tame the Tories. Lee also tried to convince the provincial congress that as long as ship-to-shore contact was permitted, the British would have complete information on every defensive measure. When the provincial congress gave no indication that it would act upon either suggestion, the general took matters into his own hands. He ordered Lieutenant Colonel Isaac Sears to administer a test oath to all suspected inhabitants on Long Island. Lee informed congress that he was prepared to suffer all the consequences should his action be reversed. But as he saw his duty, "When the enemy is at your door, forms must be dispensed with."[28] Sears cheerfully set about searching for Tories. Within a short time he was sending back gleeful reports to Lee: "I arrived at Newton, and tendered the oath to four of the grate Torries [sic], which they swallowed as hard as if it was a four pound shot. . . ."[29]

Except for a motion to have Isaac Sears come before congress and explain his action, the New York Whigs suffered General Lee's high-handed action in silence.[30] Perhaps the provincial congress deemed it wise to let the matter drop as General Lee was then proceeding southward to assume command of the newly created Southern military district. A more likely explanation is that the provincial congress simply realized that it was powerless to halt such proceedings and accepted this state of affairs with reasonable equanimity. Although staunch Whigs like Alexander McDougall and John Jay still clung to the hope that "the day is not very distant—when this Colony will act as decisive as any of its neighbors," by March the pace of events had made this unobtainable.[31] Whether New Yorkers liked it or not they had become almost a protectorate of the Continental Congress.

On the heels of Lee's departure General Stirling assumed command of the 9,000 troops in the city and carried on the defensive preparations begun by his predecessor. The Continental Congress even appointed a special three-man committee on March 11 to confer with General Washington on additional

defensive measures to protect the city. On February 25 a letter
from James Duane gave the provincial congress a good indication of how the attitude of Congress was changing. Duane
scolded the provincial congress for burdening General Schuyler with the job of recruiting the battalion intended for
Canadian service and for neglecting to submit the officer
recommendations for the four battalions the province was to
raise. Duane reported that the prevailing mood in Congress
was that "while everything was done for New York at the
publick expense that could be wished or asked, they neglected
their own defence. . . ."[32]

In the wake of the unauthorized roundup of Tories conducted by Sears the provincial congress became more resolute.
On March 9 its members voted to take over the provincial
treasury. Five days later the provincial congress approved
Lord Stirling's proposal to bring in additional militia units
from Pennsylvania and New Jersey. At the same time congress issued a general order for all healthy male residents of
the city to begin working on the barricades and fortifications.
Governor Tryon, sensing the changing mood of the New York
congress, directed a letter to the inhabitants of the province
on March 16. In his letter he praised Britain's moderate spirit
and predicted the commissioners would soon be on hand to
restore harmony. Tryon warned New Yorkers, however, that
should they become too zealous in their military preparations
Britain would be even more unmerciful in its response. The
provincial congress even endorsed the March 14th recommendation of the Continental Congress to disarm all nonassociators. But it was not until General Washington arrived
in the city in mid-April that all intercourse with the British
warships in the harbor was permanently curtailed.

By mid-April New York was still not ready for independence. To be sure the extensive congressional assistance

during the early months of 1776 had made the Whigs more the masters of their house than at any time previously. And yet the radical Whigs in the Continental Congress were still reluctant to place their full trust in the province. According to one New Englander, New York was still a "moth."

None of the other Middle Colonies required congressional intervention to untangle their affairs during the winter of 1775-1776. Pennsylvania's internal affairs were quite turbulent, nonetheless. When the newly elected members of the Pennsylvania assembly gathered in Philadelphia on October 4, 1775, many of them must have felt that "Dreadful Times" had come at last to the City of Brotherly Love.[33] Rumors of British warships at the mouth of the Delaware were commonplace. Scores of families had already moved out of the city. Attendant with the growing expectation that Philadelphia would soon be under British guns was the radicals' insistence that all aspects of the military program be made compulsory. One of their primary objectives was military conscription regardless of religious views. On October 20 the Philadelphia committee memorialized the assembly for mandatory militia service. They requested that conscientious objectors be forced to pay a suitable tax in lieu of actual service so that all citizens in one way or another would help bear the defense burden. The radical-dominated committee of privates voiced similar sentiments in a separate memorial to the assembly. A remonstrance from the Chester County committee pointed out that the refusal of many conscientious objectors to join the military association was creating a serious morale problem, because those who possessed tender consciences were usually "Men of considerable Property and influence. . . ."[34]

At this juncture the Quaker elders decided to break their public silence on the issue. In an address laid before the assembly on October 26, they protested that a provision in

Penn's Charter protected citizens from being forced "to do or
suffer any Act or Thing contrary to our religious Persuasion."[35]
They construed this to include payment of monetary assess-
ments. The Quaker address closed with a prayerful plea for
reconciliation. The appearance of the Quaker address made
the supporters of a conscientious objector tax even more determined to carry their point. Within a week the assembly was
bombarded by anti-Quaker petitions. A remonstrance from
the powerful Philadelphia committee charged that the Quaker
address "bears an Aspect unfriendly to the Liberties of America, and maintains Principles destructive to all Society and
Government. . . ."[36] In an effort to intensify public pressure on
the assembly, members who were sympathetic to the radical
demands sought to have the doors of the chamber thrown
open. When this proposal was defeated sixty-six members of
the Philadelphia committee staged a protest march to the State
House.

    Although reluctant to clamp down on the Quakers and
"Sectarian" Germans the conservative assemblymen realized
that if they failed to accede to the demands of the radicals and
moderate Whigs, a provincial congress might be called to do
what they would not. Accordingly on November 8, the assembly voted to tax all nonassociators a sum equivalent to
actual service. On the same day they also approved an issuance
of £80,000 in bills of credit to finance provincial military
programs.

    Before the exponents of strong military measures could
celebrate their achievement, the assembly approved a rather
surprising set of instructions for the congressional delegation.
It contained an explicit prohibition against voting for any
measures pointing toward independence. The Pennsylvania
radicals howled in indignation but were powerless to reverse
this action. John Dickinson's prominence and public opposi-

tion to independence stayed the hands of the radicals.[37] They could only lament that the new instructions tarnished Pennsylvania's reputation and had a profound influence on the other Middle Colonies. Gilbert Barkly noted that Pennsylvania ". . . is the Center of all the Collonies [sic], and the fountain from which they are in great degree supplied, in military stores, money, and provisions etc. . . . ." He envisioned that a British military occupation of the province might well bring on the collapse of the anti-imperial movement.[38] The alacrity with which New Jersey and New York sought to follow Pennsylvania's example lent credence to the assertion by Anthony Wayne that "Whatever may be our Unanimous Determinations . . . will be Readily Adopted by our neighboring Colonies."[39]

Although Pennsylvania had little difficulty influencing its sectional partners, the Connecticut settlers in the Wyoming Valley were not as pliant. An unsuccessful attempt by the Connecticut men early in October to engross more land in the valley brought the dispute to the brink of open warfare. When private conferences between the congressional delegations from both colonies failed to head off the clash, the two antagonists each drafted peace plans and laid them before Congress. The Connecticut proposal centered on a temporary truce as a means of averting hostilities. Pennsylvania would have none of this. The Pennsylvania assembly insisted that they be given civil jurisdiction over the entire valley. Both sides did agree to accept a cooling-off period based on existing boundaries until the Continental Congress should resolve the dispute. Congress then proceeded to appoint a committee to look into the Wyoming Valley dispute, but its report on November 4 merely referred the problem back to the respective assemblies.[40]

The failure of Congress to impose a settlement led to another flurry of violence in December. Already in November there had been talk that the land speculators in Philadelphia were planning to raise a substantial body of armed men to drive the "Yankees" from Pennsylvania soil.[41] On December 25 a force of 500 Pennsylvanians attacked a group of well-entrenched Connecticut settlers under Captain Zebulon Butler. The encounter proved to be very short and only one Pennsylvanian was killed. Less than a week before, the Continental Congress had finally agreed to adjudicate the dispute. After lengthy debates on December 18 and 20, Congress decided by a vote of six colonies to four to impose the Connecticut plan. That Congress sided with the Connecticut "Yankees" was not easy for the Pennsylvania delegates to accept.[42]

The truce imposed by Congress kept the two parties from further hostilities. But Pennsylvanians could not help thinking that the foothold that the New Englanders held in the Wyoming Valley might only be a prelude to further encroachment should the colonies embrace independence. Many inhabitants of Pennsylvania had long held latent suspicions about the "Yankees." The intransigent position taken by Connecticut in the Wyoming Valley dispute, however, helped to further reinforce these feelings at a time when the Central Provinces were already very concerned about the intentions of the New Englanders.

The year 1776 opened on a sour note for John Dickinson and his Whig followers. Thomas Wharton's own pessimistic outlook no doubt reflected their state of mind as well:

We are now entered into a New Year and I pray to the great disposer of events that he may so change the hearts of those in power in England . . . to withdraw their armies and treat with the Americans on terms becoming to both of us.[43]

Yet the tide of events still had not dislodged the conservative–moderate coalition from control of the assembly. The radicals were not without their difficulties either. The news of Montgomery's decisive defeat before Quebec cast serious doubt upon the effectiveness of American forces. Dunmore's burning of Norfolk was another painful reminder of colonial naval inferiority. A British sympathizer reported from Philadelphia early in February that ". . . many people here are tired of our great ones knight errantry; for I am afraid on a formidable appearance of the King's troops, the Congress will not find so many friends as they imagined."[44] In his mind the actions of the Continental Congress were comparable to those of the Spanish Inquisition. Evidence of intensified Tory activity forced the council of safety to devote much of its time in January to uncovering and punishing these enemies of the country. In Bucks County, for example, the local militia commander, Colonel Daniel Roberdeau, received several threatening letters. The mysterious correspondents demanded the immediate release of Dr. John Kearsley, who had been imprisoned the preceding fall. The Tory writers warned that the Congressional resolve of January 2 to disarm and arrest all suspected Tories

. . . has served to stir up the people to arm themselves, and will make such a stand that you will want no other Enemy to engage but those of our Country, if that Resolve is not Repealed and that very soon.[45]

When the assembly reconvened in late February effective mobilization was again the foremost order of business. A memorial from the council of safety urged the house to raise an additional 2,000 troops to aid in the defense of the city and to adopt the recommendations of the committee of privates for improving the military association.[46] "As every Day brings with it fresh Proof of the Violence of the British Ministry, and of their fixed Purpose to subdue the free spirit of America . . ." warned the council of safety, "it truly becomes us to prepare seriously for the Storm gathering over the Colonies, and which, in the Uncertainty of its Course, may, in a few Weeks, fall

upon this province."[47] On February 28 the assembly appointed
a committee headed by John Dickinson and Joseph Reed to
examine all of the suggested changes offered by the various
groups.

Early in March as the assembly continued its dilatory
habits, the members were shocked to learn that the Philadelphia committee had issued a call on March 4 for a provincial
convention. The task of this assemblage would be to review
the present military conditions of the province. The conservative Whigs in the assembly were caught unawares by this
maneuver. Their surprise was no doubt owing to the fact the
semi-annual election for the members of the Philadelphia
committee on February 16 had been preceded by no special
electioneering on the part of the radicals and over two-thirds
of the incumbents were returned to office. The nascent independence party headed by James Cannon, Christopher Marshall, Timothy Matlack, Thomas Paine, Benjamin Rush and
Thomas Young had hidden their intentions expertly.[48] Faced
with the prospect of being superseded by a convention, Dickinson and Reed managed to convince the conservative Whigs
in the assembly to offer concessions to the radicals. Accordingly on March 14 the house passed a resolution to expand
its membership by seventeen to provide more equitable representation for the western counties and the city of Philadelphia.
Since the balance of power would be held by whichever Whig
faction captured the May 1st elections for the new representatives, both groups set about campaigning at once. Because the
questions of independence and reconciliation were bound up
so tightly in the election, the campaign spawned a great debate
over the future course of the colonial union. For the next two
months writers in the public press engaged in a free-wheeling
war of words.

On the eve of the great debate five newspapers were published regularly in Philadelphia. Both the *Pennsylvania Gazette* and the *Pennsylvania Journal* had served the colony for more than two decades, while the *Pennsylvania Packet* first appeared in 1771. Two other newspapers, the *Pennsylvania Evening Post* and the *Pennsylvania Ledger,* were only in their second year of publication.

Despite the absence of modern editorial techniques, the political sentiments of all five papers in the great debate are clearly discernible. The *Gazette, Packet, Evening Post* and the *Journal* all supported the radical Whigs. William Bradford, the editor of the *Journal* who was frequently referred to as the "Patriot Printer," along with Benjamin Towne, the irascible editor of the *Evening Post,* published the strongest Patriot organs. Neither editor displayed the least impartiality in selecting articles. The *Gazette* and *Packet* pursued a less partisan editorial policy that perhaps manifested closer adherence to the ideal of unbiased reporting of the news. John Dunlap, the Scottish editor of the *Packet,* and David Hall and William Sellers, the co-editors of the *Gazette,* published almost as many essays by conservative Whig authors as they did pieces from radical Whigs.

The *Pennsylvania Ledger* was the only paper that consistently catered to the conservative Whig essayists. Edited by James Humphreys, Jr., a former apprentice to William Bradford, the *Ledger* offered the most complete coverage of English news and such extras as a poets' corner and an occasional short story. The inception of the debate over independence apparently encouraged Humphreys to abandon the strict impartiality that his paper had displayed since its founding in January, 1775. He endeavored to print any and all news items that illustrated conciliatory sentiment in England and opposition to the ministerial course. Proposals for reconciliation advanced by Edmund Burke and others, along with conservative Whig essays, received front-page treatment. Likewise, petitions from London, Bristol, and the Irish House of Commons critical of the coercive plans of the ministry appeared in profusion.

The main protagonist for the conservative Whigs in the great debate was Dr. William Smith, Provost of the College of Philadelphia and an Anglican churchman. Egotistical and cynical, Smith had not endeared himself to the city's intellectual elite during his years in Philadelphia. Yet the radical Whigs who ridiculed him clearly respected his intellectual abilities. "Rationalis," "Cato" and "Candidus" were the three pen names under which he put forth his various pamphlets and essays. His opening essay in the debate over independence was published in the *Pennsylvania Gazette* under the pseudonym of "Rationalis."[49] Intended as a rebuttal against *Common Sense,* Smith strove to extol peaceful reconciliation as the best course for America while deprecating the virtues of independence. He shrewdly covered himself against the anticipated "Tory" epithet by admitting his willingness to support independence should Britain make all other peaceful measures untenable. The British Constitution and its great monarchial component were vigorously defended in an attempt to refute Paine's captious attack. Most of the basic arguments developed in this essay Smith reiterated many times during the course of the great debate, for he was painfully aware that the central issue was whether peace was still a genuine alternative.

The first serious pamphlet to appear in response to *Common Sense* was printed by Robert Bell in mid-March. *Plain Truth* by "Candidus" was dedicated to John Dickinson. The Pennsylvania leader was exhorted to "STEP then forth; exert those talents with which Heaven had endowed you; and cause the Parent, and her children to embrace and be foes no more."[50] In the body of the pamphlet Smith presented a very disparaging view of America's military potential. On the question of possible military assistance from France or Spain, he cogently argued that both of these monarchial states would be foolish to endanger their precarious domestic positions by risking possible infection from American liberalism. Even if substantial aid could be wrung from these powers they would certainly not be satisfied without pledges more inhibiting on American rights than Great Britain had ever proposed. Smith also sought to arouse distrust amongst the American Patriots by referring to New England's traditional religious intolerance and more recent expansionistic inklings. As he gazed into the future Smith was convinced that a Cromwellian style of dictatorship would soon emerge from the confusion of war and independence.

Overall, Smith's work was inferior to *Common Sense*. Lacking the directness and vibrancy of Paine's work, it was also very discursive. In his private correspondence Smith sadly admitted that everything rested on the peace commissioners. Already in mid-March he realized that "The mouths of the most zealous Friends of Peace will then be shut," if the commissioners did not arrive soon.[51]

Plain Truth did not circulate as widely as *Common Sense*. By means of an aggressive advertising campaign Bell managed to sell enough copies to warrant a second edition, but the 2,000 copies sold could hardly match the influence of 100,000 copies of *Common Sense*.

Imitating the radical Whigs' supplements to *Common Sense*, Smith wrote a pamphlet entitled *Additions to Plain Truth*, which Bell published early in April. Although the pamphlet was more effectively written than its predecessor, it was essentially a revised rendition of *Plain Truth*. Smith did, however, inculcate a few new argumentative twists. He was more vociferous in his attacks upon the author of *Common*

Sense, accusing him of being a spokesman for the rabble. The most sensational charge in the pamphlet was that

... the author of Common Sense for some time past has been anxiously busied in negotiating a match between Mademoiselle Borgio, a descendant of Pope Alexander the Sixth, vulgarly called the scarlet Whore of Babylon, and a great grandson of John Calvin.[52]

Another new slant taken by Smith was his comparison of the present censorship of the press to the relative freedom prevalent under the old order. In conclusion he implored his fellow Americans to await the arrival of the commissioners before plunging into the maelstrom of independence. Although Robert Bell conducted an aggressive advertising campaign for *Additions to Plain Truth,* sales were not sufficient to warrant a second edition.

There is no question that Smith achieved his most pervasive influence as "Cato." Published serially in Philadelphia papers during March and April, these letters were intended to examine the great question solely in relation to Pennsylvania. Many of the arguments and tactics that Smith previously relied upon, including his attempts to incite the people against the "Yankees," were reiterated with special reference to the Quaker Colony. The only new arguments he developed were a somewhat superficial distinction between formal and informal independence and the ludicrous charge that the author of *Common Sense* was actually a hireling of the British ministry. The influence that *"Cato's Letters"* had with the general public was doubtless heightened by the vitriolic counterattacks launched by radical Whig penmen such as "Cassandra" and "The Forester." The apparent moderation of the seemingly highminded "Cato" must have evoked considerable sympathy if not support.

One of the radical Whig writers presented a mock dialogue between "Cato" and "Plain Truth" to expose the tactics of the former. "Cato" was depicted as lecturing his colleague on the necessity of remaining uncommitted to any one position and upon the advantages inherent in the letter-to-the editor technique. He was reputed to have said, "You can thus keep the minds of the people in constant suspense and prevent them from determining anything, this is our business."[53] Although Smith was not as eclectic as this writer maintained, his primary purpose was to fight a delaying action against independence. What he lacked in the way of tangible evidence concerning Britain's desire for a peaceful settlement, he tried to counteract by sowing seeds of disunity among the people.

As the great debate raged the assembly continued to exercise its authority over the resistance movement. Early in April the committee that the house had appointed late in February to recommend alterations in the military association finally brought in its report. The changes made in the military association on April 5 fulfilled some of the more substantial demands of the radical military organizations. The nonassociator tax was raised to three pounds ten shillings, provision was made for speedy naturalization of German associators and the death penalty was affixed for such offenses as mutiny, sedition and deserters who served with the enemy.[54] On April 6 the Pennsylvania assembly reluctantly voted to implement the March 14th recommendation of the Continental Congress to disarm all nonassociators. Adoption of these measures brought Pennsylvania abreast of the other Middle Colonies. The question still to be resolved was whether the radical or conservative Whig faction would be in power when the time came to decide on independence.

"It is with extreme concern I observe the Necessity His Majesty is now under of having Recourse to a military Force to secure His Dominions in America," declared New Jersey's

governor early in October.[55] The recently elected delegates to
the second provincial congress, who were meeting at the time,
no doubt shared Franklin's discomfiture but their task was to
ready the province to withstand the British forces. With only
three duly elected delegates absent the congress addressed
itself to three major items of business: raising funds to finance
mobilization, reforming the military regulations and implementing the request of the Continental Congress to raise several battalions. The difficulties which the previous congress
experienced in trying to collect the defense tax led the second
congress to seek less troublesome fund-raising methods. On
October 14 President Samuel Tucker applied to the Continental Congress for a grant to enable New Jersey to complete its military preparations. When Congress refused this
request the delegates took the next expeditious course—the
issuance of proclamation money in the amount of £30,000.[56]

Although the second congress shied away from adopting
any new taxes, it refused to allow the June tax to become a
dead letter. Citizens who were delinquent in their payment
were given until December 5 to pay up or they would be
liable to confiscation and sale of their goods. Having thus
dispensed with fiscal matters the delegates next spent several
days debating a set of new military regulations. Under the
updated regulations adopted on October 28, the New Jersey
militia was to be governed more like an army than a disjointed
home guard. The October regulations laid a four shilling per
month tax on all conscientious objectors backed up by a confiscation clause. A plan for total mobilization in the event of
a British attack was also adopted. While the other Middle
Colonies continued to strengthen and revise their military
regulations in the months ahead, New Jersey's rules needed
only minor changes.

In addition to financial and military matters the suffrage

issue raised by the previous congress came before the second congress. Petitions from Sussex and Hunterdon counties called upon the delegates to extend the suffrage to all taxpayers. On October 25 a motion introduced by the delegates from Salem County to dissolve the existing provincial congress and to elect a new body with all householders or men possessing a minimum personal estate of fifty pounds eligible to vote put congress in an uproar. Since the second congress was close to adjournment a motion to table the entire suffrage question until the next session won approval by a vote of seven counties to six.[57] The rationale for this decision was that each delegate would thus have time to assay the sentiments of his constituents before casting his vote on the question. Democratic reform may have suffered a momentary setback, but the closeness of the vote almost guaranteed that some meaningful reform would be made in the next session.

Several weeks after the provincial congress adjourned Governor Franklin launched what would prove to be his last serious attempt to check New Jersey's drift towards revolutionary collaboration with the other provinces. As we have already seen Governor Franklin came very close to succeeding. Although the assembly did not dispatch a separate petition to the King, it did forbid the delegates in Congress from acceding to independence, passed a support bill for the civil list and gave the governor strong assurance that his person and family were in no danger.[58]

The governor had caught the Whigs napping and they would not be fooled again. When a band of Tories in Sussex County began to meet openly and flout the Association in support of the governor, the Whigs lost no time in taking remedial action. On December 26 a force of 400 militiamen swept through the county and forced forty suspected Tories to disavow all inimical sentiments and sign the Association.

When two of the leaders refused to disavow their Tory sentiments they were sent to the committee of safety for further
action. The committee ordered Robert Ellison and assemblyman Nathaniel Pettit to post a fifty pound bond for good
conduct and branded both men as traitors to the cause.[59] As
for Governor Franklin, his dutiful messages to Lord Dartmouth on the state of the resistance movement prompted the
Whigs to place him in protective custody. On January 5 Lord
Stirling's troops came across a packet containing some of
Franklin's dispatches while they were searching a British
supply vessel. Acting on his own initiative Stirling sent a
militia company to arrest the governor. After some initial
indecision the Whigs allowed Franklin to remain in his house
at Perth Amboy on his own recognizance. Though technically
under arrest, Franklin tried his best to keep up the appearance
of being governor.

When the second provincial congress opened its second
session in New Brunswick on February 1, the delegates could
hardly have anticipated the extensive demands that were soon
to be placed upon New Jersey's military resources. First, the
New Jersey battalion scheduled for service in Canada could
not embark because of a serious shortage of arms. In order to
hasten the departure of Colonel William Maxwell's brigade
the delegates ordered all other militia units in the province to
proffer their arms. Within a week and a half the second
congress received a request from the New York committee of
safety that Colonel Heard's regiment be dispatched at once
to Staten Island to protect livestock and provisions from
British raiders. On February 12 a communication from
President Hancock arrived from Philadelphia asking that a
battalion of minutemen be immediately sent to New York City
as

The arrival of troops off New-York, the importance of that place to the welfare of America, and the necessity of throwing up a number of works to prevent our enemies from landing and taking post there, render it necessary that a number of troops should immediately join General Lee.[60]

The provincial congress promptly ordered Colonel Charles Stewart to take detachments equal to a battalion and proceed to New York City. When the Continenal Congress learned that the militiamen under Stewart were almost devoid of arms because of the transfer of weapons to Colonel Maxwell's battalion, they rescinded the call.

New Jersey's demonstrated inability to put even a battalion of minutemen into the field led the provincial congress to redouble its efforts to secure additional arms from the Continental Congress. Rather than justify its application by alluding to the popular uneasiness about the defenseless state of the province, the provincial congress stressed the importance of properly defending the portions of the colony adjacent to New York City and Philadelphia.[61] Both Perth Amboy and the east bank of the Delaware River below Philadelphia might be attacked by the British if there were no strong defenses. The New Jersey delegates regretted having to apply to the Continental Congress for assistance,

but as this will be an expense too great for this Colony to support on its own bottom, and as the area to be guarded at all points is a matter of utmost importance to the common cause, more especially the Cities of Philadelphia and New York. . . . [62]

In spite of the subsequent refusal of the Continental Congress to supply the necessary arms and supplies, New Jersey continued to devote itself to the task of assisting Pennsylvania and especially "a lame Brother of ours in the Liberty Schuffle," as one Jerseyite tabbed New York.[63] Late in April General Washington complimented the Jerseyites on their willingness to provide New York with military assistance whenever a request was forthcoming. He concluded that their ready commitment of troops "are sufficient proofs of the important service the Province of New-Jersey is capable of rendering in support of the great cause of American liberty. . . ."[64]

From the governor's mansion in Perth Amboy, Franklin still managed to supply Dartmouth with reports on colonial developments. Late in March the governor revealed that the supporters of independence in New Jersey were gaining ground with each passing day. He still believed that a majority of the people would not countenance the measures of the provincial congress if they knew that the measures were designed to break the ties with the Empire rather than restore them. As for his own situation Franklin promised that he would not leave the province and allow the Whigs to use his departure as a pretext to establish an independent government, "tho' it has been often recommended to me to retreat in Time."[65]

Once again Governor Franklin's unerring powers of observation proved to be sharp for New Jersey did take a noticeable turn towards independence during the first three months of 1776. The ease with which the few active Tories were suppressed and the absence of any serious cleavage between the various Whig factions enabled New Jersey to take a more positive view of separation than her less stable neighbors to the immediate south and north. "This Country is too much on their guard, too well prepared, and too much exasperated to attend to anything but plain English," was how Captain Robert Erskine of Morris County described the mood of most Jerseymen early in February.[66]

While no one can doubt that *Common Sense* helped to shake the attachment of many Jerseyites to the Empire, the Reverend Jacob Greene of Morris County also provided his fellow citizens with a well-conceived set of arguments in favor of independence. Published in January, *Observations On The Reconciliation Of Great Britain And The Colonies* was intended to blast the arguments being raised in opposition to separation and offer a sound rationale for taking the final step. According to Greene, the thirteen colonies could only achieve their true greatness if the shackles imposed by Britain were ripped away. Although this pamphlet lacked the compelling logic of Paine's effort, it must have influenced many Jerseymen who had a liking for home-grown products.

Other Whig writers also joined in. "Essex" contributed an essay early in March which applauded *Common Sense*. He proposed that in forming an independent government representation should be apportioned on the basis of one delegate for each 1,000 troops under arms. In advancing this proposition "Essex" was no doubt cognizant that New Jersey had a very high percentage of its able-bodied men serving under arms.[67]

The slowly emerging groundswell of support for independence also found expression in the action of the provincial congress in February. On February 15 this body selected Jonathan Sergeant to represent New Jersey in the Continental Congress. Since late November when Kinsey and De Hart resigned their seats the three remaining delegates, William Livingston, Stephen Crane and Richard Smith, had been struggling to carry out their responsibilities. With one of the three frequently absent for personal reasons, New Jersey was on occasion unable to cast a vote on important matters because the two delegates present were at odds. "I can assure you that nothing but my Devotion to the Public, has kept me here this long," wrote William Livingston, and "I scorn to quit my Colours thro impatience or Discouragement but I think it reasonable that the Burden should be divided."[68] The selection of Sergeant to bolster the delegation was highly

significant. Several delegates spoke against his candidacy because he was known to favor independence. But when his
nomination came to a vote eleven counties supported him and
only one opposed.[69]

Congress did not stop with the selection of a pro-independence delegate. In a businesslike manner it proceeded
to draft a set of instructions which in effect superseded the
instructions laid down by the assembly in November. The new
instructions did not specifically mention independence, but
the provincial congress did remove the prohibition levied by
the assembly. The provincial congress noted that it did not
have access to firsthand news and information like the delegates in Congress, and thus did not wish to confine them to any
one mode of action: "We, therefore, only request that you
would join in the general voice of the United Colonies, and
pursue such measures as you may judge most beneficial for
the publick good of all the Colonies."[70] Despite the addition
of Sergeant, the New Jersey delegation was not yet ready to
cast a vote for independence. But the Whig leaders back
home were giving notice that if a solid majority of the colonies
decided upon secession they might join in regardless of what
Pennsylvania decided.

The heightened incidence of active Toryism that beset
the other Middle Colonies, especially New York, during the
winter of 1775-1776 was also evident in Delaware. The
colony's most notorious Tory, Thomas Robinson, remained
at large and continued his activities with impunity. Robinson
shrewdly played upon the divisions among the Sussex County
committee members to hinder the Whigs. In a letter published
in the *Pennsylvania Journal* early in October, he claimed that
the charges leveled against him in July were trumped up in
order to deny him his assembly seat. Robinson produced the
names of five Sussex committee members who supported his

assertion. The inability of the Whigs in Sussex to overawe the Tories was further demonstrated in November when a certain "J.C." was brought before the committee for having openly derided Congress and the cause. After much vacillation the committee did not mete out any penalty, and an irate Whig sadly concluded, "All the friends of Liberty here in Sussex may as well give up as contend any longer, for we are too weak to oppose the Ministerial tools."[71] The few staunch Whigs in Sussex were hopeful that the provincial committee of safety or Kent County might come to their assistance, but no help was forthcoming.

When the committee of safety did convene in January it was forced to deal with the results of Robinson's influence in Sussex. To the members' chagrin, they discovered that the inhabitants of Sussex had not even learned of the military arrangements prescribed for the colony as a whole in September, 1775.[72] Before recessing the body empowered seven of its members from Sussex County to handle the commissioning of officers for the western battalion and to decide upon a proper division between the two other battalions still to be formed.

In March when the assembly convened, Delaware belatedly altered the instructions for her congressional delegation. Although the new instructions did not specifically mention independence, the delegates were ordered to work for reconciliation with the mother country. If, however, the delegates found that military measures were a necessary prelude to negotiations, they were to concur in such as they deemed essential. The three lower counties on the Delaware, or at least two of them, had followed Pennsylvania thus far and if the Quaker Colony went for independence, undoubtedly they would accede as well.

Late in April, 1776, Sam Adams surveyed the positions of the colonies on the independence question and concluded

that the Middle Colonies were still the major holdouts. He
conceived that Pennsylvania and New York were certain to be
the primary stumbling blocks when the time for a decision
arrived. As for New Jersey Adams realized that "it is with
them rather a Matter of Prudence whether to determine till
some others have done it before them. . . ."[73] Nonetheless, he
was assured by one zealous Jerseyite that fully half the inhabitants were of New England descent. Adams also admitted
that much more favorable auspices existed in Pennsylvania
than New York, for he fully expected the independence party
candidates to sweep the provincial elections on May 1. New
York, however, remained sphinxlike. "[I]t is uncertain what
they will do," Sam Adams wrote in disgust, for ". . . they are
at least as unenlightened in the Nature & importance of our
political disputes as any one of the united Colonies."[74]

In wider view Adams' faint optimism about the temper
of the Middle Colonies testifies to the transformation wrought
in their attitudes by the course of events during the winter of
1775-1776. Few could question that by the spring of 1776 independence had become a viable alternative for the Middle
Colonies to adopt. Although his assessment did not spell it
out, Sam Adams was doubtless aware that once Pennsylvania
went for independence the Middle Colonies would quickly
fall in line. The New Jersey Whigs would no longer have to
bide their time and Delaware must follow suit as well. If all
this transpired only New York would be left. But New York
could not stand alone. Besides, during the winter months the
Whig party's limited capacity for trenchant decision making
had been weakened further by a series of events that gave
credence to their previously unsubstantiated fears of New England. The New York Whigs could hardly interpret Sears' Raid,
General Lee's actions in New York City and the attempt by
the New England delegates in Congress to have New York in-

cluded in the Northern military district as anything less than conclusive evidence of New England's designs. As a result, the New York Whigs foresaw not just one invasion threat but two. If New York did not agree to independence, troops from New England would certainly descend on the province to force the issue and the British already had designated New York as their major military objective. Even before the First Congress the New York Whigs had never been ones to rush to judgment, and they were certainly in no hurry in the spring of 1776.

chapter eight

THE LAST OUTPOST OF RESISTANCE TO INDEPENDENCE

The Middle Colonies

By the middle of April even the most stolid conservative Whig would have grudgingly agreed with Benjamin Franklin that

> every day furnished us with new cause of increasing enmity, and new reasons for wishing for an eternal separation; so that there is a rapid increase of the formerly small party, who were for an independent government.[1]

To admit the inevitability of withdrawal from the Empire was one thing, but setting a date quite another. It was on this question that the Middle Colonial bloc and the New England radicals clashed in their final struggle. Wise heads like Joseph Reed and George Washington recognized that this last hurdle was most formidable. "Nothing but disunion can hurt our cause," warned Washington. "This will ruin it, if great prudence, temper, and moderation is not mixed in our counsels."[2] Joseph Reed likened the united colonies to an orchard that would only yield pleasing fruit if the sun and the elements were given ample time to work their magic.[3] No one knew better than John Adams that thirteen clocks could never be synchronized to chime for independence at the same moment. "Some people must have time to look around them; before, behind, on the right hand, and on the left; then to think and after this resolve: on such a momentous question as independence," observed Adams while "Others see at one intuitive glance into the past and the future, and judge with precision at once."[4] The Middle Colonies went one better for they looked twice in every direction before they leaped.

For men like John Jay and John Dickinson, independence might well be the last act of the resistance movement. But before it could be proclaimed there was much that had to be accomplished. Stable governments would have to be established, a workable confederation set up to govern the colonial union and foreign alliances secured. Although most Middle Colonial leaders avowed their doubts that the long-awaited commissioners could offer any reasonable terms, they were reluctant to cut the few remaining ties with the Empire until their suspicions were confirmed. In early April Jay faced up to the need "to erect good & well ordered governments in all Colonies, and thereby exclude that anarchy which already too much prevails," but he could not see New York taking such action ". . . till the business of the Commissioners is over. . . ."[5] Likewise, John Dickinson wished to wait for the commissioners. In his *Remarks on a Late Pamphlet Entitled Plain Truth* published in May, Dickinson sought to show that his sentiments were not far removed from those expressed by the author of *Common Sense*. By means of some circular argumentation, however, he managed to make his support for Paine's position contingent upon a hearing for the commissioners on their arrival.

Impatient radicals frequently lampooned the supporters of reconciliation for their determination to delay the final stroke until the commissioners were heard from. John Adams likened the unshakeable belief that the commissioners would smooth over all Anglo-American differences to the Tales in London Papers and Magazines, a few years ago concerning the Cock Lane Ghost, and others concerning a Man of six feet high, who leapt into a Quart Bottle and Corked himself up.[6]

That the conservative Whigs in the Central Provinces refused to turn their back on the commissioners, despite the growing evidence that they would shoot first and ask questions later, was not a sign of myopia but rather an indication of their political astuteness.[7] The leaders of the Middle Colonial bloc in Congress like Dickinson, Willing, Duane, Jay, Wm. Livingston and Read dreaded independence because it would end forever their section's favored position and fully expose them to New England's exploitation.[8] They all recognized that only the faint hope held out by the commissioners stood in the way of separation. Many of the conservative Middle Colonial leaders could not bear to take this step until the commissioners themselves had proven that they came to treat with vassals not Englishmen.[9]

Early in May the Middle Colonial bloc in Congress made a move to assure the commissioners a reception befitting their station. Acting upon General Washington's request of March 24 concerning the mode of conduct he should pursue if the commissioners communicated their arrival to him, the Middle Colonial leaders moved that the general be empowered to grant them safe conduct passes and present their credentials to Congress. This motion also contained an expression of congressional interest in peace. The radical majority easily tabled this motion. Nonetheless, the significance of the encounter was not lost on John Adams:

It was one of those delusive Contrivances by which the Party in Opposition to Us endeavoured, by lulling the People with idle hopes of Reconciliation, into Security, to turn their hearts and thoughts from independence.[10]

Having dispensed with the Middle Colonial bloc's bid to forestall independence, the radicals resumed their search for the means to hasten the final break. Central to their task was the need to unseat Dickinson's party. Although the independence Whigs had picked up a number of seats in the May 1st election the conservative Whigs still controlled the Pennsylvania assembly. Men like John and Sam Adams knew that if Pennsylvania took to the independence road "the Middle Way" would be no more.[11]

On May 10, the day after rumors of foreign mercenaries were at last confirmed by the publication of the actual treaties, John Adams moved that Congress recommend the formation of new governments in all the provinces. John Adams scarcely had time to sit down before John Dickinson rose to express his hearty support for the measure. The radicals were shocked by Dickinson's endorsement. But they soon discovered that the Pennsylvania leader was willing to support the resolution because he considered the existing Pennsylvania government as sufficient to meet the needs of the people. Confident that he had disarmed Adams' resolution, Dickinson departed for Delaware to immerse himself in rural pursuits for a few days.

With Dickinson absent, John Adams hit upon the idea of using the preamble customarily attached to resolutions to void Pennsylvania's exemption from the new government resolution. Accordingly on May 15 Congress took up the preamble which unequivocally affirmed that all governments under the Crown must be dismantled. Whether the Middle Colonial bloc was completely surprised by this strategem is unlikely since James Duane sent out a call for help on May 11. "A business of still greater moment is on the Carpet," he informed John Jay in an effort to bring him to Philadelphia to bolster the peace forces.[12] Jay, however, never saw fit to

leave New York and the Middle Colonial bloc lacked both
the voices and the votes to prevent the preamble's acceptance.
James Wilson warned that the measure would plunge Pennsylvania into anarchy. He urged Congress to shelve the preamble at least until the Pennsylvania assembly met on May
20. Since the radicals were trying to undermine this body,
however, his entreaties were ignored. Duane also spoke out
against the preamble, arguing that Congress lacked the authority to intervene in provincial matters. He warned that Congress
should not slam the door on reconciliation until the commissioners had been heard from.

Immediately after the affirmative decision on the preamble, by a vote of six colonies to four, the entire Maryland
delegation walked out of Congress in protest.[13] Bound by
their instructions to oppose all measures that looked toward
independence, the Marylanders wished to lay the entire matter before the provincial congress before proceeding further.[14]
Whether Maryland's action would prove to be a serious setback to the drive toward independence was a question that
both the radical and conservative Whigs sought to fathom.
John Jay concluded that "The Proceedings of Maryland will
probably check the ardor of some people."[15] John Adams,
however, did not believe that Maryland's example would have
any great influence on the course of events in the Middle
Colonies. For as Adams saw it, Maryland was an enigma unto
itself:

That is so eccentric a Colony—sometimes so hot, sometimes so
cold; now so high, then so low—that I know not what to say
about it or to expect from it. I have often wished it could exchange Places with Hallifax. When they get agoing I expect some
wild extravagant Flight or other from it. To be sure they must go
beyond every body else when they begin to go.[16]

Adams and Jay did concur on one major point—Pennsylvania would be the bellwether for the Middle Colonies.

Passage of the preamble on May 15 galvanized the radical cabal in Philadelphia into immediate action. James Cannon and Benjamin Rush, who directed the steering committee of the Philadelphia committee, moved quickly to take advantage of the opportunity which Congress had provided. A town meeting on May 20 called by the city committee brought out over 7,000 people who concurred wholeheartedly with the "Protest" that was read to them. Essentially the "Protest" was intended to scuttle the assembly. It demanded the immediate repeal of the instructions against independence, declared the assembly to be ". . . a Body of Men bound by Oaths of Allegiance to our Enemy . . ." and called upon all county committees to send delegates to a provincial convention on June 18.[17] Confronted with an open challenge to its authority, the conservative Whigs in the assembly quickly drafted a "Remonstrance" justifying the authority and legality of their body. During the remainder of May, Dickinson's group sent numerous agents into the backcountry to secure support for the "Remonstrance." This bid for popular approval was countered in every county by the network of militiamen which James Cannon had put together in the spring. Where persuasion proved unsuccessful the military associators resorted to mild intimidation to prevent the distribution of the "Remonstrance." By the end of May Benjamin Rush joyously proclaimed "Our cause prospers in every county in the province, The hand of heaven is with us."[18]

Despite Rush's optimism, the conservative Whigs did not simply vanish. Cheered by the presence of 6,000 signatures on the "Remonstrance" and an address from the Philadelphia County committee endorsing their position, Dickinson and his cohorts tried to keep the assembly in business. Once again, however, Congress came to the aid of the independence party. In light of the fact that Congress had set June 7 as the day for taking up the Virginia resolution calling for a declaration of independence, the radicals threatened to stop the proceedings of the Pennsylvania assembly by staying away unless the instructions for the congressional delegation were changed. On June 5 the conservative Whigs bowed to pressure and voted to appoint a committee to draft new instructions. Three days later, as the debate in Congress on the Virginia resolutions entered its second day, the Pennsylvania assembly adopted new instructions. Although this set of instructions did not explicitly authorize the delegates to vote for separation, there was enough flexibility in the language to allow for this result. They were empowered

to concur with the other Delegates in Congress, in forming such further Compacts between the United Colonies, concluding such Treaties with foreign Kingdoms and States, and in adopting such other Measures as, upon a View of all Circumstances, shall be judged necessary for promoting the Liberty, Safety and Interests of America.[19]

Meanwhile in Congress, Dickinson, Wilson, Robert R. Livingston and Edward Rutledge were leading the fight of the reconciliation forces against "the power of N. England, Virginia & Georgia. . . ."[20] They raised numerous objections to the immediate acceptance of the Virginia resolves, ranging from the need to secure foreign alliances and hammer out a workable confederation before leaving the Empire, to the danger of colonial disunion should the Middle Colonies be coerced into acting. The best that the Middle Colonial bloc could do was to win a three week postponement of the vote on the Virginia resolves. The radicals in Congress made it quite clear that the delay was granted because the Middle Colonies, along with South Carolina and Maryland, needed just a little more time to bring in a favorable decision on this paramount question.[21] To insure that the reprieve did not extend beyond July 1 the radicals saw to it that Congress appointed a committee to take up each of the Virginia resolves (independence, foreign alliances, confederation).

Whatever hope John Dickinson and his supporters had of using the three-week grace period to make over the assembly so that it could continue to serve as the legal government of the province was quickly dashed by the radical assemblymen. They stayed away from their seats from June 10 to June 14 and thus forced the house to expire for want of a quorum. With the assembly out of the way, James Cannon and the city radicals had no trouble convincing the provincial conference to entrust the government of the colony to the council of safety until the new constitution came into being. The provincial conference also went on record in support of the Virginia resolves. "The revolution is now begun and must be supported" was the cry of the triumphant radicals.[22]

In the months ahead the radical clique that had brought the old political order to its knees would construct a new constitution placing effective control of government in the hands of the people. By refusing to bend with the wind, the established political leadership in Pennsylvania became so isolated that new men with new ideas easily shunted them aside. Late in the summer of 1776, after reading Pennsylvania's thoroughly democratic constitution, John Dickinson affirmed that he stood blameless for this amazing document. His old friend Charles Thomson, however, gently chided him for his unwillingness to compromise his principles in the months before independence was declared: ". . . I cannot help regretting that by a perseverence which you were fully convinced was fruitless, you have thrown the affairs of this

state into the hands of men totally unequal to them."[23] In the
other Middle Colonies the veteran politicos tacked before the
wind and thus were able to perpetuate their ascendance in
large part beyond July 2.

Delaware was the first of the Middle Colonies to follow
Pennsylvania's lead in providing for a new government and
modifying the instructions for her delegates in Congress.
Caesar Rodney, who was on hand to observe the proceedings
in Philadelphia in May, recognized that the formation of a
new government was a very ticklish business. If the people
were left without government, for even a short time, there
was danger that they would develop licentious habits. But to
form a weak government in haste was also unthinkable.[24]
Taking note of the heated contest raging in Pennsylvania and
the reports that the Sussex Tories were preparing for hostilities,
Caesar Rodney determined that Delaware could ill afford
cleavage among its Whigs.[25] After much discussion the Whig
leaders decided to have the assembly implement the call for a
new government. On June 15 speaker Rodney and assemblyman McKean saw to it that the Delaware assembly ended its
own existence and provided new instructions for the congressional delegation. By simply substituting the authority of the
people for that of the King, the government was empowered to
carry on its functions until a new constitution was drafted. The
new instructions for the delegates to Congress more or less
copied the recent counsel extended by the Pennsylvania assembly to its delegates. Delaware thus went no further down the
road to independence than the Pennsylvania assembly.

Within seven days of Delaware's affirmative action the
New Jersey provincial congress expressly ordered its new
congressional delegation to vote for independence. In view of
the favorable attitude toward separation that the second

provincial congress displayed in March, one might have expected New Jersey to have climbed down off the fence sooner than it did. That the province did not was the result of a surprising change of heart in April. This dramatic shift in sentiment was first evident at an unofficial meeting of county committee members. Apparently, the Reverend John Witherspoon and a handful of radical Whigs had planned this meeting, unbeknownst to the participants, to secure an affirmative referendum on independence. Elias Boudinot arrived unexpectedly shortly after the meeting began. When he perceived what was going on he tried to persuade the committeemen that the delegates in Congress

were the only proper Judges of the Measures to be pursued and that we had no right to involve them in Distress & Trouble by plunging ourselves into a Measure of so delicate a Nature until they should advise us in what Manner to Proceed. . . .[26]

When a poll was taken at the meeting's close, thirty-six men indicated they wished to wait for congressional action before declaring for separation. Only four men sided with Witherspoon in favor of provincial initiative on this question.

The disinclination of the ad hoc conference to express support for independence while Pennsylvania was still agitating over the great question no doubt prompted Governor Franklin to issue a call on May 13 for the assembly to convene on June 20. This bit of strategy by Franklin, two weeks before the date set for the election of delegates to the third provincial congress, merely underscored that the upcoming vote was to be a mandate on independence. Jonathan Sergeant resigned his seat in Congress early in May to work for the election of pro-independence men. Staunch Whigs like Witherspoon, William Paterson and Richard Stockton were also engaged in the same pursuit. When the results were in, it was immediately apparent that the advocates of independence would have an overpowering majority in the third provincial congress when that body met on June 10.[27]

Before the new congress could turn its attention to the independence question, Governor Franklin and the New Jersey assembly had to be dealt with. In light of the May 15th preamble, allowing the assembly to meet would be equivalent to opposing the Continental Congress. Accordingly on June 15 the delegates ordered all inhabitants to disregard the governor's proclamation of May 13, stopped payment of his salary and declared him to be "an enemy to the liberties of this Country. . . ."[28] Colonel Heard was then ordered to take his excellency into custody or secure his parole. When Franklin refused to sign the parole tendered to him he was taken to Burlington and confined.

Still full of fight the governor composed a lengthy epistle defending his conduct and condemning the actions of the provincial congress. When Franklin requested Isaac Collins to print his remarks the printer declined on the grounds that he was not anxious to put his life in jeopardy. Undeterred, the governor verbally communicated the sentiments contained in his epistle to the members of the provincial congress when they examined him on June 21. The wily Franklin informed the delegates that he desired to remain in the province so that he could assist the royal commissioners when they arrived to negotiate a settlement. "Depend upon it you can never place yourselves in a happier situation than in your ancient constitutional dependancy on Great-Britain," warned the governor. He also conjured up the threat of New England imperialism: "Let me exhort you to avoid, above all things, the traps of independency and Republicanism now set for you, however temptingly they may be baited."[29] Two days before Franklin was examined, the provincial congress requested the Continental Congress to remove him from the province. After his interview the New Jersey congress asked that he be expelled as soon as possible.[30]

Following the promulgation of the resolves against Governor Franklin on June 15, the provincial congress focused attention on the questions of independence and a new government. The delegates were doubtless aware that the Pennsylvania assembly had modified its instructions without completely committing the province to independence. Meanwhile, in New York, the call had gone out for a new provincial congress, but the election was weeks away. The resignation of Richard Smith from his seat in Congress in mid-June along with William Livingston's military duties, left the way open for the appointment of an entirely new delegation. Jonathan Sergeant was so confident of a favorable outcome that he informed John Adams on June 12 that New Jersey "will vote plump!"[31] The provincial congress did just that but not until June 22. By then it was apparent that the Pennsylvania provincial conference would shortly decide for independence. The appointment of Richard Stockton, Abraham Clark, John Hart, Francis Hopkinson and John Witherspoon as delegates to Congress made New Jersey a certain supporter of the Virginia resolves, for the new members were "all independent souls. . . ."[32]

New Jersey, like Delaware, had followed in Pennsylvania's footsteps. There was a difference, however. The three lower counties on the Delaware took their action prior to the meeting of the Pennsylvania provincial conference. Whereas, before New Jersey came out so strongly for independence, the Pennsylvania provincial conference already had put the Quaker Colony into the independence column.

When the news of New Jersey's action reached William
Whipple of New Hampshire he happily concluded that the
vote on July 1 would be unanimous for "The Middle Colonies
are getting in a good way."[33] In drawing his conclusion he
somehow failed to consider New York. The northernmost
Central Province was moving in a very leisurely fashion
towards implementing the May 15th resolution and reaching
a decision on independence. John Adams would have been
more than happy to have pointed out to Mr. Whipple that his
omission was a serious one. In a moment of exasperation
Adams inquired of a friend if he knew what troubled New
York:

> What is the reason that New York must continue to embarass the
> Continent? Must it be so forever? Have they no politicians
> capable of instructing and forming the sentiments of their people?
> Or are their people incapable of seeing and feeling like other
> men?[34]

If John Adams had not been blinded by his strong attachment
to his section he might have been able to answer his own
question.

Events in New York during April and early May closely
paralleled developments in Pennsylvania. After the acceptance
of the May 15th preamble, however, New York's internal
situation took a different turn. Just as the May 1st assembly
elections in Pennsylvania offered a popular referendum on
independence, the April 24th elections for delegates to the
third provincial congress provided New Yorkers with a similar
chance. In both colonies the voters generally opted for candidates who opposed any precipitous declaration of independence. Even in New York City, where the radical organization
headed by the committee of mechanics was quite strong, the
conservative Whig ticket won out. As we have already seen,

the radical group in Pennsylvania, with assistance from the Continental Congress, was able to deliver the *coup de grâce* to the Pennsylvania assembly. In New York a far different set of circumstances combined to permit the conservative Whigs, led by John Jay, Gouverneur Morris and Philip Livingston, to hold onto the reins of power and make a more deliberate exit from the Empire.

In the first place the three men who had built and maintained the formidable radical organization in New York City were no longer at the helm in the spring of 1776. Without the capable leadership of Isaac Sears, John Lamb and Alexander McDougall the radicals did not pose a serious threat to the conservative leadership.[35] The intermittent war with Britain had also greatly altered the face of New York City and the outlook of its inhabitants. By the end of May no one doubted any longer that Lord Howe's fleet was destined for New York City. The remaining inhabitants braced for the clash.[36] Since the evacuation of Boston, New York City had become the base camp of the Continental Army and life in the city took on military overtones:

You would no longer know your native city, without reconoiteering well the Batteries and Barriers which block up every street & avenue to its approach, while all the Eminencies of the Environs are converted into Forts, and lines, breastworks and redoubts stare you in the face from every shore. In short we are a Garrison Town & the very Dogs (or Doctors I mean) dare not stir out after Tatoo beating, without the countersign; and Rumteetoodlee wou'd shoot, even his mothers breading sow, as was she to show her nose after nine o'clock without squeaking Virginia or New Jersey.[37]

James Duane was no doubt reflecting upon the precarious position of the province when he warned the conservative Whigs in the provincial congress to exercise the utmost care

in putting the May 15th resolution into effect. Hasty action
might open the gates for the mechanics to form a new government with unmistakable democratic overtones. "But, above
all," pleaded Duane, "let us see the conduct of the middle
colonies before we come to a decision: it cannot injure us to
wait a few weeks: the advantage will be great for this trying
question will clearly discover the true principles & extent of
the Union of the Colonies."[38] New York's behavior since the
"Intolerable Acts" had been marked by a high degree of opportunism, and Duane saw no reason to change the pattern especially with New York under threat of a double invasion.
Apparently a majority of the third provincial congress shared
Duane's sentiments for this body proved unwilling to come to
any decision on a new government or separation.

It was largely through the efforts of John Jay that an
intricate plan was worked out. It allowed the third provincial
congress to shunt the new government issue off onto its
successor, the fourth provincial congress. The resolution
adopted by the third provincial congress on May 31 called
upon the voters to select delegates to a fourth congress and
thereby express their sentiments on the new-government
issue. Whether the fourth congress, to be elected late in
June, was to consider itself duly authorized to bring a new
government into being was left unclear, although Jay apparently intended it to have this power.[39]

Having disposed of one explosive issue the third congress showed no disposition to grapple with the even more
momentous question of independence. On June 4 the committee of mechanics petitioned the provincial congress to
authorize the New York delegation to vote for a formal
declaration of independence. The delegates thanked the
mechanics for their concern, but refused to take any action

on their petition. The provincial congress claimed that the matter was of such consequence that the Continental Congress would have to be the initiatory body. But on June 8 an urgent request from the New York delegation asking for advice on the Virginia resolutions invalidated this evasive tactic. Undeterred, the provincial congress justified its inaction by claiming it possessed insufficient authority. The New York delegation was thus constrained from voting on the Virginia resolves until the fourth provincial congress convened early in July.

The question that naturally arises from the preceding narration is why the New York provincial congress deliberately ducked the two questions which the other twelve colonies answered in time for the July 1 vote.[40] The answer seems to be that the New York Whigs preferred to be dragged out of the Empire rather than march out on their own two feet, even though the other Middle Colonies were certain to be in the revolutionary procession. With the British Army set to pounce on the province even the most zealous Patriot must have mulled over the thought that should the province be overrun, British justice might be less severe if independence had not been formally declared. Moreover, the New England radicals were not about to permit New York to remain outside the new nation. With their property and even their lives at stake the New York Whigs did not abandon their opportunism; they only clutched it more tightly.[41]

As the time for taking up the Virginia resolutions grew nearer, the suspense over the outcome began to wane. An occasional congressman still expressed uncertainty as to what the conclusion of the affair would be but most were like Joseph Hewes of North Carolina who asserted, "It will be carried, I expect, by a great majority and then, I suppose we

shall take upon us a new name. . . ."[42] A few men like
Edward Rutledge of South Carolina were still trying to
round up enough votes to prevent acceptance of the Virginia
resolutions. On June 29 he appealed to John Jay to come
at once to Philadelphia to bolster the dwindling group of
peace advocates. Rutledge tried to heighten the impact of
the letter by alluding to the danger that a plan of confederation presently under consideration would give virtual control
of the new government to the despicable New England men.[43]

The crucial session of the Continental Congress began
on Monday morning, July 1, with only New York and Maryland as doubtful supporters of the Virginia resolutions. Before
the morning hours were well along word reached the chamber
that the Maryland convention had voted unanimously for
independence.[44] The radicals were convinced that this was
the final stroke but not so John Dickinson. In a chamber
filled with more hostile than friendly faces, he delivered a
brilliant speech against the timing of independence. Dickinson
spoke of the need for a stable confederacy and a handful of
victories in the field before a declaration of independence
would be either safe or advantageous. Whether his words
were the deciding factor will never be known, but the vote
taken on July 1 momentarily upset the calculations of the
radicals. While nine colonies saw their way clear to voting
for independence, South Carolina and Pennsylvania voted
no, Delaware was divided and New York abstained for want
of instructions. In counting the votes before the balloting
began the radicals had too readily assumed that both Pennsylvania and Delaware would vote for the resolve since their
instructions no longer prohibited such action.

Quick thinking by Edward Rutledge helped Congress
avoid the dangerous question of whether the nine supporters

of independence should proceed without the undecided colonies. He suggested that the final vote be postponed until the morrow. After a night of persuasive argument, doubtless over free-flowing cups, the South Carolina delegation changed its vote and the Pennsylvania delegation with Dickinson and Morris abstaining also came around. This, coupled with Caesar Rodney's dramatic all-night ride which put Delaware in the independence column, served to make passage of the Declaration of Independence unanimous—except, of course, for New York. On July 9 the fourth provincial congress, faced with a *fait accompli,* declared for independence and brought the slowest sailor of the thirteen into the new nation. When the news was proclaimed in New York City in mid-July, "The Equestrian Statue of George III erected in year 1770, was thrown from its pedestal, and broken into Pieces; and we hear the lead wherewith this Monument was made is to be run into bullets."[45]

The Middle Colonies were the most reluctant of an entire contingent of blenching revolutionaries, but the British ministry saw to it that the greater attachment they felt for the Empire was never used as a lifeline to save the thirteen colonies. While the ministry dimly perceived that pro-British sentiment was strongest in the Central Provinces, they never understood how it could be utilized to forestall rebellion. Lord North's attempt in the spring of 1775 to retain the loyalty of New York and Delaware by exempting them from the Commercial Restraining Act was a miserable failure. After Lexington the British made no further effort to single out any of the Middle Colonies for special treatment except to arm Tory contingents in Delaware and New York. It is doubtful that any British leader was aware that the Middle Colonies had allied themselves between 1774 and 1776 because they believed in the Empire. If at any time before June, 1776, the ministry had requested a truce or expressed interest in beginning serious negotiations, the Middle Colonies would have quickly accepted. Even as late as June, 1776, the Central Provinces might have been able to round up enough Southern support to have postponed acceptance of the Declaration of Independence. But Britain never thought of the Americans as anything more than wild frontiersmen and rude farmers. Even before the First Continental Congress was fairly into its work, King George III had already made up his mind about the ultimate outcome of the Anglo-American dispute. On September 11, 1774, he resolutely informed Lord North, "The dye is now cast, the Colonies must either submit or triumph. . . ."[46]

In some ways it was a strange ending. To be sure the New York Whigs outwaited all the other colonies and fulfilled the dictum laid down by James Duane. In the same vein the New Jersey and Delaware Whigs moved to embrace independence only after it became apparent that the radical Whigs in Pennsylvania were gaining ascendancy over Dickinson's party. But what of John Dickinson? Why did he carry the fight against independence to the point where his political power was destroyed and his name maligned? Dickinson was certainly an accomplished politician, but in this instance his convictions held sway. In his final speech before Congress he set forth all of the hopes and fears that the Middle Colonies had shared as they had worked to save the Empire. If Joseph Galloway was in Philadelphia on July 1 he no doubt perceived the irony of the moment. For in the fall of 1774 he too had stood before Congress extolling the virtues of the Empire and condemning the motives of those who would destroy it. Now John Dickinson was cast in the same role. He tried to convince his fellow congressmen that he was not against independence per se but only wished to wait for a more propitious moment. But he could not conceal his abiding affection for the Empire. Dickinson, despite all his illusions, still clung to the hope that Britain might yet offer concessions to the colonies. He closed with a stinging rebuke of the New England delegates. Dickinson charged that while they publicly avowed a desire for reconciliation during the last twelve months, they were secretly working for independence all the time. He admitted that if the New England states formed a separate "Commonwealth" in the years ahead, it would come as no great surprise to him.[47]

EPILOGUE:

The Long Dawn of Independence

> Prudence, indeed, will dictate that governments long established, should not be changed for light and transient causes; and, accordingly all experience hath shown, that mankind are more disposed to suffer, while evils are sufferable than to right themselves by abolishing the forms to which they are accustomed.

This phrase in the Declaration of Independence effectively summarizes the sentiment in the Middle Colonies from 1774 to 1776. During the preliminary stages of every human revolution some of the participants have always shown themselves to be more favorably inclined toward change within the system than the destruction of existing forms. And so it was with the Middle Colonies. Throughout the duration of the Anglo-American dispute the dominant Whig groups in New York, New Jersey, Pennsylvania and Delaware displayed an almost unshakeable faith in the Empire and an inordinate capacity to tolerate all manner of threats to their liberties.

Before the meeting of the First Continental Congress the Middle Colonies shared a community of interest. All four of the provinces were bound together in a regional economy that provided more general prosperity and stability than either New

210

England or the Southern Colonies enjoyed. Although a sense of subconscious regionalism affected the well-to-do classes to some degree in all four provinces, the merchants and landed gentry of New York and Pennsylvania were the primary cultivators of this feeling. Ever since mid-century relations between these two influential provinces had been steadily improving. By 1774 men like John Dickinson and James Duane had come to realize that while their two provinces might always compete for the rewards of the Empire, it was in their common interest to see that nothing disturbed their bounteous relationship with Great Britain. This appreciation of the unlimited future economic possibilities of the "Flour Colonies," or nabob mentality, was so compelling that many leading men in New Jersey and Delaware were also caught up in it.

In 1774 when the Anglo-American dispute shifted from a sporadic feud to a struggle of major proportions the four Central Provinces found good reason for drawing together. For a time the struggle between Galloway and Dickinson in the First Congress kept the Middle Colonies from deepening their sectional attachment. But during the first six months of 1775 the moderate Whigs in Pennsylvania, New Jersey and Delaware became as alarmed as the conservative Whigs in New York about the intentions of the New Englanders. The growing suspicion in the Middle Colonies that the "Yankees" would not be satisfied until they destroyed the Empire transformed their long-standing antipathy into an obsession. The insidious message of the Tory pamphleteers helped a great deal to bring about this change in attitude. When the Second Congress convened in May, 1775, John Dickinson was able to unite the delegates from the four Middle Colonies because sectional feeling born of fear was breaking into the conscious realm.

In the Second Congress the Middle Colonial bloc sought to have Congress take the initiative to secure peace. Through

their unstinting efforts Congress reluctantly approved the
Olive Branch Petition to the King early in July. In forcing
Congress to take this action the supporters of reconciliation
inadvertently mortgaged the future by setting a time limit on
British good will. If the the ministry failed to respond to this
peace bid, the Middle Colonial bloc would be forced to shift
its *raison d'être*. They could no longer rely on the prospect of
peaceful accord as their rationale for opposing the steady
assumption of sovereign powers by Congress and the provinces.
Instead they would have to base their opposition solely upon
the defects in the doctrine of separation. Early in November
when word reached Congress that the Olive Branch Petition
had been curtly rejected, this is precisely what happened.
Dickinson quickly prodded the Pennsylvania assembly into
issuing a new set of instructions which enjoined the congressional delegation from acceding to any declaration of
secession. New Jersey quickly followed suit and New York
acknowledged that it shared the spirit which prompted the
Quaker Colony's preemptive action.

The willingness of New York to follow Pennsylvania's
lead reflected a significant demise in the former's capacity for
sectional leadership. During the summer and fall of 1775 New
York's Whigs had been beset by a host of problems such as the
recurring threat of British invasion, an active Tory movement
and a disinterested citizenry. Plagued by uncertainty about
their ability to control events in New York and apprehensive
about New England's constant attention, the New York Whigs
found it expedient to let Pennsylvania provide the leadership
for the Middle Colonies.

It is extremely unlikely that the Middle Colonial bloc
could have held out against independence as long as it did
were it not for the new life, which the reports early in 1776
that British commissioners were coming, breathed into the

prospects for reconciliation. While spokesmen for the Middle Colonial position like Dickinson, Duane, and Wilson continued to point out the disastrous consequences that would follow a hasty declaration of independence, they also used the commissioners as evidence of Britain's ultimate good intentions. Yet it is not an easy task to work for peace while engaged in a bloody civil war, and this was the dilemma of the Central Provinces. As they continued to hope against hope that Britain would come to her senses before it was too late, they were forced during the winter of 1775-76 to agree to measures that laid the groundwork for the ultimate transfer of power from the Empire to the new confederation of states.

With the onset of spring the dominant Whig groups in all the Middle Colonies save New Jersey still recoiled from independence. The seemingly favorable inclination of New Jersey can be traced to the absence of any serious factional disputes among its Whig leadership and the relatively weak condition of the Tories in the province. But despite being blessed with a far greater degree of internal harmony and security than the other three Central Provinces, New Jersey never openly challenged the sectional leadership of Pennsylvania. The Jersey delegates in the Second Congress voted down the line with the Middle Colonial bloc. One must surmise that more than a half century of dependence upon its two large neighbors could not easily be undone. The military implications of New York's weakness also played a part. For a month after the New Jersey provincial congress had sent a pro-independence delegate to Congress and lifted the restrictions on independence, New Jersey retreated from this advanced position. In the end the province adopted independence only after the question was resolved in Pennsylvania.

That the Middle Colonies were the last outposts of resistance to independence during the final months before separation is unquestioned. But by dwelling on this final performance

historians have failed to perceive the inchoate sectional feeling
that drove the Middle Colonies to resist the demands of the
New England radicals from May, 1775, to July, 1776. If the
Middle Colonies had not drawn together as they did, independence might have come as early as January, 1776. Such
an event could have shattered the colonial union, if the Middle
Colonies and a few Southern Colonies had defected.

The pivotal role played by Pennsylvania in fostering and
maintaining sectional solidarity was again underscored during
the final weeks before independence. Having failed throughout the winter months to enervate the new-found sectional
unity of the Central Provinces, the New England radicals decided to concentrate their attack on Pennsylvania. With the
May 15th preamble as their mandate, the radical Whigs
quickly overthrew the government of Pennsylvania and effectively stripped the Middle Colonies of their key sectional
leaders. Only by means of this maneuver were the New England radicals able to break the back of the Middle Colonial
sectional movement and at last achieve independence. After
separation the sense of regional peril that had brought the
Middle Colonies closer to a conscious sectional identity than
at any other time in their history was quickly dispelled by the
trials of war and New England's patently nonaggressive
behavior.

NOTES and REFERENCES

Introduction

1. Jensen, "Historians," *Reinterpretation*, 102.
2. Tolles, "Historians," *ibid.*, 65.
3. Mood, "Sectional Concept," *Regionalism*, 6-7.
4. *Letters on the Am. Rev.*, 11.

Chapter One

1. Adams, *History of the U.S.*, I, 108.
2. *Burnaby's Travels*, 117.
3. John Adams to Abigail Adams, July 7, 1775; *Adams Family Correspondence*, I, 242.
4. "Patrick M'Roberts Tour," *Pa. Mag. Hist. & Biog.*, 148.
5. O'Callaghan, *Documentary History of N.Y.*, I, 748.
6. Harrington, *New York Merchant*, 242.
7. "Patrick M'Roberts Tour," *Pa. Mag. Hist. & Biog.*, 139-140.
8. Greene, "Old Empire," *History of N.Y.*, III, 140.
9. Shearer, "Church," *History of N.Y.*, II, 69.
10. *Burnaby's Travels*, 56.
11. *American Husbandry*, 91.
12. Bidwell and Falconer, *History of Agriculture*, 72.

13. Bridenbaugh, *Cities in Revolt,* 272.

14. Hawke, *Revolution,* 76.

15. Williamson, *American Suffrage,* 34.

16. Kraus, *American Culture,* 24.

17. Bridenbaugh, *Cities in Revolt,* 263.

18. "Heads of Inquiry Report, 1774," *N.J. Archs.,* X, 442.

19. Scott, "Early Cities," *Procs. N.J. Hist. Soc.,* 151.

20. Witherspoon, *Works,* IV, 408.

21. Main, *Social Structure,* 25.

22. *American Husbandry,* 98.

23. Woodward, *Ploughs and Politicks,* 231.

24. "Heads of Inquiry Report, 1774," *N.J. Archs.,* X, 440.

25. McCormick, *History of Voting,* 63.

26. Rutherford, "Notes," *Procs. N.J. Hist. Soc.,* 88.

27. Pomfret, "West New Jersey," *W. & M. Quar.,* 502.

28. *Burnaby's Travels,* 87.

29. Main, *Social Structure,* 32.

Chapter Two

1. Sachs, "Agricultural Conditions," *Jour. Econ. Hist.,* 284.

2. *New York Gazette & Weekly Mercury,* August 21, 1775.

3. Both Pennsylvania and Philadelphia enjoyed general prosperity from the end of the Seven Years War until 1775. Only the import merchants in the English trade suffered any marked economic distress. Jensen, *Maritime Commerce,* 126. Conditions in New York City were not as good during the same period. From 1763-1770 the City economy was somewhat depressed although the early 1770's saw a resumption of prosperity. Harrington, *New York Merchant,* 316 and 343.

4. Williams, *Contours,* 85-93.

5. Dickinson, *Writings,* 402-403.

6. *Ibid.*

7. Livingston, *Memoir,* 184.

8. Dickinson, *Writings,* 473.

9. *New York Gazette & Weekly Mercury,* May 23, 1774.

10. Thomas Mifflin informed Sam Adams on May 21 that merchant opposition to a trade stoppage was so strong in Philadelphia that the best the popular leaders could hope for would be to secure a commitment for a general congress. Rossman, *Thomas Mifflin,* 23.

11. Alexander McDougall contended that the DeLancey–merchant coalition was made up of men who feared a civil war, opponents of New England republicanism, Episcopalians who hated Eastern men, merchants who did not wish to have their commerce interrupted and men who desired government patronage. Adams, *Diary and Autobiography,* II, 106.

12. Cadwallader Colden to Lord Dartmouth, June 1, 1774, "Colden Papers," *N.Y. Hist. Soc. Colls.,* X, 340.

13. Jensen, *Founding a Nation,* 481. McDougall and Sears evidently noted the success of the June 18th mass meeting in Philadelphia and decided to employ the same tactic in their city to break the hold of the conservatives.

14. "Wharton Letter-Book," *Pa. Mag. Hist. & Bio.,* 433-434.

15. Governor John Penn to Earl of Dartmouth, July 5, 1774; L. C. Transcripts, PRO, Col. Off. Papers, Class 5, Vol. 1285.

16. Immediately after the Pennsylvania delegation was announced, radical Whigs in Philadelphia began to apprise their comrades in other provinces of this unfortunate result. William Bradford, Jr., bemoaned the fact that ". . . several of those appointed for this ·province are known to be inimical to the Liberties of America. I mean Galloway the author of the detestable piece signed Americanus in the time of the Stamp Act; & one Humphries an obscure assemblyman, who but the moment before he was appointed voted against having a Congress at all." William Bradford, Jr., to James Madison, August 1, 1774; William Bradford Collection, Hist. Soc. Pa.

17. "Votes of Assembly," *Pa. Archs.,* VIII, 7100.

18. Cadwallader Colden to Governor Tryon, September 7, 1774; "Colden Papers," *N.Y. Hist. Colls.,* X, 361.

19. *New York Journal,* June 30, 1774; in *N.J. Archs.,* XXIX, 408-410.

20. Governor Franklin's surprising aloofness from the course of events during the summer of 1774 was apparently the result of a basic miscalculation on his part. Late in May he asserted

that little could be accomplished by the rabble rousers in the provinces as long as he and his fellow governors refused to call the assemblies into session. Governor Franklin to Earl of Dartmouth, May 31, 1774; "Franklin Correspondence," *N.J. Archs.,* X, 457-59.

21. *Pennsylvania Gazette,* June 22, 1774.

22. "Kent County Loyalists," *Del. Hist.,* 98.

23. *Journals of the Cont. Cong.,* I, 22.

24. William Bradford, Jr., to James Madison, October 17, 1774; William Bradford Collection, Hist. Soc. Pa.

25. *New York Journal,* August 4, 1774; in *N.J. Archs.,* XXIX, 437.

26. Livingston, *Memoir,* 173-174.

27. Silas Deane to Mrs. Deane, September 1-3, 1774; *Letters of the Cont. Cong.,* I, 4.

28. Joseph Galloway to Governor William Franklin, September 3, 1774; *ibid.,* 5.

29. John Adams, *Diary and Autobiography,* II, 106-107.

30. Joseph Galloway to Governor William Franklin, September 5, 1774; *Letters of the Cont. Cong.,* I. 9.

31. *Ibid.,* 9-10.

32. John Adams to Abigail Adams, September 18, 1774; *Adams Family Correspondence,* I, 159.

33. In 1773 as young Josiah Quincy, Jr., of Massachusetts journeyed from South Carolina to New York he learned firsthand that New Englanders were not revered in either the Southern or Middle Colonies. In Charles Town a British visitor denounced him and his province because they coveted the territory of all the other colonies. During his stay in Philadelphia he found that there was ". . . a general disliking, not to say antipathy among the Quakers against New England, and this aversion has its influence in their judgement of men and things of that country, especially in their opinions concerning the pubic transactions of the Massachusetts Bay." Quincy, Jr., "Journal," *Mass. Hist. Soc. Procs.,* 445-447.

34. Cadwallader Colden to Earl of Dartmouth, December 7, 1774; "Colden Papers," *N.Y. Hist. Soc. Colls.,* X, 374.

35. Alexander, *James Duane,* 103.

36. *Journals of the Cont. Cong.,* I, 32.
37. Reverend Charles Inglis to Dr. Charles G. Ridgely, October 26, 1774; Ridgely Family Papers, Del. Pub. Arch. Com., Del. Hall of Records.
38. *Journals of the Cont. Cong.,* I, 44.
39. Burnett, *Continental Congress,* 50.
40. The sectional tendencies of the delegates to the First Congress were readily perceived by astute Philadelphia observers. In one of his last letters to Lord Dartmouth, Joseph Reed warned him that if the colonial economic measures failed to have their desired effect, "the northern colonies will try the last resort, while the middle and southern will secretly, if not openly assist them." Joseph Reed to Earl of Dartmouth, September 25, 1774; Reed, *Correspondence,* I, 79.
41. South Carolina Delegates Report to the Provincial Congress, November, 1774; *Letters of the Cont. Cong.,* I, 86 and Jensen, *Founding a Nation,* 497.
42. John Dickinson to Arthur Lee, October 27, 1774; *Letters of Cont. Cong.,* I, 83.
43. After Congress had been in session for three weeks, during which time the conduct of the New England delegates was most exemplary, Sam Adams sadly admitted that "There is however a certain Degree of jealousy in the Minds of Some that we aim at a total independence not only of the Mother Country but of the Colonies too: and that as we are a hardy and brave People we shall in time overrun them all." Sam Adams to Joseph Warren, September 25, 1774; Samuel Adams Papers, N.Y. Pub. Lib.

Chapter Three

1. Thomas Young to Samuel Adams, October 12, 1774; Samuel Adams Papers, N.Y. Pub. Lib.
2. John Dickinson to Samuel Ward, January 29, 1775; John Dickinson Papers, Hist. Soc. Pa.
3. *New York Gazette & Weekly Mercury,* October 24, 1774.
4. *Ibid.,* January 16, 1775.
5. Thomas Wharton to Samuel Wharton, January 31, 1775; "Wharton Letter-Books," *Pa. Mag. Hist. & Biog.,* 41-43.

6. *New York Gazette & Weekly Mercury,* February 6, 1775.

7. *New York Journal,* February 9, 1775.

8. William Lee to John Dickinson, January 7, 1775; John Dickinson Papers, Lib. Co. Phila.

9. A London correspondent noted on January 4 that "The Petition of Congress has been presented to the King, and received with a better Grace than might have been expected." *Pennsylvania Gazette,* March 15, 1775.

10. Bancroft, *History of U.S.,* VII, 201.

11. Thomas Rodney to Caesar Rodney, March 19, 1775; Rodney, *Letters,* 54-55.

12. Donoughue, *British Politics,* 284.

13. Joseph Galloway to Samuel Verplanck, April 1, 1775; "Galloway Letters," *Pa. Mag. Hist. & Biog.,* 481-482.

14. Charles Lee of Virginia urged his friend Benjamin Rush to encourage the Philadelphia Whigs to use their good offices with the New York Whigs in pushing for ratification of the proceedings of Congress. Charles Lee to Benjamin Rush, December 15, 1774; "Lee Papers," *N.Y. Hist. Soc. Colls.,* I, 143-144.

15. Thomas Wharton to Samuel Wharton, January 31, 1775; "Wharton Letter-Book," *Pa. Mag. Hist. & Biog.,* 41-43.

16. *New York Gazette & Weekly Mercury,* December 26, 1774.

17. William Bradford, Jr., to James Madison, January 4, 1775; William Bradford Collection, Hist. Soc. Pa.

18. William Bradford, Jr., believed that the ". . . . provincial convention was called (it is thought) principally for the purpose of setting on foot independent companies & appointing officers," William Bradford, Jr., to James Madison (no date) 1775; William Bradford Collection, Hist. Soc. Pa.

19. John Dickinson to Samuel Ward, January 29, 1775; John Dickinson Papers, Hist. Soc. Pa.

20. Charles Lee to Robert Morris, January 27, 1775; "Lee Papers," *N.Y. Hist. Soc. Colls.* I, 168.

21. *Rivington's New York Gazetteer,* December 1, 1774.

22. *N.J. Archs.,* X, 539-541.

23. Governor William Franklin to Joseph Galloway, March 12, 1775; "Franklin Correspondence," *ibid.,* 575.

24. *Pennsylvania Chronicle,* July 9-16, 1770; in *N.J. Archs.,* XXVII, 197.

25. One Jersey essayist used an incident involving the ducking of two New York merchants to impugn their motives. "How enormous must be the Guilt of those who would betray the liberties of the Public, to advance their private Fortunes, when even a public Bridge is not able to support the Weight of their Eniquities [sic]? May this be the Fate of every Wretch who would sell his Country for a Mess of Pottage." *New York Gazette & Weekly Post Boy,* August 13, 1770; in *ibid.,* XXVII, 225.

26. *New York Gazette & Weekly Mercury,* January 30, 1775.

27. Livingston, *Memoir,* 169.

28. Governor William Franklin to Joseph Galloway, March 12, 1775; "Franklin Correspondence," *N.J. Archs.,* X, 577.

29. The assembly was very candid about the provincial applicability of the list of grievances they copied from the Congressional papers such as the burden of a standing army and arbitrary changes in judicial procedures. They noted that "Although all the grievances above enumerated do not immediately affect the people of this Colony, yet as in their consequence, they will be deeply involved we cannot remain silent and unconcerned." Force, *Am. Archs.,* II, 1132-1133.

30. Charles Beatty to Erkurius Beatty, January 28, 1775; "Beatty Letters," *Procs. N.J. Hist. Soc.,* 31-32.

31. Fox, *Yankees and Yorkers,* 1.

32. Samuel Seabury to Dr. Hinde, December 29, 1776; L. C. Transcripts, SPG Records, Series B, Vol. 11, Part 2.

33. Seabury, *Free Thoughts,* 11.

34. *Ibid.*

35. Seabury, *A View of the Controversy,* 17.

36. Chandler, *A Friendly Address,* 48.

37. *Ibid.,* 53.

38. A prime example of Rivington's Whig-baiting was his account of the Sons of Bacchus chapter in Woodbridge, New Jersey. Apparently the staunchly patriotic members of this group

became inebriated while erecting a liberty pole and when they arose from their stupor, they found that a nimble Tory had cut the pole in half. "It is thought that their pole, under its present contemptible appearance will not strike even the rabble, either with complaceny or awe that was intended." *Rivington's New York Gazetteer,* March 30, 1775.

39. The editor of the *New York Gazette & Weekly Mercury,* Hugh Gaine, was also considered by some of the more ardent Whigs to have been a British sympathizer. It appears that he incurred the Patriot wrath because of his penchant for impartiality. He wished to give both sides a hearing. Gaine, *Journals,* 53.

40. *New York Gazette & Weekly Mercury,* January 23, 1775.

41. *New York Journal,* February 20, 1775.

42. *Ibid.,* April 6, 1775.

43. *Ibid.*

44. Thomas Young to John Lamb, November 18, 1774; John Lamb Papers, N.Y. Hist. Soc.

45. *New York Gazette & Weekly Mercury,* November 14, 1774.

46. Becker, *Political Parties,* 167.

47. James Duane to Samuel Chase, December, 1774; James Duane Papers, N.Y. Hist. Soc.

48. Seabury, *Alarm to the Legislature,* 11.

49. Cadwallader Colden to General Gage, January 29, 1775; "Colden Papers," N.Y. Hist. Soc. Colls., X, 398.

50. Cadwallader Colden to Governor Tryon, April 5, 1775; *ibid.,* 381.

51. *New York Gazette & Weekly Mercury,* February 20, 1775.

52. *New York Journal,* April 20, 1775.

53. Arthur Lee to Sam Adams, February 24, 1775; Samuel Adams Papers, N.Y. Pub. Lib.

54. Governor William Tryon to Earl of Dartmouth, April 12, 1775; L. C. Transcripts, PRO, Col. Office Papers, 5/1106.

55. Force, *Am. Archs., II,* 389.

56. Alexander McDougall to Thomas Young, February 16, 1775; Samuel Adams Papers, N.Y. Pub. Lib.

57. Dr. John Jones to John Dickinson, March 20, 1775; John Dickinson Papers, Lib. Co. Phila.

58. Samuel Adams to Arthur Lee, March 4, 1775; S. Adams, *Writings,* III, 194-198.

59. Broadside Collections, Hist. Soc. Pa.

60. Galloway, *A Candid Examination,* 41-42.

61. Joseph Galloway to Samuel Verplanck, February 14, 1775; "Galloway Letters," *Pa. Mag. Hist. & Biog.,* 480-481.

62. John Dickinson to Samuel Ward, January 29, 1775; John Dickinson Papers, Hist. Soc. Pa.

63. *Ibid.*

64. *Maryland Journal and the Baltimore Advertiser,* March 29, 1775.

65. *Pennsylvania Gazette,* December 28, 1774.

66. *Pennsylvania Ledger,* February 11, 1775.

67. Thomas Tilton to Dr. Charles Ridgely, February 28, 1775; Ridgely Family Papers, Del. Pub. Archs. Comm., Del. Hall Records.

68. *Ridgely Family Letters,* 37.

69. *Pennsylvania Gazette,* March 15, 1775.

70. Force, *Am. Archs.,* II, 127.

71. Joseph Reed to Dennys De Berdt, February 13, 1775; Reed, *Correspondence,* I, 96.

72. Kemmerer, *Path to Freedom,* 223.

73. Reverend Charles Inglis to Dr. Charles G. Ridgely, October 26, 1774; Ridgely Family Papers, Del. Pub. Archs. Comm., Del. Hall Records.

Chapter Four

1. *Pennsylvania Gazette,* April 12, 1775.

2. The Restraining Act, passed by Parliament on March 9, initially did not apply to New York, Delaware, North Carolina or Georgia because the ministry believed that these colonies were not in sympathy with the program of the First Congress. Jensen, *Founding a Nation,* 582. James Duane thought that the ministry had misjudged the American temper, for neither economic sanctions nor bribery would lead the Middle and

Southern Colonies to affirm their loyalty to the Empire. If anything, this clumsy measure would have the opposite effect of forcing these colonies into closer union with New England. James Duane to Col. Livingston, June 7, 1775; Livingston Family Papers, Hyde Park Lib.

3. Robert R. Livingston to Col. Livingston, May 13, 1775; *ibid.,*

4. "Minutes of the Council of New York," "Colden Papers," *N.Y. Hist. Soc. Colls.,* VII, 289.

5. Curwen, *Journal and Letters,* 26.

6. Governor William Franklin to Earl of Dartmouth, May 6, 1775; "Franklin Correspondence," *N.J. Archs.,* X, 590-597.

7. William Hooper to Samuel Johnson, May 23, 1775; *Letters of the Cont. Cong.,* I, 96.

8. Thayer, *Pennsylvania Politics,* 166, and Becker, *Political Parties,* 192.

9. John Adams to Abigail Adams, June 17, 1775; *Adams Family Correspondence,* I, 216.

10. Nettels, *George Washington,* 111; and Henderson, "Political Factions," 80.

11. *Ibid.*

12. Henderson, "Political Factions," 64-65.

13. Head, *A Time to Rend,* 16.

14. Only Delaware occasionally wavered in its sectional allegiance. This was due in large part to the peculiar makeup of its delegation. With George Read supporting the Dickinson faction and Thomas McKean the New England radicals, Delaware's vote was often determined by Caesar Rodney, who steadfastly refused to be aligned with any faction.

15. Resolutions three and four, which embodied the essential peace planks of the Middle Colonial faction, gave encouragement to the conservatives outside of Congress. Lieutenant Governor Colden for one was optimistic: "In this gloomy Prospect of Affairs the Friends of Government have received a glimpse of Hope upon hearing that Mr. Duane, a Delegate from New York, has moved in the Continental Congress to introduce a Plan of Accommodation which produced warm debate, but was carried in favour of the motion." Lieutenant

Governor Colden to Earl of Dartmouth, June 7, 1775; "Colden Papers," *N.Y. Hist. Soc. Colls.*, VII, 421.

16. Jacobson, *John Dickinson*, 88.

17. *Ibid.*, 91. Dickinson suggested to his fellow delegates that they consider a redress of all the grievances enumerated by the First Continental Congress as a *quid pro quo* for colonial recognition of the right of Parliament to regulate colonial trade and the grant of a fixed income for the King.

18. John Dickinson did not actually introduce either of the two resolutions that embodied his program. John Jay presented the resolutions for a petition to the King, and James Duane offered the negotiation resolution. Bancroft, *History of U.S.*, VII, 361, 379.

19. Samuel Chase to John Dickinson, April 29, 1775; John Dickinson Papers, Lib. Co. Phila.

20. John Adams, *Diary and Autobiography*, III, 318.

21. Bancroft, *History of U.S.*, VII, 362.

22. John Adams to James Warren, July 6, 1775; "Warren-Adams Letters," *Mass. Hist. Soc. Colls.*, I, 76-77.

23. Gordon, *History of U.S.*, II, 38.

24. William Smith, a member of the governor's council and an eventual Loyalist, was actively promoting a peace plan during May and June. He contacted at least two of the New York delegates, Philip Schuyler and Lewis Morris, in hopes of convincing them that the adoption of such a plan was a surer road to peace than military preparations. Smith, *Memoirs*, 187.

25. "Minutes of the N.Y. Prov. Cong.," Force, *Am. Archs.*, II, 1316.

26. *Ibid.*

27. *Ibid.*, 1318.

28. *Rivington's New York Gazetteer*, June 15 & June 22, 1775.

29. New York Delegates to New York Congress, July 6, 1775; Force, *Am. Archs.*, II, 1591.

30. Gilbert Barkly to Grey Cooper, June 6, 1775; Barkly, "British Spy," *Pa. Mag. Hist. & Biog.*, 9.

31. Benjamin Franklin to Joseph Priestly, July 7, 1775; Franklin, *Works*, VII, 155-156.

33. John Adams to James Warren, July 6, 1775; *ibid.*, 152. *Cont. Cong.*, I, 157.
33. James Adams to James Warren, July 6, 1775; *ibid.*, 152.
34. *Ibid.*
35. John Adams to Abigail Adams, July 7, 1775; *Adams Family Correspondence*, I, 242.
36. Fulmer Mood contends that the tripartite arrangement for Indian, military and naval affairs was simply a reflection of the three distinct sectional interests in Congress. The inclusion of New York in the Northern Indian district and Virginia in the Middle Indian district calls into question his assertion. It appears that Congress was simply trying to establish controlling agencies that matched up with the significant Indian concentrations. Mood has the right idea about sectional divisions in Congress but marshalled poor supportive evidence to prove his case. Mood, "Sectional Concept," *Regionalism,* 27.
37. *Journals of the Cont. Cong.*, II, 187.
38. William Bradford, Jr., to James Madison, June 24, 1775; William Bradford Collection, Hist. Soc. Pa.
39. John Adams to Abigail Adams, July 23, 1775; *Adams Family Correspondence*, I, 252.
40. Gilbert Barkly to Grey Cooper, June 7, 1775; Barkly, "British Spy," *Pa. Mag. Hist. & Bio.*, 10.
41. George Cuthbert to Lieutenant-General John Dalling, April 1, 1775; "Notes, April, 1775," *Pa. Mag. Hist. & Biog.*, 206.

Chapter Five

1. *Pennsylvania Gazette,* April 26, 1775.
2. Marshall, *Diary,* 26.
3. Jacobson, *John Dickinson,* 85.
4. "Votes of Assembly," *Pa. Archs.*, VIII, 7320.
5. Governor John Penn to Earl of Dartmouth, June 5, 1775; L. C. Transcripts, PRO, Col. Off. Papers, 5/1286.
6. *Pennsylvania Gazette,* May 10, 1775.
7. Pennsylvania's overwhelming response to the call-to-arms was not solely confined to local militia units. On June 10 the

Continental Congress requested that Pennsylvania raise 800 riflemen to reinforce the Continental Army outside Boston. In the space of a few days about 1,430 Pennsylvanians signed up and the first company reached Cambridge on July 25, with eight more arriving two weeks later. *Newport Mercury,* September 25, 1775.

8. "Votes of Assembly," *Pa. Archs.,* VIII, 7237-7240.

9. "Minutes of the Council of Safety," *Col. Recs. of Pa.,* X, 287.

10. *Journals of the Cont. Cong.,* II, 128.

11. William Lee to John Dickinson, June 8, 1775; John Dickinson Papers, Lib. Co. Phila.

12. *Pennsylvania Gazette,* August 2, 1775.

13. William Lee to John Dickinson, July 12, 1775; John Dickinson Papers, Lib. Co. Phila.

14. An anonymous London correspondent reported in the September 25th issue of the *New York Gazette & Weekly Mercury* that the ministry was not only negotiating with German princes but also the Russian government in hopes of obtaining 30,000 soldiers. Another correspondent recounted the signing of a treaty for 10,000 German troops in the October 5th issue of *Rivington's New York Gazetteer.* The *Pennsylvania Gazette* printed an unsigned letter on October 11 to the effect that British transports recently embarked for Emden to take on Hanoverian troops for the colonies.

15. John Adams to Abigail Adams, July 11, 1775; *Adams Family Correspondence,* I, 215.

16. Metzger, *Catholics,* 118.

17. *Pennsylvania Packet,* July 10, 1775.

18. James Lloyd to William Tilghman, September 2, 1775; Gratz Collection, Old Congress Case, Hist. Soc. Pa.

19. William Cox to Joseph Reed, September 9, 1775; Joseph Reed Papers, N.Y. Hist. Soc.

20. John Adams, *Diary and Autobiography,* I, 177.

21. *Pennsylvania Journal,* September, 1775; in Force, *Am. Archs.,* III, 172-176.

22. John Armstrong to James Wilson, September 19, 1775; Gratz Collection, Generals of the Revolution Case, Hist. Soc. Pa.

23. Connecticut Delegates to Zebulon Pike and others, August 2, 1775; *Letters of the Cont. Cong.*, I, 186.

24. "Minutes of the Council of Safety," *Col. Recs. of Pa.*, X, 336.

25. That the political friendships built up over decades did not die easily was borne out by Benjamin Franklin's efforts to entice Joseph Galloway back into the Whig camp. Franklin apparently visited Galloway on two separate occasions during the early months of the summer, but his entreaties were of no avail. Hutchinson, *Diary and Letters,* II, 237.

26. *New York Gazette & Weekly Mercury,* May 1, 1775.

27. Early in May, New York City went through what was to be the first of many invasion scares. The committee of one hundred wrote a frantic letter to Congress asking advice and two days later appealed to Governor Trumbull to station some Connecticut militia units on the border between the two colonies. New York Committee to Jonathan Trumbull of Connecticut; Force, *Am. Archs.,* II, 636.

28. Lieutenant Governor Colden to Earl of Dartmouth, May 3, 1775; O'Callaghan, *Docs. Relative to Col. Hist. of N.Y.,* VIII, 571-572.

29. *New York Gazette & Weekly Mercury,* May 8, 1775.

30. *Ibid.,* June 5, 1775.

31. Resolutions of the Committee of Tryon County, May 21, 1775; Force, *Am. Archs.,* II, 665.

32. New York Provincial Congress to Governor Jonathan Trumbull, May 24, 1775; *Ibid.*

33. New York Provincial Congress to New York Delegation in Congress, June 7, 1775; *ibid.,* 1281.

34. James Duane to Colonel Livingston, June 7, 1775; Livingston Family Papers, Hyde Park Lib.

35. General Schuyler to President of Congress, July 2, 1775; Force *Am. Archs.,* II, 1530.

36. New York Provincial Congress to New York Delegation in Congress, July 20, 1775; James Duane Papers, N.Y. Hist. Soc.

37. Christopher Tappan to George Clinton, June 10, 1775; Clinton, *Public Papers,* I, 201.

38. John Holt to Joseph Reed, August 24, 1775; Joseph Reed Papers, N.Y. Hist. Soc.

39. New York Committee of Safety to the New York Delegation in Congress, July 15, 1775; Force, *Am. Archs.,* II, 1788-1789.

40. Labaree, "William Tryon," *Dictionary of Am. Biog.*, XIX, 26.

41. William Smith, *Memoirs*, 232.

42. General George Washington to Major General Philip Schuyler, June 25, 1775; Washington, *Writings*, III, 302.

43. Governor Tryon to Earl of Dartmouth, July 4, 1775; O'Callaghan, *Docs. Relative to Col. Hist. of N.Y.*, VIII, 589.

44. Robert R. Livingston to Colonel Livingston, August 26, 1775; Livingston-Redmond Family Correspondence, Hyde Park Lib.

45. Frederick Smyth to Elias Boudinot, May, 1775; Edwin A. Ely Collection, N.J. Hist. Soc.

46. Bergen County Declaration, May, 1775; Broadside Collection. Rutgers Univ.

47. *Rivington's New York Gazetteer*, June 6, 1775.

48. Gordon, *History of N.J.*, 162.

49. "Minutes of the New Jersey Provincial Congress," Force, *Am. Archs.*, II, 691.

50. Governor Franklin to Earl of Dartmouth, June 5, 1775; "Franklin Correspondence," *N.J. Arch.*, X, 601-606.

51. Daniel Coxe to Cortlandt Skinner, July 4, 1775; *ibid.*, 654-655.

52. Governor Franklin to Earl of Dartmouth, August 2, 1775; *ibid.*, 652-653.

53. Woodbridge Committee to the several committees of Massachusetts, May 1, 1775; Force, *Am. Archs.*, II, 459.

54. "Minutes of the New Jersey Provincial Congress," Force, *Am. Archs.*, III, 42.

55. Pole, "Suffrage Reform," *Procs. N.J. Hist. Soc.*, 181.

56. Nevertheless, New Jersey was still a far safer place than Philadelphia or New York City, at least in terms of mob violence and the British military threat. A schoolmaster in Morris Town, New Jersey, sought to boost his enrollments by depicting his school as a safe haven ". . . a distance from probable sudden change and confusion. . . ." *New York Gazette & Mercury*, July 3, 1775.

57. *Pennsylvania Journal and Weekly Advertiser*, September 27, 1775.

58. John Adams to Isaac Smith, Sr., June 7, 1775; *Adams Family Correspondence*, I, 212-213.

59. Caesar Rodney to Thomas Rodney, May 8, 1775; *Letters,* 57.
60. *Pennsylvania Packet,* July 24, 1775.
61. Hancock, *Delaware Loyalists,* 7.
62. Hancock, "Kent County Loyalists," *Del. Hist.,* 118-119.
63. *Ibid.,* 119-120.
64. "Minutes of Broad Creek Meeting," Force, *Am. Archs.,* II, 1032.
65. Scharf, *History of Delaware,* I, 223.
66. "Council of Safety Minutes," *Del. Hist.,* I.
67. Benjamin Franklin to a Friend in England, October 3, 1775; Franklin, *Works,* VIII, 161-163.

Chapter Six

1. John Adams' Diary, *Letters of the Cont. Cong.,* I, 198.
2. John Adams to James Warren, July 24, 1775; *ibid.,* 176.
3. Samuel Adams to James Bowdoin, November 16, 1775; S. Adams, *Works,* III, 234.
4. Thomas Lynch to George Washington, November 13, 1775; *Letters of the Cont. Cong.,* I, 253.
5. Edward Rutledge to John Jay, June 29, 1776; Jay, *Correspondence,* I, 67.
6. Robert Morris to _____, December 9, 1775; *Letters of the Cont. Cong.,* I, 271.
7. Edward Shippen, Jr. to Jasper Yeates, March 11, 1776; Shippen Family Papers, Hist. Soc. Pa.
8. The one recorded occasion when John De Hart chose to enter the lists he was unable to find a second for a motion to prohibit all assemblies and conventions from issuing any more paper money. Richard Smith's Diary, *Letters of the Cont. Cong.,* I, 206.
9. John Patterson to Governor Tryon, November 20, 1775; L. C. Transcripts PRO, Col. Off. Papers, 5/1107. In this letter Patterson provided his excellency with a colony-by-colony breakdown of the sentiments of the delegates in the fall of 1775. His evaluation points up the individual delegates and colonies from whom the Middle Colonial bloc often sought support:

Moderate Delegates:

Mass.—Cushing and Payne "pretty moderate" Adams and Hancock "Violent"

Rhode I. Hopkins–Ward "Violent"

N.Y. All moderate save one

N.J. All moderate

Penna. Save for Franklin and Wilson all moderate

Del. Read and Rodney

Md. Johnson, Hall, the rest "pretty moderate"

Virginia—Jefferson and Nielson [sic], remainder of Del. "violent"

N.C. All moderate

S.C. All Violent

Georgia—Moderate perhaps but largely unknown.

Although Patterson gave no hint as to his sources it was apparently not too difficult to obtain information on the political alignment of the delegates if one traveled in the right circles. Gilbert Barkly, who was a merchant in the pay of the ministry, made it a point to cultivate an acquaintanceship with John Dickinson. In June Barkly conversed with him about the state of the Anglo-American dispute and found that he held a very low opinion of the New England Colonies. In the fall when the support for independence seemed to be growing rapidly, he implored Dickinson to do everything in his power to prevent the "Incendiarys" from leading the colonies out of the Empire. Gilbert Barkly to John Dickinson, October 12, 1775; John Dickinson Papers, Hist. Soc. Pa.

10. Mason, "Robert R. Livingston," *N.Y. Hist. Soc. Quar.,* 298.

11. John Adams, *Diary and Autobiography,* II, 204.

12. *Ibid.,* 219.

13. John Adams to James Warren, September 19, 1775; *Letters of the Cont. Cong.,* I, 200.

14. The report that the commission brought back to Congress bore the unmistakable stamp of General Washington. The recommendations for a 20,361-man army, long-term enlistments and a scale of punitive sentences for breaches of the military code were in keeping with Washington's ideas on revamping the Continental Army. Nettels, *George Washington,* 166.

15. During the course of the debate on this expedition the subject of a continental fleet was apparently brought up. John Adams

sadly concluded from the voices raised in opposition that
sectional and personal interests were the primary stumbling
blocks: "They agree that a Fleet, would protect and secure
The Trade of New England but deny that it would that of the
Southern colonies." John Adams to James Warren, October
19, 1775; *Letters of the Cont. Cong.*, I, 236.

16. John Adams, *Diary and Autobiography*, III, 356.

17. General Washington to the President of Congress, October 24,
    1775; Washington, *Writings*, IV, 40.

18. *New York Gazette & Weekly Mercury*, November 6, 1775.

19. *Pennsylvania Ledger*, November 18, 1775.

20. John De Hart to the New Jersey Assembly, November 13,
    1775; Force, *Am. Archs.*, III, 1876.

21. *Pennsylvania Ledger*, November 17, 1775.

22. Charles Lee to Benjamin Rush, December 12, 1775; "Lee
    Papers," *N.Y. Hist. Soc. Colls.*, 227.

23. In mid-May of 1776 as the radicals prepared the way for in-
    dependence, Elbridge Gerry of Connecticut placed the major
    share of blame for delaying the final separation on Pennsyl-
    vania. He charged that the anti-independence instructions set
    forth by the Pennsylvania assembly in November ". . . induced
    the Middle Colonies and some of the Southern to backward
    every measure which had the appearance of independence."
    Elbridge Gerry to James Warren, May 20, 1776; *Letters of
    the Cont. Cong.*, I, 460.

24. "Minutes of the New Jersey Assembly," Force, *Am. Archs.*,
    III, 1857.

25. *Ibid.*, 1851.

26. *Ibid.*, 1875.

27. Mason, *Road to Independence*, 120-121.

28. Joseph Hewes to Samuel Johnston, December 1, 1775; *Letters
    of the Cont. Cong.*, I, 266.

29. Sectional friction was not solely confined to the formation of
    the Continental Navy. When it came time to set the pay scale
    for soldiers in the remodeled Continental Army Congress
    refused to offer a bounty as an enlistment enticement and only
    reluctantly set the monthly rate at forty shillings. John Adams
    ascribed this meager wage to the fact that the delegates from

the Southern and Middle Colonies were "habituated to higher notions of themselves, and the distinction between them and the common people." John Adams to Joseph Hawley, November 25, 1775; *ibid.*, 260. General Nathaniel Greene of Rhode Island was also highly critical of Congress for its miserliness in setting wage rates because enlistments were proceeding miserably. Greene was especially unhappy about the rumor that New England harbored secret designs against the property and rights of the other colonies. When Thomas Lynch and Benjamin Harrison sought to convince him that such calumny carried no weight whatsoever in the halls of Congress, Greene still maintained that "the cement between the Northern and Southern Colonies is not very strong, if forty thousand lawful, will induce the Congress to give us up." General Nathaniel Greene to Samuel Ward, December 31, 1775; Force, *Am. Archs.*, IV, 483.

30. *Journals of the Cont. Cong.*, III, 425.

31. Richard Smith's Diary, *Letters of the Cont. Cong.*, I, 280.

32. *Journals of the Cont. Cong.*, III, 412.

33. James Duane to Cornelius Duane, December 9, 1775; "Duane Letters," *Pubs. So. Hist. Assoc.*, 177.

34. *Journals of the Cont. Cong.*, IV., 20.

35. Edward Shippen, Jr., to _____, January 19, 1776; Shippen Family Papers, Hist. Soc. Pa.

36. William Smith, *Memoirs*, 258.

37. *Pennsylvania Gazette,* January 10, 1776.

38. Richard Smith Diary, *Letters of the Cont. Cong.*, I, 304.

39. Samuel Adams to John Adams, January 15 & 16, 1776; S. Adams, *Writings*, III, 259.

40. Richard Smith's Diary, *Letters of the Cont. Cong.*, I, 317.

41. General Schuyler vented his sorrow over the death of his friend Montgomery by charging that the defeat at Quebec was the result of the wholesale desertion of the New England troops before the battle. This biased interpretation was, nevertheless, popular with many Southern and Middle Colonial men, who had little respect for New Englanders in general. Philip Schuyler to Alexander McDougall, January 25, 1776; Alexander McDougall Papers, N.Y. Hist. Soc.

42. Thomas Lynch to Philip Schuyler, January 20, 1776; *Letters of the Cont. Cong.,* I, 322.

43. George Read to Caesar Rodney, January 19, 1776; *ibid.,* 320.

44. Governor Franklin to Lord Dartmouth, January 5, 1776; "Franklin Correspondence," *N.J. Archs.,* X, 677.

45. Extract of a letter from an officer in the expedition on Long Island, January 26, 1776; Force, *Am. Archs.,* IV, 858.

46. Richard Smith's Diary, *Letters of the Cont. Cong.,* I, 348.

47. Smith, *James Wilson,* 76.

48. Edward Tilghman, a reconciliation-minded delegate from Maryland, took time early in February to inform his father of the political balance sheet in Congress. His analysis revealed that the alignment of the delegates was virtually unchanged since Congress resumed its labors in September: "There is reason to believe that the disposition of Congress (a majority) are in favor of reconciliation and abhorrent from independence. The division is this: Rhode Island frequently loses a vote, having only two members, and they differing: New Hampshire, Massachusetts, Connecticut, and the Ancient Dominion, hang very much together. They are what we call violent, and suspected of independency. All the others breathe reconciliation, except that the Lower Counties [Delaware] are sometimes divided by the absence of Rodney or Read. Colonel McKean is a true Presbyterian, joins the violents." Edward Tilghman to his father, February 4, 1776; Stillé, *Dickinson,* 173-174.

49. Richard Smith's Diary, *Letters of the Cont. Cong.,* I, 369.

50. *Ibid.,* 350.

51. *Ibid.,* 366.

52. General Washington to Joseph Reed, January 31, 1776; Washington, *Writings.,* IV, 297.

53. John Adams, *Diary and Autobiography,* III, 367.

54. "James Allen's Diary," *Pa. Mag. Hist. & Biog.,* 185.

55. Richard Smith's Diary, *Letters of the Cont. Cong.,* I, 383.

56. New York's unexpected support for the measure seems to have resulted from John Jay's strong efforts in its behalf. His resistance to independence was apparently weakening at this time, and he also viewed the privateer resolution as an opportunity

for New York to redeem itself. He recalled that in 1757 New York privateers were the scourge of the seas, and he hoped for a smilar outpouring of support in 1776. John Jay to Alexander McDougall, March 27, 1776; John Jay Papers, Miscellaneous, N.Y. Hist. Soc.

Chapter Seven

1. William Smith, *Memoirs,* 239.
2. Robert Morris to Horatio Gates, April 6, 1776; *New York Gazette & Weekly Mercury,* April 6, 1776.
3. "Minutes of the New York Provincial Congress," Force, *Am. Archs.,* III, 1280.
4. General Washington alerted the New York provincial congress on October 5 that a sizable British flotilla with 600 troops on board recently left Boston for an unknown southern destination. General Washington to the Committee of the City of New York, October 5, 1775; Washington, *Writings,* IV, 16.
5. Alexander McDougall to General Schuyler (no date), 1775; Alexander McDougall Papers, N.Y. Hist. Soc.
6. "The Intelligencer" (pseud. of Hugh Hughes) to Sam and John Adams, October 17, 1775; Samuel Adams Papers, N.Y. Pub. Lib.
7. Letter from the Deputies in attendance to the Committees of some of the Counties whose delegates were not present, December 1, 1775; Force, *Am. Archs.,* III, 1755. According to Mason the inability of the second congress to secure a quorum was due in large part to the failure of the delegates from the nascent counties (Tryon, Charlotte, Cumberland and Gloucester) to report on time and the successful Tory campaign in Queens and Richmond counties against the selection of delegates. Mason, *Road to Independence,* 117. In advancing this interpretation he diverges sharply from Becker's contention that the shaky start experienced by the second congress was due to a powerful Loyalist reaction occasioned by the growing encroachment of the resistance movement upon personal freedom and the steadily diminishing prospects for reconciliation. Becker, *Political Parties,* 228. Mason argues quite convincingly that only the conduct of Queens and Richmond counties can be ascribed to Tory machinations and even here

their anti-Whig campaign extended back to the summer
months. John Jay perhaps came closest to the true state of
affairs. He was not at all disappointed by the tardiness with
which the congress organized for he had been quite fearful
that with the crisis darkening, the lack of backbone among
the Whigs coupled with the swan songs of the Tory publicists
might have combined to prevent any meeting of the body
whatsoever. John Jay to Alexander McDougall, December
(undated), 1775; John Jay Papers, Miscellaneous, N.Y. Hist.
Soc.

8. Isaac Sears to Roger Sherman, Eliphalet Dyer & Silas Deane,
    November 28, 1775; Sol Feinstone Collection, Am. Phil. Soc.,
    Phila.

9. John Morin Scott to Colonel Richard Varick, November 15,
    1775; Dawson, *New York City,* 84.

10. Sears ostensibly took this action because he was no longer able
    to influence policy in New York from within. The radical
    triumvirate of Alexander McDougall, John Lamb and Sears
    that had played such a conspicuous part in bringing New York
    into the resistance movement began to fall apart during the
    summer of 1775. Alexander McDougall became more and
    more identified with the moderate Whigs while Scott and Sears
    were shunted into the background. Champagne, "New York's
    Radicals," *Jour. Am. Hist.,* 31-34.

11. John Jay to Colonel Woodhull, November 26, 1775; Jay,
    Correspondence, I, 38.

12. Alexander Hamilton to John Jay, November 26, 1775; Ham-
    ilton, *Papers,* I, 177.

13. New York Provincial Congress to Governor Jonathan Trum-
    bull, December 12, 1775; Force, *Am. Archs.,* IV, 401.

14. John Jay to Colonel Woodhull, November 26, 1775; Jay,
    Correspondence, I, 38.

15. William Smith, *Memoirs,* 244-245.

16. Alexander Hamilton to John Jay, January 4, 1776; Hamilton,
    Papers, I, 181. A majority of the Whigs in congress did not
    want to burn all their bridges behind them. Although John
    Jay was not a member of the provincial congress at the time
    he contended that "To declare absolutely against having any
    more assemblies would be dangerous, because the People are

too little informed to see the Propriety of such a measure."
John Jay to Alexander McDougall, December (undated),
1775; John Jay Papers, Miscellaneous, N.Y. Hist. Soc.

17. New York Committee of Safety to Provincial Congress Delegation, January 8, 1776; Force, *Am. Archs.,* IV, 1028.

18. Hugh Hughes to Samuel Adams, January 8, 1776; Samuel Adams Papers, N.Y. Pub. Lib.

19. Gilbert Potter to New York Provincial Congress, December 10, 1775; Force, *Am. Archs.,* IV, 404.

20. Even Hugh Hughes counseled against using New York City militia units to subjugate the Long Island Tories. He did, however, favor employing militiamen from Suffolk County along with Connecticut troops. Despite his fervent desire for New York to show more spirit, he apparently recognized that it was more prudent to call for outside help rather than take the chance of holding the Whig cause up to ridicule should the New York troops prove unable or unwilling to subdue the Tories. Hugh Hughes to Samuel Adams, January 8, 1776; Samuel Adams Papers, N.Y. Pub. Lib.

21. Several weeks before the Tory roundup on Long Island General Schuyler led a much larger expedition against Col. Guy Johnson's Tory enclave in Tryon County. Prompted by intelligence from Washington that Johnson was actively recruiting Indian warriors for British service Schuyler disarmed some 600 Highlander tenants, took numerous prisoners and forced Col. Johnson to post a £1600 personal bond. This highly successful raid removed for a time the Indian threat to the western counties that had worried New Yorkers during the summer and fall of 1775. Governor Tryon to Earl of Dartmouth, February 7, 1776; O'Callaghan, *Docs. Rel. to Col. Hist. N.Y.,* VIII, 663, & General Washington to General Philip Schuyler, December 24, 1775; Washington, *Writings,* IV, 663.

22. Hugh Hughes to Samuel Adams, December 22, 1775; Samuel Adams Papers, N.Y. Pub. Lib.

23. General Washington to the President of Congress, January 11, 1776; Washington, *Writings,* IV, 229. John Adams, who was in Cambridge at the time, expressed concern about the political ramifications that the Lee expedition might have. Washington neatly sidestepped Adams' objection by main-

taining that this was strictly a military matter. General Washington to John Adams, January 7, 1776; *Ibid.,* 220.

24. "Minutes of the New York Committee of Safety," Force, *Am. Archs.,* IV, 1962.

25. New York Committee of Safety to General Lee, January 21, 1776; *ibid.,* 1063.

26. General Charles Lee to the New York Committee of Safety, January 23, 1776; *ibid.,* 1075-1076.

27. General Charles Lee to General Washington, February 14, 1776; "Lee Papers," *N.Y. Hist. Soc. Colls.,* 295-296. It is doubtful that Lee's interpretation of the incident was the one shared by most inhabitants. Alexander McDougall no doubt expressed the thoughts of a large number of New Yorkers when he condemned the New England men for trifling with the well-being of the city, and he noted further that too many of their leaders seemed to be enamored with expansionism as was evidenced by the Wyoming Valley affair. William Smith, *Memoirs,* 265.

28. General Charles Lee to New York Provincial Congress, March 6, 1776; Force, *Am. Archs.,* 347.

29. Isaac Sears to Charles Lee, March 17, 1776; "Lee Papers," *N.Y. Hist. Soc. Colls.,* 359.

30. Upon the urging of the New York delegation the Continental Congress decreed on March 8 that no test oaths should henceforth be administered by military officers. It is doubtful that this mild, *ex post facto* censure of General Lee had any enduring significance. New York Delegation in Congress to New York Provincial Congress, March 10, 1776; Force, *Am. Archs.,* IV, 392.

31. Alexander McDougall to General Charles Lee, December 29, 1775; Alexander McDougall Papers, N.Y. Hist. Soc.

32. James Duane to New York Provincial Congress, February 25, 1776; Force, *Am. Archs., V,* 312-313.

33. "James Allen's Diary," *Pa. Mag. Hist. & Biog.,* 185.

34. "Votes of Assembly," *Pa. Archs.,* VIII, 7323-7324.

35. *Ibid.,* 7326-7328.

36. *Ibid.,* 7334-7336.

37. Governor Franklin was still convinced early in October that

"Were the People, even now, left to judge for themselves, and the Avenues of information not obstructed, I have no Doubt but their natural good Sense would prevent their engaging ir the Support of the present hostile and destructive Measures." Governor Franklin to Earl of Dartmouth, October 3, 1775; "Franklin Correspondence," *N.J. Archs.,* X, 662-665.

38. Barkly, "British Spy," *Pa. Mag. Hist. & Biog.,* 23.

39. Address delivered by Anthony Wayne in 1775; Anthony Wayne Papers, Hist. Soc. Pa.

40. "Votes of Assembly," *Pa. Archs.,* VIII, 7330-7331; *Journals of the Cont. Cong.,* III, 321.

41. Edward Shippen, Jr., to his father, November 1, 1775; Shippen Family Papers, Hist. Soc. Pa.

42. Richard Smith Diary, *Letters of the Cont. Cong.,* I, 281.

43. Thomas Wharton to Samuel Wharton, January 1, 1776; "Wharton Letter-Book," *Pa. Mag. Hist. & Bio.,* 52-53.

44. Extract of a letter from Philadelphia brought by way of New York, February 13, 1776; *Letters on the Am. Rev.,* 259-260.

45. Letter to Colonel Roberdeau, January 22, 1776; *Pa. Archs.,* I, 570-571.

46. Popular resentment toward the Quakers also picked up noticeably in January as the Philadelphia Monthly Meeting published a strong anti-independence address. After expounding upon the many benefits which Pennsylvanians received from membership in the British Empire, the address condemned all actions which in any way threatened to sever this bountiful relationship. "The Ancient Testimony and Principles of the People Called Quakers, Renewed with Respect to the King and Government; and Touching the Commotions now Prevailing in these and other Parts of America, Addressed to the People in General." Broadside Collection, Hist. Soc. Pa.

47. "Votes of Assembly," *Pa. Archs.,* VIII, 7425.

48. Hawke, *Revolution,* 19, 102.

49. *Pennsylvania Gazette,* February 28, 1776.

50. Smith, *Plain Truth,* 1.

51. Gegenheimer, *William Smith,* 178.

52. Smith, *Additions to Plain Truth,* 112.

53. *Pennsylvania Packet,* March 25, 1776.

54. "Votes of Assembly," *Pa. Archs.*, VIII, 7485.

55. Governor Franklin to Earl of Dartmouth, October, 3, 1775; "Franklin Correspondence," *N.J. Archs.*, X, 662-665.

56. New Jersey Provincial Congress to the Continental Congress, October 14, 1775; Force, *Am. Archs.*, III, 1051. After indicating that the Continental Congress could not supply any funds, President Hancock went on to suggest that the plan to maintain a force of 4,000 minutemen was far too ambitious for a colony of New Jersey's size. John Hancock to the New Jersey Provincial Congress, October 25, 1775; *ibid.*, 1236.

57. "Minutes of the New Jersey Provincial Congress," Force, *Am. Archs.*, III, 1233.

58. "Minutes of the New Jersey Assembly," *ibid.*, 1861-1862.

59. "Minutes of the New Jersey Committee of Safety," *ibid.*, IV, 664.

60. President Hancock to the New Jersey Provincial Congress, February 12, 1776; *ibid.*, IV, 1013.

61. The chairman of the Morris County committee informed Lord Stirling in mid-March that many members were unhappy that their militia units were being called upon to defend New York City. Concern was expressed that farms were being left untended and should the British invade Perth Amboy there would be few troops available to repel the attackers. Alexander Carmichal to Lord Stirling, March 16, 1776; Stirling Papers, N.Y. Hist. Soc.

62. New Jersey Provincial Congress to the Continental Congress, Force, *Am. Archs.*, IV, 1490-1491.

63. William Churchill Houston to Professor John Winthrop, December 27, 1775; André de Coppet Collection, Princeton Univ.

64. General Washington to the New Jersey Committee of Safety, April 24, 1776; Force, *Am. Archs.*, V, 1052.

65. Governor Franklin to Earl of Dartmouth, March 28, 1776; "Franklin Correspondence," *N.J. Archs.*, X, 705.

66. Robert Erskine to Walter Ewing, February 10, 1776; in Tuttle, "Morris County," *"Procs. N.J. Hist. Soc.,* 34.

67. *New York Journal,* March 7, 1776.

68. William Livingston to a Friend in New Jersey, December 22, 1775; Gratz Collection, Old Congress Case, Hist. Soc. Pa.

69. *Pennsylvania Evening Post,* March 7, 1776.

70. "Minutes of the New Jersey Provincial Congress," Force, *Am. Archs.,* IV, 1608.

71. Samuel McMasters to Dr. James Tilton, November 14, 1775; *ibid.,* III, 1550-1551.

72. "Council of Safety Minutes," *Del. Hist.,* 69.

73. Samuel Adams to Samuel Cooper, April 30, 1776; S. Adams, *Writings,* III, 282-283.

74. *Ibid.*

Chapter Eight

1. Benjamin Franklin to Josiah Quincy, April 15, 1776; *Letters of the Cont. Cong.,* I, 422.

2. George Washington to Joseph Reed, April 15, 1776; Washington, *Writings,* IV, 483.

3. Joseph Reed to Charles Pettit, March 25, 1776; Joseph Reed Papers, N.Y. Hist. Soc.

4. John Adams to Benjamin Kent, June 22, 1776; Adams, *Works, IX,* 401-402.

5. John Jay to Alexander McDougall, April 11, 1776; John Jay Papers, Miscellaneous, N.Y. Hist. Soc.

6. John Adams to Horatio Gates, April 27, 1776; Horatio Gates Papers, N.Y. Hist. Soc.

7. During the early months of 1776 the flow of news from London regarding the powers of the commissioners provided no definitive account of what their status would be. Reports that the commissioners would have extensive bargaining authority were countered by other reports that they would only be able to grant pardons and institute military government. *Pennsylvania Ledger,* March 9, 1776; *New York Gazette & Weekly Mercury,* April 15, 1776. It is easy to understand how the pro- and anti-commissioner colonials were able to maintain their respective positions by believing only half of what they read.

8. Many Middle Colonial inhabitants no doubt held the same prejudice that Captain Persifor Frazer of Pennsylvania did

before he saw service with the Continental Army on the New York frontier. "No man was ever more disappointed in his expectations respecting New Englanders in general than I have been," Frazer informed his wife. "They are a set of low, dirty, griping, cowardly, lying rascals. . . . You may inform all your acquaintances not to be afraid that they will ever Conquer the other Provinces (which you know was much talked of,) 10,000 Pennsylvanians I think sufficient for ten times that number out of their Country." "General Persifor Frazer," *Pa. Mag. Hist. & Biog.,* 135.

9. Joseph Reed believed that Pennsylvania would not commit itself to independence until the commissioners presented their terms. As he described the state of mind in Pennsylvania, "Notwithstanding the Act of Parliament for seizing our property, and a thousand other proofs of a bitter and irreconcilable spirit, there is a strange reluctance in the minds of many to cut the knot which ties us to Great Britain. . . ." Joseph Reed to George Washington, March 3, 1776; Reed, *Correspondence,* 163.

10. John Adams, *Diary and Autobiography,* III, 381.

11. John Adams to Horatio Gates, March 23, 1776; Horatio Gates Papers, N.Y. Hist. Soc.

12. James Duane to John Jay, May 11, 1776; *Letters of the Cont. Cong.,* I, 444.

13. While North Carolina, New Jersey, Delaware and New York voted nay, both Pennsylvania and Maryland surprisingly abstained. Hawke, *Revolution,* 124.

14. After treating the Maryland walkout in a rather ho-hum manner, Carter Braxton expressed great alarm over the prospect that the Pennsylvania assembly might bow to the preamble. Putting this contingency in rather apocalyptic terms he asked, "What then will be the consequence God only knows." Carter Braxton to Landon Carter, May 17, 1776; *Letters of the Cont. Cong.,* I, 454.

15. John Jay to James Duane, May 29, 1776; James Duane Papers, N.Y. Hist. Soc.

16. John Adams to James Warren, May 20, 1776; *Lettters of the Cont. Cong.,* I, 461. For one thing Maryland had already demonstrated its capacity to be a maverick. Piqued by the

attempt of General Charles Lee to stick his nose into their internal affairs, the Maryland convention had refused to seize Governor Robert Eden as the Continental Congress directed in April. Klingelhofer, "Cautious Revolution," *Md. Hist. Mag.*, 278. But Maryland's perversity stemmed from a far more fundamental source. The Whigs were frightened by the social and class antagonism which was threatening to overwhelm the old order. On the Eastern shore scattered, small-scale insurrections by blacks and poor whites were under way and paramilitary Tory bands were also active. Hoffman, "Revolution in Maryland," 369.

17. "Votes of Assembly," *Pa. Archs.*, VIII, 7514-7516.

18. Benjamin Rush to Mrs. Rush, May 29, 1776; Rush, *Letters*, I, 99-100.

19. "Votes of Assembly," *Pa. Archs.*, VIII, 7542-7543.

20. Edward Rutledge to John Jay, June 8, 1776; Jay, *Correspondence*, I, 66.

21. Jefferson, *Writings*, I, 25.

22. *Pennsylvania Gazette*, June 26, 1776.

23. Hawke, *Revolution*, 178.

24. Caesar Rodney to John Haslet, May 17, 1776; Rodney, *Letters*, 79.

25. Caesar Rodney to Thomas Rodney, May 22, 1776; *ibid.*, 82-83. Emboldened by the proximity of British forces and the continued vacillation of the Whig committees, the Delaware Tories were in readiness when the May 15th resolution was promulgated. Led by Robinson, the Tories circulated a counter-petition, which was a revised version of the Pennsylvania "Remonstrance." The Delaware "Remonstrance" charged that the Patriots purposely misconstrued the intentions of Congress regarding the institution of new governments and that the present system of government in Delaware was still supported by a majority of the populace. It also condemned the Whigs for seeking to shift the basis of American opposition from redress to total separation. According to Robinson over 5,000 Delawareans affixed their signatures to the "Remonstrance," while only 300 signed the Whig petition calling for implementation of the May 15th resolution. John Clark, Esq., was commissioned to deliver the "Remonstrance" to Congress. He was captured enroute by supporters of the

American cause and the "Remonstrance" destroyed. Hancock, "Thomas Robinson," *Del. Hist.*, 3. This arbitary act inflamed the British sympathizers. On Saturday, June 1, at the Mispillon Muster, Clark and some of his followers circulated copies of the "Remonstrance" and caused a minor riot. Colonel Haslet informed Caesar Rodney on June 5 that he considered the muster disturbance a definite Tory plot, but warned that an insurrection might well occur in Sussex County. Within a week his prediction was fulfilled. On June 13 1,000 or more British sympathizers gathered at Broad Creek with the intention of joining the British forces on board the *Roebuck*. Militia units from Kent and New Castle were immediately dispatched to the trouble spot along with 3,000 Continental soldiers. With this impressive show of force, and the British failure to supply the insurgents with arms, they were quickly dispersed. Several of the Tory leaders were captured, including Robinson, and forced to post bond. "It's thought this trick of the Tories was concerted in this place in order to give disturbance and break our measures," was how Christopher Marshall in Philadelphia interpreted the insurrection, "but they will find I hope, that the pit they dug, they themselves will fall into." Marshall, *Diary*, 87.

26. Boudinot, *Addresses*, I, 17.

27. Erdman, *New Jersey Constitution*, 22-26.

28. New Jersey Provincial Congress to Governor Franklin, June 15, 1776; "Franklin Correspondence," *N.J. Archs.*, X, 720.

29. *Ibid.*, 726.

30. New Jersey Provincial Congress to President of Congress, June, 1776; Force, *Am. Archs.*, VI, 1010.

31. John Adams to Samuel Chase, June 14, 1776; *Letters of the Cont. Cong.*, I, 492.

32. John Adams to Samuel Chase, June 24, 1776; *ibid.*, 503.

33. William Whipple to John Langdon, June 24, 1776; *ibid.*, 504.

34. John Adams to Samuel H. Parsons, June 22, 1776; Adams, *Works*, IX, 406.

35. Champagne, "New York Politics," *N.Y. Hist. Soc. Quar.*, 281-282.

36. On June 3 the Continental Congress issued requests to various

colonies asking them to immediately send their allotments of
the 14,000 additional troops assigned to help in the defense
of New York. *Journals of the Cont. Cong.,* IV, 412-413.

37. John Jones to James Duane, April 14, 1776; "Duane Letters,"
    Procs. So. Hist. Assoc., 254.

38. James Duane to John Jay, May 18, 1776; Jay, *Correspon-
    dence,* I, 61.

39. Jensen, *Founding a Nation,* 697, & Becker, *Political Parties,*
    269.

40. Late in June when congressmen were counting noses to deter-
    mine how the July vote would turn out, Elbridge Gerry finished
    his tally and noted that only New York and Maryland were
    in the doubtful column. He did not consider this state of affairs
    to be critical. "These will not impede us a moment. I do not
    affirm that either of these are of the neuter gender; but on
    the other hand am persuaded the people are in favour of a
    total and final separation, and will support the measure, even
    if the conventions and Delegates of those Colonies vote
    against it." Elbridge Gerry to James Warren, June 25, 1776;
    Letters of the Cont. Cong., I, 500.

41. Becker contends that determination of the conservative Whigs
    to maintain complete control of the governmental machinery
    and their refusal to have internal policy dictated by outside
    forces accounts for New York's case of indecisiveness. It
    seems strange, however, that the conservative Whigs who
    controlled the third provincial congress did not take advantage
    of the May 15th resolution and construct a government to
    their liking while at the same time securing the approval of the
    Continental Congress. As for Becker's state rights argument,
    it seems to be inapplicable for if the New York Whigs were
    really desirous of avoiding congressional interferences they
    should have marched in step with the other colonies rather
    than fallen out of line. Becker, *Political Parties,* 274-275.
    Mason's assessment differs from that of Becker in that it places
    greater emphasis on the fear of mob rule and loss of personal
    property while ignoring the state rights argument. The speed
    with which many prominent Whigs such as Philip Livingston,
    Lewis Morris and Governeur Morris, to name only a few, fled
    the danger areas with their effects lends credence to the charge
    of opportunism. Mason, *Road to Independence,* 173-176.

42. Joseph Hewes to James Irdell, June 28, 1776; *Letters of the Cont. Cong.,* I, 514.

43. Edward Rutledge to John Jay, June 29, 1776; Jay, *Correspondence,* I, 67.

44. The news that all of the Middle Colonies save New York would support independence and the effective politicking of Samuel Chase turned the tide. Klingelhofer, "Cautious Revolution," *Md. Mag. Hist.,* 303-304.

45. *New York Gazette & Weekly Mercury,* July 15, 1776.

46. King George III to Lord North, September 11, 1774; Hanover, *Correspondence,* III, 131.

47. "John Dickinson," *Pa. Mag. Hist. & Biog.,* 481.

BIBLIOGRAPHY

Unpublished Manuscript Collections

Samuel Adams Papers, New York Public Library, New York, New York.

William Bradford Collection, Historical Society of Pennsylvania, Philadelphia, Pennsylvania.

Broadside Collection, Historical Society of Pennsylvania, Philadelphia, Pennsylvania.

Broadside Collection, Rutgers University, New Brunswick, New Jersey.

André de Coppet Collection, Princeton University, Princeton, New Jersey.

John Dickinson Papers, Historical Society of Pennsylvania, Philadelphia, Pennsylvania.

John Dickinson Papers, Library Company of Philadelphia, Philadelphia, Pennsylvania. (Collection housed in the Historical Society of Pennsylvania.)

James Duane Papers, New York Historical Society, New York, New York.

Edwin A. Ely Collection, New Jersey Historical Society, Newark, New Jersey.

Sol Feinstone Autograph Collection, American Philosophical Society, Philadelphia, Pennsylvania.

247

Benjamin Franklin Papers, American Philosophical Society, Philadelphia, Pennsylvania.

Horatio Gates Papers, New York Historical Society, New York, New York.

Gratz Collection, Historical Society of Pennsylvania, Philadelphia, Pennsylvania. (Papers of James Wilson, Anthony Wayne, William Livingston and Robert Morris.)

John Jay Papers, Columbia University, New York, New York.

John Jay Papers, Miscellaneous, New York Historical Society, New York, New York.

John Lamb Papers, New York Historical Society, New York, New York.

Library of Congress, Transcripts, Colonial Office Papers, Great Britain, Public Record Office, 1774-1776.

Library of Congress, Transcripts, Society for the Propagation of the Gospel, Great Britain, 1774-1776.

Livingston Family Papers, Hyde Park Library, Hyde Park, New York.

Livingston-Redmond Family Correspondence, Hyde Park Library, Hyde Park, New York.

Alexander McDougall Papers, New York Historical Society, New York, New York.

Joseph Reed Papers, New York Historical Society, New York. New York.

Ridgely Family Papers, Delaware Public Archives Commission, Delaware Hall of Records, Dover, Delaware.

Philip Schuyler Papers, New York Public Library, New York, New York.

Shippen Family Papers, Historical Society of Pennsylvania, Philadelphia, Pennsylvania.

Lord Stirling Papers, New York Historical Society, New York, New York.

Anthony Wayne Papers, Historical Society of Pennsylvania, Philadelphia, Pennsylvania.

Published Manuscript Collections and Sources

Adams Family Correspondence. Vol. I, ed. Lyman H. Butterfield, Cambridge: The Belknap Press, 1963.

Adams, John. *Diary and Autobiography of John Adams.* Vols. II & III, ed. Lyman H. Butterfield, Cambridge: The Belknap Press, 1961.

Adams, John. *The Life and Works of John Adams.* Vol. IX, ed. Charles Francis Adams, Boston: Little Brown and Company, 1850-56.

Adams, Samuel. *The Writings of Samuel Adams.* Vols. II & III, ed. Henry A. Cushing, New York: G. P. Putnam's Sons, 1904-1908.

Allen, James. "Diary of James Allen, Esq., of Philadelphia, Counsellor-At-Law, 1770-1778," *Pennsylvania Magazine of History and Biography,* IX (1895) 176-196, 278-296.

American Husbandry. Ed. Harry J. Carmen, New York: Columbia University Press, 1939.

Barkly, Gilbert. "A British Spy in Philadelphia 1775-1777," ed. Geoffrey Seed, *Pennsylvania Magazine of History and Biography,* LXXXI (January, 1961), 3-37.

"Beatty Letters, 1773-1782," ed. Joseph M. Beatty, *Proceedings of the New Jersey Historical Society,* LXXXI (January, 1963), 21-46.

Boudinot, Elias. *The Life, Public Services, Addresses of Elias Boudinot, LL.D.* Vol. I, ed. Jane J. Boudinot, Boston & New York: Houghton Mifflin and Company, 1896.

Burd, Neddie. *Neddie Burd's Reading Letters.* Ed. Nolan J. Bennet, Reading: Berks County Bar Association, 1927.

Burke, Edmund. *Edmund Burke, New York Agent with his Letters to the New York Assembly and Intimate Correspondence with Charles O'Hara, 1761-1776.* Ed. Ross J. S. Hoffman, Philadelphia: American Philosophical Society, 1956.

Burnaby, Andrew. *Burnaby's Travels Through North America,* Ed. Rufus Rockwell Wilson, New York: A. Wessels Company, 1904.

Clinton, George. *Public Papers of George Clinton, First Governor of New York 1777-1795.* Vol. I, ed. Hugh Hastings, New York & Albany: State of New York, 1899-1911.

"Papers of Cadwallader Colden," *New York Historical Society Collections for the Year 1877.* Vol. X, New York: Printed for the Society, 1878.

"Papers of Cadwallader Colden," *New York Historical Society Collections for the Year 1923.* Vol. VII, New York: Printed for the Society, 1923.

"Council of Safety Minutes," ed. Leon de Valinger, *Delaware History,* I (January, 1946).

Curwen, Samuel. *Journal and Letters of the Late Samuel Curwen.* Ed. George Atkinson Ward, New York: Leavitt Trow & Co., 1845.

Cuthbert, George. "Notes and Documents: Philadelphia, April 1775," ed. Arthur P. Watts, *Pennsylvania Magazine of History and Biography,* LXII (April, 1942), 205-215.

Dawson, Henry B. *New York City during the American Revolution.* New York: Privately printed for the New York Mercantile Library Association, 1861.

"Papers of Silas Deane," *Collections of the New York Historical Society for the Year 1886.* Vol.I, New York: Printed for the Society, 1887.

Dickinson, John. *The Writings of John Dickinson.* Ed. Paul Leicester Ford, *Memoirs of the Historical Society of Pennsylvania,* Vol. XIV, Philadelphia: Historical Society of Pennsylvania, 1895.

Dickinson, John. "Speech of John Dickinson Opposing the Declaration of Independence, 1 July, 1776," ed. John H. Powell, *Pennsylvania Magazine of History and Biography,* LXV (October, 1941), 458-481.

Duane, James. "The Duane Letters," *Publications of the Southern History Association,* VII (May & July, 1903), 170-187, 247-268.

Fithian, Philip Vickers. *Journal and Letters of Philip Vickers*

Fithian. Ed. Hunter Dickinson Farish, Willamsburg: Colonial Williamsburg Incorporated, 1957.

Force, Peter (ed.). *American Archives: Consisting of a Collection of Authentick Records, State Papers, Debates, and Letters*. 4th Series, Vols. I-VI, Washington: M. St. Clair Clarke and Peter Force, 1837-1853.

Franklin, Benjamin. *The Works of Benjamin Franklin*. Vols. VII & VIII, ed. Jared Sparks, New York: Tuppan, Whittemore and Masson, 1836-1840.

"Correspondence of Governor William Franklin," *New Jersey Archives*. 1st Series, Vol. X, eds. Frederick W. Ricord & Wm. Nelson, Newark: Daily Advertiser Printing House, 1886.

Frazer, Persifor. "Some Extracts from the Papers of General Persifor Frazer," *Pennsylvania Magazine of History and Biography*, XXXI (1907), 129-144.

Gage, Thomas. *The Correspondence of General Thomas Gage with the Secretaries of State, and with the War Office and the Treasury*. Vol. II, ed. Clarence Edward Carter, New Haven: Yale Universiy Press, 1933.

Gaine, Hugh. *The Journals of Hugh Gaine, Printer*. Vol. I, ed. Paul Leicester Ford, New York: Dodd, Mead & Company, 1902.

Galloway, Joseph. "Some Letters of Joseph Galloway, 1774-1775," *Pennsylvania Magazine of History and Biography*, XXI (1897), 477-485.

Hamilton, Alexander. *The Papers of Alexander Hamilton*. Vol. I, ed. Harold C. Syrett, New York: Columbia University Press, 1961.

Hanover, George. *The Correspondence of King George the III, From 1760 to December, 1783*. Vol. III, ed. Sir John Fortescue, London: Frank Cass Co., Ltd., 1967. Reprint.

Hiltzheimer, Jacob. *Extracts from the Diary of Jacob Hiltzheimer of Philadelphia 1765-1798*. Ed. Jacob Cox Parsons, Philadelphia: Press of Wm. I. Fell & Co., 1893.

Hutchinson, Thomas. *The Diary and Letters of His Excellency*

Thomas Hutchinson Esq. Vol. I, ed. Peter Orlando Hutchinson, Boston: Houghton Mifflin & Co., 1886.

Jay, John. *The Correspondence and Public Papers of John Jay.* Vol. I, ed. Henry P. Johnston, New York: G. P. Putnam's Sons, 1890-1893.

Jefferson, Thomas. *The Writings of Thomas Jefferson, 1743-1826.* Vol. I, ed. Albert Ellery Burgh, Washington, D.C.: Thomas Jefferson Memorial of the United States, 1905.

Journals of the Continental Congress, 1774-1789. Vols. I-IV, ed. Worthington Chauncy Ford, Washington, D.C.: Government Printing Office, 1904-1937.

"The Kent County Loyalists, Part II, Documents," ed. Harold Bell Hancock, *Delaware History,* VI (September, 1954), 92-140.

"Papers of Charles Lee," *New York Historical Society Collections for the Year 1871.* Vol. I, New York: Printed for the Society, 1872.

Letters of Members of the Continental Congress. Vols. I & II, ed. Edmund Cody Burnett, Washington, D.C.: Carnegie Institute Press, 1921-1936.

Letters on the American Revolution, 1774-1776. Ed. Margaret Wheeler Willard, Boston: Houghton Mifflin Company, 1925.

Livingston, Robert R. "Robert R. Livingston and the Non-Exportation Policy: Notes for a Speech in the Continental Congress, 1775," ed. Bernard Mason, *New York Historical Society Quarterly,* XLIV (October, 1960), 295-311.

Livingston, William. *A Memoir of the Life of William Livingston.* Ed. Theodore Sedgewick, Jr., New York: J. & J. Harper, 1833.

Marshall, Christopher. *Passages from the Diary of Christopher Marshall, 1774-1777.* Ed. William Duane, Philadelphia: Hazard & Mitchell, 1849.

"Minutes of the Council of Safety of the Province of Pennsylvania," *Colonial Records of Pennsylvania.* Vol. X, Harrisburg: Theo. Ferm & Company, 1822.

M'Roberts, Patrick. "Tour Through Part of the North Provinces of America, 1774-1775," ed. Carl Bridenbaugh, *Pennsylvania Magazine of History and Biography,* LIX (April, 1935), 134-180.

"Extracts from American Newspapers Relating to New Jersey," *New Jersey Archives.* 1st Series, Vol. XXVII, ed. William Nelson, Paterson: Press Printing and Publishing Co., 1905.

"Extracts from American Newspapers Relating to New Jersey," *New Jersey Archives.* 1st Series, Vol. XXIX, ed. A. Van Doren Honeyman, Paterson: Call Printing and Publishing Co., 1917.

O'Callaghan, Edmund B. (ed.). *Documents Relative to the Colonial History of the State of New York.* Vols. VIII & IX, Albany: Weed, Parsons & Co., 1853-1887.

_____. *The Documentary History of the State of New York.* Vol. I, Albany: Weed, Parsons & Co., 1849.

Pennsylvania Archives. 1st Series, Vol. IV, ed. Samuel Hazard, Philadelphia: Joseph Severn & Co., 1853.

"Journal of Josiah Quincy, Junior, 1777," *Massachusetts Historical Society Proceedings,* IL (1915-1916), 424-481.

Reed, Joseph. *Life and Correspondence of Joseph Reed.* Vols. I-II, ed. William B. Reed, Philadelphia: Lindsay and Blakiston, 1847.

Read, George. *The Life and Correspondence of George Read.* Ed. William Thompson Reed, Philadelphia: J. B. Lippincott & Company, 1870.

A Calendar of the Ridgely Family Letters 1742-1879. Ed. Leon de Valinger, Jr., Dover: Published privately, 1948.

Rodney, Caesar. *Letters to and from Caesar Rodney 1756-1784.* Ed. Herbert Ryden, Philadelphia: Published for the Historical Society of Delaware by the University of Pennsylvania Press, 1933.

Rush, Benjamin. *Letters of Benjamin Rush.* Vol. I, ed. Lyman H. Butterfield, *Memoirs of The American Philosophical Society.* Princeton: Princeton University Press, 1951.

Rutherford, John. "Notes on the State of New Jersey, 1776."
    Proceedings of the New Jersey Historical Society, 2nd
    Series, I (1868), 79-90.

Smith, William. *Historical Memoirs of William Smith from
    16 March 1763 to 9 July 1776.* Ed. William Henry Sabine,
    New York: New York Public Library, 1956.

*Timoleon's Biographical History of Dionysius, Tyrant of
    Delaware.* Ed. John A. Munroe, Newark: University of
    Delaware Press, 1948.

"Votes of Assembly," *Pennsylvania Archives.* 8th Series. Vol.
    VIII, ed. Charles F. Hoban, Harrisburg: Pennsylvania Bu-
    reau of Publications, 1935.

Washington, George. *The Writings of George Washington
    from the Original Manuscript Sources, 1745-1799.* Vols.
    III & IV, ed. John C. Fitzpatrick, Washington. D.C.: U.S.
    Government Printing Office, 1931-1944.

"Warren-Adams Letters, 1743-1777," *Massachusetts Histori-
    cal Society Collections,* Vol. I, Boston: Published by the
    Society, 1917.

Wharton, Thomas. "Selections from the Letter-Book of
    Thomas Wharton of Philadelphia 1773-1783," *Pennsyl-
    vania Magazine of History and Biography,* XXXIII (Oc-
    tober, 1909), 432-453.

Witherspoon, John. *The Works of the Reverend John With-
    erspoon.* Vol. IV, Philadelphia: William W. Woodward,
    1802.

Newspapers

Maryland Gazette. (Annapolis), 1775-1776.

Maryland Journal and the Baltimore Advertiser. 1774-1776.

Newport Mercury. (Rhode Island), 1775-1776.

New York Gazette & Weekly Mercury. (New York), 1774-
    1776.

New York Journal. (New York), 1774-1776.

Pennsylvania Evening Post. (Philadelphia), 1776.

Pennsylvania Gazette. (Philadelphia), 1774-1776.

Pennsylvania Journal and Weekly Advertiser. (Philadelphia), 1776.

Pennsylvania Ledger. (Philadelphia), 1775-1776.

Pennsylvania Packet. (Philadelphia), 1774-1776.

Rivington's New York Gazetteer. (New York), 1774-1775.

Pamphlets

Chandler, Thomas Bradbury. *A Friendly Address to all Reasonable Americans.* New York: James Rivington, Printer, 1774, in *American Culture Series* (Microfilm, Reel 252), Ann Arbor: University of Michigan Microfilms.

_____. *What Think Ye of the Congress Now?* New York: James Rivington, Printer, 1775.

Galloway, Joseph. *A Candid Examination of the Mutual Claims of Great Britain and the Colonies.* New York: James Rivington, Printer, 1775.

_____. *Historical and Political Reflections on the Rise and Progress of the American Rebellion,* in *American Culture Series* (Microfilm, Reel 18), Ann Arbor: University of Michigan Microfilms.

Inglis, Charles. *The True Interest of America Impartially Stated, in Certain Strictures on a Pamphlet entitled Common Sense,* in *American Culture Series* (Microfilm, Reel 252), Ann Arbor: University of Michigan Microfilms.

Seabury, Samuel. *A View of the Controversy Between Great Britain and Her Colonies.* New York: James Rivington, Printer, 1774.

_____. *An Alarm to the Legislature of the Province of New York.* New York: James Rivington, Printer, 1775.

_____. *Free Thoughts on the Proceedings of the Continental Congress at Philadelphia Sept. 5, 1774.* New York: James Rivington, Printer, 1774.

Smith, Dr. William. *Additions to Plain Truth: Addressed to the Inhabitants of America, Containing Further Remarks on a late Pamphlet, entitled Common Sense,* in *American Culture Series* (Microfilm, Reel 252), Ann Arbor: University of Michigan Microfilms.

——————. *Plain Truth: Addressed to the Inhabitants of America Containing Remarks on a late Pamphlet, entitled Common Sense,* in *American Culture Series* (Microfilm, Reel 195), Ann Arbor: University of Michigan Microfilms.

Books

Abernethy, Thomas Perkins. *Western Lands and the American Revolution.* New York: D. Appleton-Century Company, 1937.

Adams, Henry. *History of the United States of America during the First Administration of Thomas Jefferson.* Vol. I, Boston: Charles Scribner's Sons, 1891-1896.

Alden, John Richard. *The First South.* Baton Rouge: Louisiana State University Press, 1961.

Alexander, Edward P. *A Revolutionary Conservative, James Duane of New York.* New York: Columbia University Press, 1938.

Bancroft, George. *History of the United States from the Discovery of the American Continent.* Vols. VII & VIII, Boston: Little Brown & Company, 1864-1868.

Becker, Carl Lotus. *The History of Political Parties in the Province of New York, 1760-1776.* Madison: The University of Wisconsin Press, 1960. Reprint.

Benton, William Allen. *Whig-Loyalism: An Aspect of Political Ideology in the American Revolutionary Era.* Rutherford: Fairleigh Dickinson University Press, 1969.

Bidwell, Percy Wells and John I. Falconer. *History of Agriculture in the Northern United States, 1620-1860.* Washington, D.C.: Carnegie Institute, 1925.

Boyd, George Adams. *Elias Boudinot, Patriot and Statesman, 1740-1821.* Princeton: Princeton University Press, 1952.

Bridenbaugh, Carl. *Cities in Revolt: Urban Life in America, 1743-1776.* New York: Capricorn Books, 1964.

Brown, Weldon A. *Empire or Independence: A Study in the Failure of Reconciliation.* New Orleans: Louisiana State University Press, 1941.

Brunhouse, Robert Levere. *The Counter-Revolution in Pennsylvania, 1776-1790.* Philadelphia: Pennsylvania Historical Commission, 1942.

Burnett, Edmund Cody. *The Continental Congress.* New York: The Macmillan Company, 1941.

Conrad, Henry C. *History of the State of Delaware.* Vol. I, Wilmington: Published by the Author, 1908.

Craven, Wesley Frank. *New Jersey and the English Colonization of North America.* New York: D. Van Nostrand Company, Inc., 1964.

Dangerfield, George C. *Chancellor Robert R. Livingston of New York, 1746-1813.* New York: Harcourt Brace, 1960.

Dillon, Dorothy R. *The New York Triumvirate: A Study of the Legal and Political Careers of William Livingston, John Morin Scott, William Smith, Jr.* New York: Columbia University Press, 1949.

Donoughue, Bernard. *British Politics and the American Revolution: The Path to War, 1773-1775.* London: Macmillan & Co., Ltd., 1964.

Edwards, George W. and Arthur E. Peterson. *New York as an Eighteenth Century Municipality.* New York: Longmans, Green & Company, 1917.

Erdman, Charles. *The New Jersey Constitution of 1776.* Princeton: Princeton University Press, 1929.

Flick, Alexander. *Loyalism in New York During the American Revolution.* New York: Columbia University Press, 1901.

Fox, Dixon Ryan. *Yankees and Yorkers.* Port Washington, New York: Kennikat Press, 1967. Reprint.

Gegenheimer, Albert Frank. *William Smith: Educator and Churchman, 1727-1803*. Philadelphia: University of Pennsylvania Press, 1943.

Gerlach, Donald R. *Philip Schuyler and the American Revolution in New York, 1733-1777*. Lincoln: University of Nebraska Press, 1964.

Gipson, Lawrence Henry. *The British Isles and the American Colonies: The Northern Plantations*, Vol. III in *The British Empire before the American Revolution*. New York: Alfred A. Knopf, 1937-1969.

Goldman, Eric F. (ed.). *Historiography and Urbanization*. Baltimore: The Johns Hopkins Press, 1941.

Gordon, Thomas F. *The History of New Jersey from its Discovery by Europeans to the Adoption of the Federal Constitution*. Trenton: Daniel Fenton, 1834.

Gordon, William. *The History of the Rise, Progress, and Establishment of the United States of America*. Vol. II, London: Charles Dilly and James Buckland, Printers, 1788.

Greene, Evarts B. *The Revolutionary Generation 1763-1790*. New York: The Macmillan Company, 1943.

Hancock, Harold Bell. *The Delaware Loyalists*. Wilmington: Hambleton Printing Co., 1940.

Hanna, William S. *Benjamin Franklin and Pennsylvania Politics*. Stanford: Stanford University Press, 1964.

Harrington, Virginia. *The New York Merchant on the Eve of the Revolution*. New York: Columbia University Press, 1935.

Hawke, David. *In the Midst of a Revolution*. Philadelphia: University of Pennsylvania Press, 1961.

Hesseltine, William B. *Sections and Politics*. Madison: The State Historical Society of Wisconsin, 1968.

Head, John M. *A Time to Rend: An Essay on the Decision for Independence*. Madison: The State Historical Society of Wisconsin, 1969.

Jacobson, David L. *John Dickinson and the Revolution in*

Pennsylvania, 1764-1776. Berkeley & Los Angeles: University of California, 1765.

Jensen, Arthur L. *The Maritime Commerce of Colonial Philadelphia.* Madison: The State Historical Society of Wisconsin, 1963.

Jensen, Merrill. *The Founding of a Nation.* New York: Oxford University Press, 1969.

Jones, Thomas. *History of New York during the Revolutionary War.* New York: *New York Times,* 1879.

Kemmerer, Donald. *Path to Freedom: The Struggle for Self-Government in Colonial New Jersey 1703-1776.* Princeton: Princeton University Press, 1940.

Kraus, Michael. *Intercolonial Aspects of American Culture on the Eve of the Revolution.* New York: Octagon Books, Inc., 1964. Reprint.

Labaree, Benjamin Woods. *The Boston Tea Party.* New York: Oxford University Press, 1964.

Lincoln, Charles. *The Revolutionary Movement in Pennsylvania, 1760-1776.* Philadelphia: University of Pennsylvania, 1901.

Lundin, Leonard. *Cockpit of the Revolution: The War for Independence in New Jersey.* Princeton: Princeton University Press, 1940.

Mackesy, Piers. *The War for America, 1775-1783.* Cambridge: Harvard University Press, 1964.

Main, Jackson Turner. *The Social Structure of Revolutionary America.* Princeton: Princeton University Press, 1965.

Mason, Bernard. *The Road to Independence: The Revolutionary Movement in New York, 1773-1777.* Lexington: University of Kentucky Press, 1966.

McCormick, Richard P. *New Jersey from Colony to State, 1609-1789.* New York: D. Van Nostrand Co., 1964.

_____. *The History of Voting in New Jersey: A Study of the Development of Election Machinery 1664-1911.* New Brunswick. Rutgers University Press, 1953.

Merritt, Richard L. *Symbols of American Community 1735-1775.* New Haven: Yale University Press.

Metzger, Charles H. *Catholics and the American Revolution.* Chicago: Loyola University Press, 1962.

Mombert, J. I. *An Authentic History of Lancaster County, in the State of Pennsylvania.* Lancaster: J. E. Barr & Co., 1869.

Monaghan, Frank. *John Jay.* New York: Bobbs Merrill Company, 1935.

Montgomery, Morton L. *History of Berks County, Pennsylvania from 1774-1783.* Reading: Chas. F. Haage, 1894.

Morris, Richard. *The American Revolution Reconsidered.* New York: Harper & Row, 1967.

Munroe, John A. *Federalist Delaware 1775-1815.* New Brunswick: Rutgers University Press, 1954.

Nelson, William. *The American Tory.* Oxford: The Clarendon Press, 1961.

Nettels, Curtis. *George Washington and American Independence.* Boston: Little Brown & Company, 1957.

Onderdonk, Henry, Jr., *Revolutionary Incidents of Suffolk and Queens Counties.* New York: Leavitt & Company, 1849.

Ramsay, David. *The History of the American Revolution.* Vol. I, Dublin: Ireland, William Jones, 1793.

Rossiter, Clinton. *Seedtime of the Republic: The Origin of the American Tradition of Political Liberty.* New York: Harcourt Brace and Company, 1953.

Rossman, Kenneth R. *Thomas Mifflin and the Politics of the American Revolution.* Chapel Hill: University of North Carolina Press, 1952.

Savelle, Max. *Seeds of Liberty: The Genius of the American Mind.* New York: Alfred A. Knopf, 1948.

Scharf, Thomas J. *History of Delaware, 1609-1888.* Vol. I, Philadelphia: T. J. Richards & Co., 1888.

Scharf, Thomas J. and Thompson Westcott. *History of Phila-delphia, 1609-1884.* Philadelphia: L. H. Everts & Co., 1884.

Smith, Charles Page. *James Wilson, Founding Father 1742-1798.* Chapel Hill: University of North Carolina Press, 1956.

Stevens, John Austin, Jr. *Colonial New York: Sketches Bi-ographical and Historical 1768-1784.* New York: John F. Trowe & Co., 1867.

Stillé, Charles J. *The Life and Times of John Dickinson, 1732-1808.* Philadelphia: The Historical Society of Penn-sylvania, 1891.

Thayer, Theodore. *Pennsylvania Politics and the Growth of Democracy, 1740-1776.* Harrisburg: Pennsylvania Histor-ical and Museum Commission, 1953.

Upton, Leslie. *The Loyal Whig: William Smith of New York and Quebec.* Toronto: University of Toronto Press, 1969.

Valentine, Alan, *Lord Stirling.* New York: Oxford University Press, 1969.

Young, Alfred F. *The Democratic Republicans of New York.* Chapel Hill: Institute of Early American History and Culture, 1967.

Williams, William Appleman. *The Contours of American History.* Cleveland: World Publishing Company, 1961.

Williamson, Chilton. *American Suffrage from Property to Democracy 1760-1860.* Princeton: Princeton University Press, 1960.

Wittke, Carl. *We Who Built America.* Cleveland: Western Reserve University Press, 1964.

Woodward, Carl Raymond. *Ploughs and Politics: Charles Read of New Jersey and His Notes on Agriculture, 1715-1774.* New Brunswick: Rutgers University Press, 1941.

Articles

Anderson, John R. "Militia Law in Revolutionary Jersey,"
Proceedings of the New Jersey Historical Society, LXXVI
(October, 1958), 280-296.

Baldwin, Ernest H. "Joseph Galloway, The Loyalist Politician," *Pennsylvania Magazine of History and Biography,*
XXVI (July, Oct., Dec., 1902), 161-191; 289-321; 417-
442.

Bernstein, David. "A Glimpse at New Jersey Colonial Politics," *The Journal of the Rutgers University Library,* XXX
(June, 1967), 53-59.

Bridenbaugh, Carl. "Baths and Watering Places of Colonial
America," *William and Mary Quarterly,* 3rd Series, III
(January, 1946), 151-182.

Brunhouse, Robert L. "The Effect of the Townshend Acts
in Pennsylvania," *Pennsylvania Magazine of History and
Biography,* LIV (October, 1930), 355-373.

Champagne, Robert J. "New York Politics and Independence,
1776," *New York Historical Society Quarterly,* XLV (July,
1962), 281-304.

_____. "New York's Radicals and the Coming of In-
dependence," *Journal of American History,* LI (June,
1964), 21-40.

_____. "New York and the Intolerable Acts of 1774,"
New York Historical Society Quarterly, XLV (April,
1961), 195-207.

Cutler, Willard W. "Historical Address on Sussex County,"
Proceedings of the New Jersey Historical Society, New
Series, VI (July, 1921), 129-142.

Fennelly, Catherine. "William Franklin of New Jersey," *William and Mary Quarterly,* 3rd Series, VI (July, 1949),
361-382.

Greene, Evarts B. "New York and The Old Empire," in *History of the State of New York.* Vol. III, ed. Alexander C.

Flick, New York: Columbia University Press, 1933, 129-145.

Hancock, Harold Bell. "Thomas Robinson, Delaware's Most Prominent Loyalist," *Delaware History,* IV (March, 1950), 1-38.

Haskett, Richard C. "William Paterson, Attorney General of New Jersey: Public Office and Private Profit in the American Revolution," *William and Mary Quarterly,* 3rd Series, VII (January, 1950), 26-38.

Klein, Milton M. "The Cultural Tyros of Colonial New York," *South Atlantic Quarterly,* LXVI (Spring, 1967), 218-232.

Klingelhofer, Herbert E. "The Cautious Revolution: Maryland and the Movement Toward Independence: 1774-1776," *Maryland Historical Magazine,* LX (September, 1965), 261-314.

Kramer, Leonard J. "Presbyterians Approach the American Revolution," *Journal of The Presbyterian Historical Society,* XXXI (September, 1953), 167-180.

Labaree, Leonard Wood. "William Tryon," *Dictionary of American Biography,* XIX, New York: Charles Scribner's Sons, 1928-1937.

McKee, Samuel, Jr. "The Economic Pattern of Colonial New York," in *History of the State of New York,* Vol. II, ed. Alexander C. Flick, New York: Columbia University Press, 1933, 247-283.

Mood, Fulmer. "The Origin, Evolution, and Application of the Sectional Concept, 1750-1900," in *Regionalism in America,* ed. Merrill Jensen, Madison & Milwaukee: The University Press, 1965. 5-98.

Munroe, John A. "The Philadelawareans: A Study in the Relations Between Philadelphia and Delaware in the Late Eighteenth Century," *Pennsylvania Magazine of History and Biography,* LXIX (April, 1945), 128-150.

Pole, J. R. "Suffrage Reform and the American Revolution," *Proceedings of the New Jersey Historical Society,* LXXIV (July, 1956), 173-194.

Pomfret, John E. "West New Jersey: A Quaker Society 1675-1776," *William and Mary Quarterly,* 3rd Series, VIII (October, 1951), 493-519.

Powell, John H. "John Dickinson, President of the Delaware State, 1781-1782," *Delaware History,* I (January, 1946), 1-55.

Quarles, Benjamin. "Lord Dunmore as Liberator," *William and Mary Quarterly,* 3rd Series, XV (October, 1958), 494-507.

Sachs, William S. "Agricultural Conditions in the Northern Colonies before the Revolution," *Journal of Economic History,* XIII (Summer, 1953), 274-290.

Scott, Austin. "The Early Cities of New Jersey," *Proceedings of the New Jersey Historical Society,* 2nd Series, IX (1886), 151-177.

Shearer, Augustus M. "The Church, the School and the Press," in *History of the State of New York,* Vol. III, ed. Alexander C. Flick, New York: Columbia University Press, 1933.

Shryock, Richard. "Historical Traditions in Philadelphia and in the Middle Atlantic Area: An Editorial," *Pennsylvania Magazine of History and Biography,* LXVI (April, 1943), 115-141.

Teeter, Dwight L. "Benjamin Towne: The Precarious Career of a Persistent Printer," *Pennsylvania Magazine of History and Biography,* LXXXIX (July, 1965), 316-330.

Tolles, Frederick B. "The Historians of the Middle Colonies," in *The Reinterpretation of Early American History,* ed. Ray Allen Billington, San Marino: The Huntington Library, 1966, 65-77.

Tuttle, Reverend Joseph F. "Reverend Jacob Greene of Hanover, New Jersey," *Proceedings of the New Jersey Historical Society,* XII (1891), 191-241.

_____. "The Early History of Morris County, New Jersey," *Proceedings of the New Jersey Historical Society,* II (1870), 17-53.

Vermeule, Cornelius C. "Number of Soldiers in the Revolution," *Proceedings of the New Jersey Historical Society,* New Series, VII (July, 1922), 223-227.

Worthen, Samuel Copp. "The Secession of New Jersey," *Proceedings of the New Jersey Historical Society,* New Series, VI (July, 1921), 142-148.

Young, Henry J. "Treason and Its Punishment in Revolutionary Pennsylvania," *Pennsylvania Magazine of History and Biography,* XC (July, 1966), 287-313.

Young, Alfred and Staughton Lynd. "After Carl Becker: The Mechanics and New York City Politics, 1774-1801," *Labor History,* V (Fall, 1964), 225-246.

Unpublished Dissertations

Calhoon, Robert McCluer. "Critics of Colonial Resistance in Pre-Revolutionary Debate, 1763-1776." Ph.D. dissertation, Western Reserve University, 1964.

Henderson, Herbert James. "Political Factions in the Continental Congress 1774-1789." Ph.D. dissertation, Columbia University, 1963.

Hoffman, Ronald. "Economics, Politics and the Revolution in Maryland." Ph.D. dissertation, University of Wisconsin, 1969.

Jenks, Major B. "George Clinton and New York State Politics 1775 to 1801." Ph.D. dissertation, Cornell University, 1936.

INDEX